ETHICAL ELEMENTS OF MAHĀBHĀRATA

Ethical Elements of MAHABHARATA

MANJU RANI VERMA

Commonwealth

ETHICAL ELEMENTS OF MAHĀBHĀRATA

Edition : 2025

ISBN 81-7169-158-7

Published by :
COMMONWEALTH PUBLISHERS (P) LTD.
4831/24, Govind Lane,
Ansari Road, Darya Ganj,
New Delhi - 110002
Ph. : 23242541, 23272541
e-mail : commonwealthpublishers2016@gmail.com

Distributed by :
ARJUN PUBLISHING HOUSE
4831/24, Govind Lane,
Ansari Road, Darya Ganj,
New Delhi - 110002
Ph. : 23242541, 23272541
e-mail : arjunbooks2001@gmail.com

Laser Typesetting by :
Dimple Computers
Delhi

Printed at :
Balaji Digital
Delhi

Preface

The approach of Indian Philosophy to Truth and Reality is essentially moral and practical. Ethics is an essential appendage of Metaphysics because one can attain Truth only by following all ethical rules and precepts prescribed for this purpose. In India, the ethical approach is not a mere intellectual approach to moral problems. It is practical through and through as the primary object of ethical teachings in India is to serve as a true guide of man in his uphill journey of life ending in the realization of the Supreme good. Morality should constitute the keynote of a man's empirical life as nobody can reach the transendental state of Moksa without making his empirical life spotlessly pure. Purushārthas are not merely to be intellectually apprehended; but these are also to be attained in life. The transcendental Truth can be realised only by the actual realisation of ethical ideas in practical life. Supra-moral is linked with the moral and the transcendental Peace and Delight with the moral purity of the empirical life.

The world is to be looked upon as positive and essential as it is based on Truth. It is our duty to respect the world, to respect the society to which we belong and also to respect all relations which exist between man and man. The harmony between the metaphysical life of spiritual freedom and the moral life of purity and peace has been depicted in a rational and convincing manner in the *Mahābhārata*.

An humble attempt has been made to explicate thoroughly and in a searching manner the ethical teachings of the

Mahābhārata to bring to light the inherent merits of this great epic in a planned and effective manner.

Chapter I is of introductory nature, giving general outline of Indian ethics. Chapter II deals with the concept of Dharma which is the pivot around which the great epic revolves. Chapter III deals with the relation of Purushārthas in the social, moral and spiritual life of man. Chapter IV discusses Varnāsramadharma emphasizing on the individual and social good. Chapter V deals with the Law of Karma as a law of justice. Chapter VI deals with the different standards of Morality as envisaged by the great epic. Chapter VII embodies the concluding remarks which have been substantiated after a perusal of the different points of view expressed by different thinkers with regard to the ethical teachings of the *Mahābhārata*. The ethical teachings of the *Mahābhārata* are of immense value for the modern man in reorienting his socio-ethical life.

The following study was undertaken under the guidance of Dr. I.N. Sinha, University Professor of Philosophy, Patna University, Patna. I am grateful to him for his encouragement, counsel and invaluable guidance in undertaking this work. I sincerely express my profound sense of gratitude to him. I am also grateful to Mrs. I.N. Sinha for she has all along been a source of inspiration and encouragement in my endeavour.

One gets help from so many people in course of writing a Doctoral Dissertation, and it is impossible to thank everyone individually. Nevertheless, without the truest affection, timely advice, inspiration and well wishes of my parents, the present state of my work and my endeavours would not have been successful. At this juncture the efforts of my in-laws Shree P.N. Prasad, Smt. Girija Devi, Dr. V.N. Prasad (Husband), Miss Rupali and Roly (daughers) are also worthy of appreciation.

I also do wish to acknowledge gratefully the financial support rendered by the University Grants Commission, New Delhi.

MANJU RANI VERMA

Contents

Transliteration Chart

अ	आ	इ	ई	उ	ऊ	ऋ
a	ā	i	ī	u	ū	r
ए	ऐ	ओ	औ	अं	अः	
e	ai	o	au	ṁ	h	
क	ख	ग	घ	ङ		
ka	kha	ga	gha	na		
च	छ	ज	झ			
ca	cha	ja	jha	na		
ट	ठ	ड	ढ	ण		
ṭa	ṭha	ḍa	ḍha	ṇa		
त	थ	द	ध	न		
ta	tha	da	dha	na		
प	फ	ब	भ	म		
pa	pha	ba	bha	ma		
य	र	ल	व			
ya	ra	la	va			
श	ष	स	ह			
śa	ṣa	sa	ha			
क्ष	त्र	ज्ञ				
ksa	tra	jṅa				

1

Introduction

Every great philosophy has the twofold task before it. On the one hand, it criticises the existing beliefs and schools of thought, and on the other, it develops and establishes certain beliefs and theories of its own. Moreover, every philosophy is the product of an age, of particular time and place. It tries to fulfil certain needs, answer certain demands and responds to certain challenges which present themselves in a given place or time. But all the same, a great philosophy tries to rise above the limits of time and place, in so far as it discusses certain questions and problems which are eternal and universal, valid for all time and place. So it has not only a historical value but is related to the very being of mankind, and hence is of interest to everybody and every age.

The author of the *Mahābhārata*[1] threw light on such perennial problems of human life. Hence right through the centuries their works have been read and reread. Those were classics for the ancient and still are classics for the moderns. The problems they deal with, are as much the problems for us as for the peoples of their own ages; and the particular suggestions they offer do not matter so much as the principles

1. Radha Kamal Mukherji, *The Culture and Art of India* (George Allen & Unwin, London, 1959), p. 73.

underlying them. The ills that they sought to diagnose and cure—ills both of human society and human character—plague our modern age no less than the ancient. All social thinkers and idealists, however, are conditioned, in so far as they have, of necessity, to take the conditions and institutions of their own times for their starting point, when they are thinking of their ideals. So, in order to understand their ideas, we must take into account the social and political set-up and the prevailing state of morals of the time.

THE PROBLEM BEFORE THE AUTHORS OF THE MAHĀBHĀRATA

The Development of the Mahābhārata from a Non-Aryan Nucleus

Although it is not possible to assign any exact date for the composition of the *Mahābhārata*, but it may fairly be assumed that it is a post-Buddhistic[2] work so far as its philosophical, ethical and didactic portions are concerned. The original epic, probably, had no connection with philosophy at all. It is a pseudo epic which contains the mixture of the philosophical doctrines.[3] According to the internal evidence of the *Mahābhārata* itself, it passed through three recitations or editions at the hands of Vyāsa, Vaisampāyana and Sauti Ugraasravā[4] before it reached the present form. These three stages were those of the 'Jaya',[5] the 'Bhārata'[6] and the 'Mahābhārata'.[7] Thus, it may fairly be

2. Though Buddhism is not directly mentioned but there are numerous indirect references to it, e.g. XII. 218. 34-35.
3. S.K. De, *History of Philosophy East and West*, p. 105 n; Hopkins also calls the present form of the Mahābhārata. As pseudo epic in his *The Great Epic of India* (New Haven, 1920).
4. *Mbh.* I. 2.21.
5. *Mbh.* I. 62.20.
6. *Mbh.* I. 1.102.
7. *Mbh.* I. 101, 107-108.

assumed that the *Mahābhārata* passed through at least three editions to reach its present shape.[8]

As already referred to,[9] there took place a renaissance of the non-Aryan culture in the first half of the first millenium B.C., as a result of which India passed through a great intellectual ferment in the middle centuries of this millenium. In early Upaniṣads, the scriptures of Buddhism and Jainism, some of which belong to this period, show that there existed a wonderful variety of speculations and theories on the origins of the universe, the nature of the soul and kindred problems. Some of those were accepted by the one or other Brahmanic schools and incorporated into orthodox belief. Others were the germinal haven of the heterodox sects.[10]

It appears as if there was a clash of cultures. The Vedic religion, ethics and philosophical ideas, crude as they were, failed to satisfy the spiritual urges of the people. Hence they leaned towards the older indigenous culture for more satisfactory religious ideas, ethical conceptions and philosophical speculations. The older culture, with its variegated beliefs and faiths, speculative ideas and philosophical systems, raised its hand and threw a strong challenge to Brahmanism. The actual course of the struggle between the two cultures, for the most part, is, however, not known to us. But this much is certain that Brahmanism had to make a great compromise with the older culture.[11] There was no alternative before the Vedic culture except "to expand and remodel its own religion to accommodate new beliefs or die and disappear."[12] And "the Aryan culture undertook, not without trouble and repugnance, the gigantic task of taking in the new beliefs and adapting itself to the moral needs of the new comers."[13] The

8. C.V. Vaidya, *The Mahābhārata: A Criticism* (Bombay, 1905) Chapt. I.
9. See Apte, pp. 52-53.
10. Basham, *op. cit.*, p. 249.
11. Belvalkar and Ranade, *History of Indian Philosophy*, Vol. II, p. 84.
12. Radhakrishnan, *Indian Philosophy*, Vol. I, p. 477.
13. *Ibid.*, p. 477.

only price it demanded was that the newer doctrines and beliefs should owe allegiance to the orthodoxitativeness of the Vedas, and accept the philosophy of sacrifice,[14] even if nominally and superficially.

The original event of the Mahābhārata seems to be non-Aryan one,[15] the memory of which must have been handed down in the forms of lays and ballads and the versified traditions of the way sung by the Sūtas and Magadhas.[16] These songs in the early stages were not fixed, because they were orally handed down from generation to generation; and it was the genius of Vyāsa,[17] who collected and edited them and brought into existence the historical epic poem 'Jaya' which must be regarded as the first literary work of the Suta tradition; and once a literary nucleus be formed, it was easy to rally round it other elements in the field of Suta tradition;[18] and further to add to it the didactic and philosophical-ethical elements to counteract the heretics. 'Jaya' was, thus, transformed into 'Bhārata', and further into the Mahābhārata by rallying round it various elements of ethics and philosophy. Thus, around the non-Aryan nucleus, which was soon converted into an Aryan story,"[19] there grew a vast treasure of legends, myths, philosophy and ethics.

The Fusion of Non-Aryan Culture

At this stage, as a result of compromise between Brahmanism and the popular faiths and beliefs, Brahmanism had to accept the traditions, thoughts, and aspirations which were not its own[20] and the Bhārata or the *Mahābhārata* was the first attempt at effecting a reconciliation between the

14. Belvalkar and Ranade, *op. cit.*, p. 84.
15. Radhakrishnan, *op. clt.*, p. 478.
16. Bhandarkar, "The Mahabharata and its Critical Edition," *Indo-Asian Culture*, Vol. XI, No. 4, pp. 41-42.
17. Cf. S.K. Chatterji, Bhartīya Ārya Bhasa Aur Hindī, (Rajkamal, Delhi, 1954), pp. 54-55.
18. Dandekar, *op. cit.*, p. 42.
19. Radhakrishnan, *op. cit.*, p. 478.
20. *Ibid.*, p. 480.

culture of the Aryan and the popular religious traditions very rich in mythology.[21] "As in the case of Bentheon, in matters of philosophy and mysticism, the *Mahābhārata* tried to Brahmanise the non-Aryan lore."[22] Further, in the hands of the protagonists of Brahmanism, it becomes a powerful instrument to counteract the challenge of heterodoxy. Due to the challenge of the heretical movements, most of the popular religions, with their variety of gods and religious practices, came to be organised into one multi-charactered whole of which Kṛṣṇaism was the most predominant. And as realists, they also accepted to avow allegiance to the Vedas and Brahmanism.[23] Most probably, all the theistic non-Aryan cults, sensing the danger from the heretical schools, made a common cause with Brahmanism to forestall the danger of heresy. It appears that the editors of the *Mahābhārata* felt that some popular hero must be made the rallying centre to counteract the growing influence of heretical sects[24] and Kṛṣṇaism was ready at hand. The religious teaching and the ethical code, as also the philosophical speculations, which came to be propagated by the epic, were derived, for the most part, from the non-Brahmanic sources but thep accepted the authority of the Vedas and the ritual of sacrifice though in a modified form. And, thus, there was a compromise between Kṛṣṇaism and Brahmanism.[25] In the epics, thus, the Vedic religion is gradually modified into Hinduism.

The Challenge of the Heretical Schools

But, in spite of the fact that Brahmanism made compromise with some of the non-Aryan cults and beliefs, and accepted many philosophical ideas of the non-Aryan culture, it could not forestall the rise of some heretical or heterodox sects and philosophical schools which were not prepared to acknowledge the supremacy of the Vedas and Vedic sacrific. These were the schools of Mahâvıra, the Buddha, and Gosala

21. *Ibid.*, p. 480; also refer to Dandekar, *op. cit* , pp. 39, 43.
22. Talwarkar, *Cultural Heritage of India*, Vol. II, p. 88 (1962 Ed.).
23. Dandekar, *op. cit*, p. 43.
24. Radhakrishnan, *op. cit.*, p. 495.
25. Dandekar, *op. cit.*, p. 44.

which, though they ignored the gods, were not thorough-going atheists and materialists. They all accepted the fundamental doctrine of transmigration, the theory of Karma and the ideal of final liberation and had an ethical system of a high order. But there were others who rejected all spiritual categories completely; and their influence appears to have been not meagre. They rejected the existence of soul, God or any other immaterial entity and denied altogether the theory of transmigration, Karma and liberation of soul. Their ethics was hedonistic. The end of human life, according to them, was enjoyment—the gratification of senses.

The materialists, skeptics and agnostics and the sophists presented a great challenge to Brahmanism. They were threatening to strike at the very root of social, moral and religious life and their challenge had to be met to ensure the stability of the social and moral system. And, therefore, when the accepted creed was challenged, naturally defenders also came forward to support it.[26] Much of the philosophical speculation and moral teachings in the *Mahābhārata* arose for the sake of defending the traditional religion and creed. But, as there were many things in the Brahmanical religion itself which could not be rationally justified, the *Mahābhārata* tried to rationalize them. It was the rallying focus in defence of Brahmanical Society and Scheme of life against the spread of heresies of materialism, Jainism, and Buddhism. The materialists, in particular, were threatening to dissipate the whole social and moral values. The *Mahābhārata*, therefore, represents, "the element of Brahmanical renaissance provoked and stimulated by moral, social, political as well as religious crisis in the history of our land."[27]

In the *Mahābhārata* we have got numerous references to these materialists which suggest that the author of the epic is very much alive to the danger from their immoral and hedonistic teachings, ordinarily, the word 'Nāstika' is used,[28]

26. *The Age of Imperial Unity*, p. 479.
27. Ghoshal, U.N., *The History of Indian Political Ideas*, (Oxford, 1959), p. 180.
28. *Mbh.* XII. 12.5, XII. 133.14, XII. 180, 49, XII. 267-69.

in the *Mahābhārata*, to connote a dissenter from the received and traditional opinion in regard, either to the existence of transcendental entities or to the authority of hallowed tradition. There is also the mention of Lokāyatikas (naturalists), Haitakas or Hatumaniah (rationalist sophists)[29] and Paṣaṇdas (reviler of the Vedas). The nāstika creed of materialism is repeated by Pamcasikha.[30] Vyāsa very forcefully criticises and refutes the doctrine of naturalism which explains the existence of the world as caused by nature itself and denies the existence of any spiritual entity other than Nature.[31] Materialists, Heretics and Hetumantah, who filled the whole land, denied the reality of soul and other spiritual categories.[32] A character in the *Mahābhārata* says that he was born a jackal, because he was counterfoil pundita, a rationalist and a critic, devoted to logic and useless science of learning, a proclaimer of logical arguments, a talker in assemblies, a reviler and opposer of priests, an unbeliever and doubter of all.[33] The Haitukas used sophistical reasonings in their discussions to disprove the immortality of soul, the existence of God and the future world; and also reviled the Vedas and the priests. The Pāṣanḍis, who are the reviler of Vedas, are also mentioned.[34]

In the Anugītā Parva[35] a bewildering picture of the conflicting views about morality, spiritual entities and dharma etc. has been given. It shows that the heretics and infidels were fairly rampant, and had brought about a state of anarchy in thought. Some say that Dharma is rewarded after this life and others deny it. Some say that Dharma is permanent and others deny it. Some deny a hereafter, some doubt all things. Some are the supporters of hedonism, some are believers in violence, some are adherents of materialism, and so on. In

29. *Mbh.* XII. 19. 23-24, XII. 180. 47-49.
30. *Mbh.* XII. 218. 23-32.
31. *Mbh.* XII. 237. 5-6.
32. *Mbh.* XII. 19. 23-24.
33. *Mbh.* XXI. 180. 47-49, XIII. 37. 12-14.
34. *Mbh.* XIII. 23. 67.
35. *Mbh.* XIV. 49. 2-12.

the "Śāntiparva",[36] Bhāradvāja says that the life-functions can be explained by purely physical and physiological reasons, and the assumption of the soul is quite unnecessary.

The Gita too is very critical of the materialists and skeptics. It says,[37] "The ignorant and the unbelieving man who has a soul of doubt is destroyed, neither this world nor the next exists, nor happiness for him who has a soul of doubt." "At another place,[38] characterising the materialists as asuras, it says that they cannot distinguish between right and wrong conduct, they have neither purity, nor good conduct, nor truth. They do not think that the world is based on any truth and reality. They do not believe in God and consider all beings to have come out from the desires of sexes and from mutual union of the two sexes. These foolish people do harm to the world, engage themselves in cruel actions and destroy their own soul because they have no faith in the other world. Full of hypocrisy, conceit and arrogance and given to insatiable passion; and, adopting false doctrines due to delusion, they take the wrong course and live an impure life. They think that existence ends finally at death and that there is nothing beyond this world and its enjoyments. Bound with innumerable desires, given over to passion, anger and attachment etc., they busy themselves in collecting materials for the enjoyment of sensuous pleasures. They always think of riches, power, glory, success, strength, enjoyment etc.

Not only in the *Mahābhārata* but in the *Upaniṣads* and the *Rāmāyaṇa* also we find references to the materialist doctrines. In the *Katha*[39] and the *Bṛhadāraṇyaka*[40] there are references to the existence of people who do not believe in the existence of consciousness after death and think that everything ends with death. In the *Chāndogya*[41] we come across Virocana who believed that the body was the ātman. In the

36. *Mbh.* XII. Chap. 186.
37. *Gita*, IV. 40.
38. *Gita*, XVX. 7-18.
39. I. 20.
40. II. 4. 12.
41. VXII 18. 4.

Śvetāśvatara[42] *Upaniṣad* we find an author of heretical schools referred to, of which Vāda (accidentalism) and Svabhāva Vāda (naturalism) are more prominent, which denied the existence of any transcendental power and regarded matter as the ultimate principle. The former denies the causation and regards the world as a chaos, and the latter ascribes, whatever order there is in the Universe, to mere chance which is a necessity inherent in the very nature of things and not imposed by any transcendental agency.

The views of the materialists, who are very much condemned as nāstikas, appear summed up in the speech of Jabali to Rāma in the *Rāmāyaṇa.*[43] He says that a creature is born and annihilated alone. Therefore, a man, who is affected by the consideration that it is his mother or father, should be looked upon as a lunatic. The father is just the imitator but it is really the seminal and menstrual fluids combined in mother's womb that leads to a man's birth. At death one meets the inevitable end and it is a pity that some people prefer virtue in the other world to the earthly goods of this world; the performance of different sacrifices for the satisfaction of the deal is only waste of food. Cleaver people wrote books praising the merit of gifts, sacrifices, invitations and asceticism. There is nothing more than what is directly perceived by the senses.

Thus, we see that in the middle centuries of the first millenium B.C., heretical views relating to materialism, atheism, ascepticism, agnosticism, naturalism, accidentalism, dualism, and sophism etc. were very much rampant. These heretics did not believe in the existence of soul, the other world, life after death, or the transmigration of souls. They identified body with soul (dehātma Vāda) and said that all consciousness ceases with death. They did not believe in any other entity, and admitted the validity of perception only. Their ethics was hedonistic, and they believed that the enjoyment, or the gratification of senses, was the end of life. The *summum bonum* of life was the pleasure of senses. They cared

42. IV. 2.
43. XV. 108. 3-17.

only for momentary sense pleasures and unrestrained enjoyment of sensual joys undisturbed by the feelings of sins and virtues, for they denied their existence. Karma, the fruits of Karma, rebirth etc. had no meaning for them. "Their whole ethical position followed from their general metaphysical doctrine that sense objects or sense pleasurers were all that existed and there was no supra sensible or transcendental reality and thus there was no gradation or qualitative difference between pleasures and no reason why any restraint should be put upon our normal tendency to indulge in sense pleasures."[44]

The editors of the *Mahābhārata* are very much alive to the danger of these disruptive doctrines of the materialists, and every now and then, as we have just seen, they preach against them. Their doctrine had really presented a great challenge, and the orthodox religion had to gird up its loins to meet this challenge. But at the same time it realized that the ritualism of the Vedas and the traditional views of morality had to be modified by incorporating into it the current metaphysical theories of the Sāmkhya and the Vedānta in order that a system of rational ethics might be evolved. The materialists discarded ascepticism and stood for the gratification of senses. They were ascetic in other-worldliness and stood for here and now; for them, the world was the be-all and end-all of life. We do not find criticism in them. They valued human life and wanted that it should be enjoyed fully. The editors of the *Mahābhārata* recognised that these ideas contained some truth and hence we find that the general tone of the *Mahābhārata* is not very favourable to too much of asceticism; but, all the same, it does not allow licentious indulgence. It stands for self-control and Niṣkāma, favours living in the world and society and not renouncing it. But at the same time, it believes that too much importance cannot be attached to the material pleasures of life. It does not sacrifice everyday life in its exuberance for the quest of life beyond. In one of its verses it says that there is nothing

44. Dasgupta, S.N., *History of Indian Philosophy* (Cambridge, 1946), Vol. III, p. 550.

higher than man on earth.[45] It takes notice of the intricacies of social life, egoistic impulses of the individual, his feelings and passions coming against society, and deprecates them; but, at the same time, it also sees that the society and the social traditions should not kill human urges and desires and consciously urges that the life here should not be sacrificed for the life hereafter. And then, it tries to strike due balance between social good and the fulfilment of individual's wants and desires, his physical needs and urges. Thus, it strikes a middle course between the spiritual and material life of man and sees that the one should not be sacrificed for the sake of the other.

"All beings desire pleasure and seek to avoid pain," says the *Mahābhārata*.[46] So the pursuit of happiness has been given an important place in it. In the Śāntiparva, it lays down that "Happiness is of two kinds viz. bodily and mental. The instincts for the possessiveness of things both in this and the other world are for the sake of happiness....There is nothing more important than happiness among the fruits of Trivarga (Dharma, Artha and Kāma). Happiness is desirable. It is an attribute of the Self. Both virtue (Dharma) and profit (artha) are sought for the sake of happiness. Hence, all acts have, for their end, happiness."[47] The *Mahābhārata*, however, allows the enjoyment of the pleasures of body provided it does not change the codes of morality and Dharma. But its ethics is anti-hedonistic. Like the Bhagavadgītā and the Manusmṛti, it says that the desires are never satisfied by their gratification. The more they are gratified, the more they increase.[48] Contentment is the root of happiness and, hence, one should control one's desires.

The heretical sects of Jainism and Buddhism too posed a challenge to the orthodox religion. Their excessive stress on asceticism and their attack on the Varṇa system were thought to be very dangerous. Too much of asceticism would lead

45. *Mbh*. XII. 299. 20.
46. *Mbh*. XII. 139. 62; XII. 295.27.
47. *Mbh*. XII. 190-9.
48. *Mbh*. I. 85. 12-13; cf. Manu. II. 94-94.

to the very extinction of man on earth and the absence of Varṇas would lead to a state of social anarchy. Moreover, their atheism, i.e., the no more cognition of God, the Creator and the ruler of the Universe, was also thought to be very dangerous.

Asceticism is not an Aryan institution. The Aryans did not take kindly to ascetics. Indra killed the Yatis.[49] Munis are mentioned in the *Ṛg Veda*,[50] but they appear to be belonging to the non-Aryan race. The ascetic idea presupposes a faith in spiritual happiness and a despair of material life. It also presupposes a dualistic concept of man, distinguishing soul from the body, the soul being immortal and real and the body mortal and unreal. It also has a pessimistic idea that all worldly joys are worthless and a source of evil, to keep the soul bound to earth and do not let it rise above and attain ultimate liberation, which is the *summum bonum* of life. Contrary to these thoughts, there is absolutely no touch of pessimism in the early Aryan outlook on life.[51] They were worldly and had a will to live and enjoy life to the full. There is no support for Nivṛtti and Sanyāsa in their approach to life. Moreover, the idea of essentially divine and human soul appears to be foreign to the thought of the early Aryans, and hence there is neither pessimism in them nor an ascetic approach to life, nor a hankering for final liberation.

Asceticism was, however, quite prevalent amongst people of the eastern regions who were mostly non-Aryans and it was associated with a particular kind of ethico-metaphysical dualism and a distinct attitude to life which regards the material body to be inherently evil and the spiritual element the soul—alone as good; and hence it lays stress on the suppression of the bodily desires so that the soul—the immortal self of man—may be free from the shackles of the transient and evil propendent body. Asceticism had a very

49. *Taittiriya Samhitā* 11. 4. 9. 2; VI. 2. 7. 5.
50. *Rg*. X. 136. 2.
51. C. Kunnan Raja, *The Cultural Heritage of India*, Vol. I, pp. 205 and 211.

powerful hold on the people of India in the middle centuries of the first millenium B.C., and Brahmanism had to compare with it by giving it a place in its scheme of the fourfold stages of life by incorporating the Vānaprastha and Sanyāsa āśramas.[52]

By the time of the Upaniṣads asceticism had become very widespread. The ascetics suffered self-inflicted tortures of hunger, thirst, heat, cold and rains, leading to various kinds of self-mortification. Some of the ascetics indulged in such practices in order to acquire magical powers, and the others did so to free the soul from the tutelage of the body, so that it may know the real truth and attain final liberation.[53]

With the rise of Jainism and Buddhism and some other minor heretical sects, asceticism assumed enormous and omitted often dangerous proportions. It was the time when the *Mahābhārata* was in the process of composition or completion. There was a wave of renunciation which may be regarded both as the cause and effect of the rise of the heterodox sects like Buddhism and Jainism, and soon it became a "menace to society. Its integrity was threatened by the growth of various ascetic orders and brotherhoods based upon renunciation of the world and social obligation."[54] Buddhism, with its exaggerated emphasis on the quiscent virtue of self-abnegation, its unwise creation of a separate class of quiescents and illumination, its sharp distinction between monks and laymen, implying an inferiority of the latter, its too fascile admission of men to monastic life and its relegation of worldly action to a position of unimportance, had created confusion, and under its influence almost half of the nation moved in the direction of "spiritual passivity and negation and the other half, by a natural reaction, plunged deep into a splendid but enervating materialism."[55] The reaction to this anti-social development is reflected in

52. C.C. Pande, *The Origins of Buddhism*, pp. 322-6.

53. Cf. Basham, *op. cit.*, pp. 545-47.

54. *The Age of Imperial Unity*, pp. 553-54.

55. Sri Aurobindo, *Vyāsa and Valmīki* (Pondicherry, 1956), pp. 50-51.

Kautilya's *Arthaśāstra* which does not at all approve of a premature renunciation of the world before the obligations of demestic life are fulfilled; and it allows the adoption of an ascetic life to a person only when he has made provision for his wife and children, and got the formal connection of the legal authorities. Kautilya even bans the entry in the rural society of unlicensed ascetics as they are disintegrating factors.[56]

The *Mahābhārata,* however, does not condemn asceticism outright. Many passages can be quoted from it in support of asceticism.[57] In fact the institution of asceticism becomes such a hallowed institution amongst the non-Aryan as well as Aryan people with the exception of the Cārvākas[58] that it could not but draw veneration from the editors of the *Mahābhārata*. The ascetic tendency in itself, if practised within limits, is not bad, rather even desirable, for a disciplined, contented and healthy society. A fully integrated personality can only be achieved by self-control, by the subjection of appetites to reason. Unbridled possessiveness and gratification of senses bring about conflicts and discontentment, selfishness and egoism often leading to the disintegration of society. The editors of the *Mahābhārata* realized it and appreciated, sometimes even encouraged, the ascetic tendency. But, when its unbridled practice became a menace to society in so far as the people of all ages and all classes began to leave their home and family forsaking their social duties and obligations, when the lure of the life beyond began to prove detrimental to the life here on this earth and the society began to disintegrate due to people's not performing their social, political, and domestic duties, there arose the need to check the growing tendency of asceticism. The tendency of Nivṛtti must be subordinated to the maintenance of social good. But the *Mahābhārata* could not prescribe the

56. Kautilya, *Arthaśāstra*, II. 1. 48.

57. *Mbh.* XII. 277; XII. 294. 2-12; XII. 261; XII. 176; XII. 177; XII. 178; XII. 179; XII. 269. 31-32.

58. It is interesting to note that even the propagators of materialist and skeptic schools were nearly all ascetion.

practice of extreme indulgence—Pravṛtti—because it too had its own dangers. Hence it, specially the Gītā, tries to chalk out a balance between the two tendencies of Nivṛtti and Pravṛtti by its principle of Niṣkāma Karma. It prescribes Karmayoga, the philosophy of action. It does not encourage inaction or renunciation of action—the Sanyāsa. It does not teach anti-social escapism. It prescribes the discharge of duties with detachment. A man should perform his duties for the sake of duty without attachment or aversion and without any desire for the enjoyment of their fruits. A man may achieve the highest good, the salvation, even while living in society and doing his duties and not by renunciation of the world. In the centuries that lay between the *Upaniṣads* and the age of *Mahābhārata*, overemphasis had been laid on quietism and renunciation. It may be said that the whole Gītā is a long sustained protest against the growing danger of too much of quietism and asceticism.[59] The *Mahābhārata* discusses two parallel trends : the one that favoured the path of renunciation embodied in Sanyāsa, and the other that supports the path of action embodied in the Gṛhastha Āśrama, and it clearly shows its preference for the latter. Dharmavyādha[60] in the Vānaparva and Tulādhāra[61] in the Śāntiparva, besides others in the epic,[62] preach the philosophy of action—the performance of one's duties while living in society. Thus the general and predominant tone of the *Mahābhārata* is in favour of activity and the life of a Gṛhastha, and disfavours Sanyāsa and renunciation. However, its activistic life is saturated with the ideal of Niṣkāma Karma and renunciation. It opposes the emphasis on asceticism laid by the heretical schools, and finds no justification for persons renouncing their homes and families and going to the forest rather supports the life of action in renunciation.

59. Sharma, B.S., *The Cultural Heritage of India*, 2nd Ed., Vol. III, p. 40.

60. *Mbh.* III. Chaps. 207-216.

61. *Mbh.* XII. Chaps. 262-263.

62. *Mbh.* XII. 12. 12-13; XII. 11. 21-22; XII. 10; XII. 18; XIV. 45. 13.

Rationalisation of Varṇa System and Sacrifices

The heretical schools were also great critics of the Varṇa Vyavasthā based on hereditary principles. The *Mahābhārata* accepts the divine origin of Varṇas and its stratification but it is also conscious of the injustice involved in such stratification based on birth.

The Ṛg Veda gives an account of the origin of Varṇas from the different organs of the cosmic Puruṣa—Brāhmanas from his mouth, Rājanyas from his arms, Vaiśyas from his thigh and śūdras from his feet.[63] The *Mahābhārata* accepts this account and mentions it at many places.[64] The Puruṣa is also identified at some places, with Kṛṣṇa or Viṣṇu as the Creator of Varṇas.[65] But this traditional theory of the origin of Varṇas and its stratification was not rationally explicable, nor could it be accepted by the critical minds.[66] Hence the *Mahābhārata* tries to give a metaphysical and rational justification for the principle of Varṇa and the social gradation involved in it, and is born in a particular Varṇa as a result of his previous Karma (action), hence there is no injustice involved in it.[67] Moreover, it also justifies the Varṇa system on the principle of Guṇa and Karma.[68] It is liberal enough sometimes to give the rational valuation to the quality and behaviour of man and not to his birth in a particular caste.[69] The *Mahābhārata*, thus, arose in a social milieu and situation in which such fundamental questions were asked, the traditional answers to which are found wanting. It, therefore, sought to provide a nationalised satisfactory answer to them.

The sacrifices were other targets of heretic criticism and the *Mahābhārata* gives a symbolical meaning to the sacrificial offerings.[70] Instead of the sacrifice of animals it prescribes the

63. *Rg*. X. 90. 2.
64. *Mbh*. XII. 72. 4-5; XII. 188. 4-5; XII. 318. 90; XII. 296. 5-6; X. 3. 18-19: XIII. 48. 3; XIII. 141. 30; also *Kane*. I. 87-93.
65. *Mbh*. XII. 47. 68; *Gītā* IV. 13.
66. *Mbh*. XII. 188. 6-9.
67. *Mbh*. XIX. 188. 10. 14.
68. *Gītā*, IV. 13, XVIII. 41.
69. *Mbh*. III. 212. 12; III. 180. 25-26 & 33, XII. 189. 8.
70. *Gītā*, IV. 24-32.

sacrifice of desires and passions of life.[71] It reintroduced Dravidian ritual of 'Pūjā' in place of the sacrificial ritual of the Vedas. "The cleansing of Vedic ritualism through the omission of animal slaughter and the fourfold metaphysical reinterpretation of sacrifice is daiva yajña, jñana yajña, sāmyama yajña and indriya yajña and the cleansing of the Dravidian Pūjā ritualism through the emphasis on love and purity of heart, are the great achievements of Śrīkṛṣṇa of the epic. But the epic clearly indicates that the new dispensation was not accepted without serious opposition."[72] Moreover, the *Mahābhārata* introduces the doctrine of Bhakti which satisfied the instinctive element in man for which there was no provision in Jainism and Buddhism.

To conclude, in the sphere of religion the Vedic rituals and sacrifices are not rejected by the *Mahābhārata* : they are shorn off their obnoxious character and invested with new symbolic meaning. New gods are incorporated in the Vedic pantheon, and they supersede the older ones. Kṛṣṇaism and Śaivism become prominent, and a sweeping current of bhakti runs through the new religious renaissance. In the sphere of philosophy there is a strong denunciation of materialism and the Sāmkhya and the Vedānta are reconciled. In the sphere of ethics, hedonism is discounted but extreme form of asceticism and renunciation too are not appreciated, and stress is laid on the observance of one's duties in a detached way. Self-control and restraint over one's appetites and desires are highly valued. The *Mahābhārata* is called by its authors an Itihāsa,[73] a Purāṇa,[74] and Ākhyāna,[75] a Samhita,[76] a Kāvya[77] and the source and basis of all legends.[78]

71. *Mbh*. XXI. 263.
72. R.K. Mukherji, *A History of Indian Civilisation*, (Hind Kitabs, Bombay, 1956), p. 262.
73. *Mbh*. Ādi, 1, 19, 26, 54, 87, 266-67. *Ibid* , II, 36, 335.
74. *Ibid*., I. 266-7. *Ibid*., II, 36.
75. *Ibid*., II, 33, 382, 384, 386, 390.
76. *Ibid*., I, 21, 102.
77. *Ibid*., Ādi I, 61, 72-3.
Ibid., II, 390.
78. *Ibid*., II, 35, 388.

It is these and even something more than these. It is the fifth Veda,[79] namely the Kārṣṇa Veda, i.e., the Veda of Kṛṣṇa Dvaipayans Vyasa[80] and the essence of other Vedas.[81] By itself it is equal to, nay, even greater than, the remaining Vedas.[82] Hence one should study the Vedas with its help.[83] One, who does not have a knowledge of this highly important work, is not a learned man even though one may be an acknowledged scholar of the Vedas and the Upaniṣads.[84]

Besides these, it is a Dharmaśāstra, an Arthaśāstra and a Kāmaśāstra.[85] There is much truth in Vyasa's challenge that "That which occurs here about Dharma, Artha, Kāma and Mokṣa (the four ends of human life) occurs elsewhere and that which does not occur here, occurs nowhere else.[86] It is really an encyclopaedia in which the divergent and even contradictory ideas on religion, morals, social and economic conditions and politics are put in close juxtaposition. It removes ignorance like sun, which removes darkness.[87] It is capable of liberating one from great sins, and of helping one in the attainment of long life, glory (here) and heaven (hereafter).[88]

The above claims should not be taken as merely the low boasts of Vyāsa. The merits of this "deathless poem"[89] have been well recognized by many modern scholars also. To

79. *Ibid.*, II, 63, 69. Vide Mullick: *Mahābhārata—As It was, Is And Shall Be*, p. 6. Cf. *Chāndogyopaniṣad*, VII. 1. 2.
80. *Mbh.* Ādi, I, 62.
Ibid., Svargarohana, V, 41.
81. *Ibid.*, Ādi, I, 62.
82. *Ibid.*, I, 271-2.
83. *Ibid.*, I, 267-8.
84. *Ibid.*, II, 382. See also *Ibid.*, Svargarohana, V, 45.
85. *Ibid.*, Ādi, II, 333.
86. *Ibid.*, LXII, 53. The same śloka occurs in *Ibid.*, Svargarohana, V, 50. See also *Ibid.*, Ādi, I, 4-3.
87. *Ibid.*, II, 84-85. See also verses 86-87.
88. *Ibid.*, I, 269-71. See also verses 94-98 of the *Mahābhārata Sravansvidhi.*
89. Sukthankar: *On the Meaning of the Mahābhārata*, p. 32.

Winternitz it is "in a certain sense, not one poetic production at all, but rather a whole literature."[90] A. Macdonell calls it an "encyclopaedia of moral teaching."[91] R.C. Datta describes it as "an encyclopaedia of the life and knowledge of ancient India"[92] and says, "No single work except the Bible has such influence in affording moral instructions in Christian lands as the *Mahābhārata* and the *Rāmāyaṇa* in India."[93] In the words of K.M. Munshi "it is a whole literature in itself, containing a code of life, a philosophy of social and ethical relations and speculative thought on human problems that is hard to rival. . . ."[94] According to C. Rajagopalachari it is "a veritable ocean, containing countless pearls and gems. It is with the *Rāmāyaṇa*, a living fountain of ethics and culture of our motherland."[95] P.C. Ray describes it as "pre-eminently the encyclopaedia of the heroic age of the Hindus . . . interspersed with weighty discourses, reflecting every system of philosophical opinion. All that is contained in the Upaniṣads, all that occurs in the innumerable treatises bearing upon the several professed systems of Hindu Philosophy, all shades of opinion on every controverted topic of religion, morals and duty may be found in some shape or other in those discourses."[96]

The *Mahābhārata* is equally valuable from the point of view of politics, because herein we get for the first time a comprehensive account of ancient Indian political thought, the highest watermark being reached in the Śānti Parva, the Rājadharmānuśāsana chapters of which presents a synthetic and systematic view of the political thought of ancient Indians.

90. *A History of Indian Literature*, Vol. I, p. 316.

91. *A History of Sanskrit Literature*, (London, 1928), p. 282.

92. *The Rāmāyaṇa and the Mahābhārata*, p. 332.

93. *Ibid.*, p. 33.

94. General Editor's Preface in A.D. Pusalkar's *Studies in the Epics and Purāṇas of India*, pp. vi-viii.

95. *Mahābhārata*, p. 3.

96. *Mbh.* Trans. Śānti Parva (1890), Notice, pp. 2-3.

Contents of the Mahābhārata

The *Mahābhārata* is divided into eighteen Parvas (books), namely the Ādi, the Sabhā, the Vana, the Virāta, the Udyoga, the Bhiṣma, the Droṇa, the Karṇa, the Śalya, the Sauptika, the Strī, the Śānti, the Anuśāsana, the Aśvamedhika, the Āśramavāsika, the Mausala, the Mahāprasthānika and the Svargarohana. These Parvas have been named after some important incidents of the main narrative of the Epic, which is connected with the Kuru dynasty and may be summarised as follows :

The first two Parvas, the Ādi and the Sabhā, inform us that Vicitravīrya, the king of Hastinapur having died, Vyāsa begot two sons with his two wives in accordance with the custom of Niyoga (levirate). The elder son Dhṛtarāṣṭra was blind from birth and hence, was passed over in favour of his younger brother Pāṇḍu, who assumed the reins of government. The former had a hundred sons, called the Kauravas, with Duryodhana as the eldest and the latter was the father of five sons, known as the Pāṇḍavas, with Yudhiṣṭhira as the eldest. At the time of the death of Pāṇḍu, Yudhiṣṭhira, the eldest, of the hundred and five cousin brothers (100 Kauravas and 5 Pāṇḍavas) was minor. Hence the sceptre temporarily went to the blind Dhṛtarāṣṭra. Reaching maturity Yudhiṣṭhira wanted to become the king, but Duryodhana would not allow him to do so. Because of his earnest desire to rule and his jealousy towards the Pāṇḍavas, Duryodhana tried his best to destroy them. They were pursuaded to go to Varanavata and to stay in the lac house (Lāksāgṛha) built with a view to be set on fire when the Pāṇḍavas, along with Kuntī, were sleeping inside so that the Pāṇḍavas would meet their end. With the help of Vidura, Yudhiṣṭhira came to know of this fraudulent plan of Duryodhana. One night when a woman and her five sons were sleeping inside the Lāksāgṛha the Pāṇḍavas set it on fire and fled to a forest through a subterranean passage, which was attached to the Lāksāgṛha and was specially built for this purpose. Duryodhana, however, became very happy at the supposed death of the Pāṇḍavas.

After some time the Pāṇḍavas heard of the Svaymvara of Draupadī and went to attend it. Arjuna fulfilled the condition made for marrying Draupadī, the daughter of Drupada, the king of Pañcala. Forced to enter the polyandrous marriage, the Pāṇḍavas married her. With the aid and backing of Drupada, their father-in-law, the Pāṇḍavas claimed the throne. This resulted in the partitioning of the kingdom. Exceedingly jealous of the growing popularity and prosperity of the Pāṇḍavas, Duryodhana devised another treacherous plan to ruin them. He invited Yudhiṣṭhira to play the game of dice with Sakuni, who was an expert in this game The latter won all the throws and ultimately, the former was deprived of his kingdom, other possessions and even his four brothers and wife, who was insulted by the winners. Dhṛtarāṣṭra, however, pacified Draupadī and asked her to wish for something. Draupadī demanded the release of her husband. Her wish was granted. Dhṛtarāṣṭra returned to Yudhiṣṭhira his lost kingdom and the Pāṇḍavas, accompanied by Draupadī, proceeded towards their capital, Indraprastha.

After the departure of the Pāṇḍavas, Duryodhana and his well-wishers pursuaded Dhṛtarāṣṭra to invite Yudhiṣṭhira to play the game of dice for a second time. This was done and Yudhiṣṭhira came back to Hastinapura. Before the beginning of the game, it was said that the defeated party would live in the forest for twelve years and would spend the thirteen year incognito (ajñātavāsa). This time also, Yudhiṣṭhira was the loser and hence he went to the forest along with Draupadī and his four brothers.

The Vana Parva describes their life in different forests. It contains discourses of Dhaumya, Mārkaṇḍeya, Lomaśa and Arstisena to Yudhiṣṭhira, and many discussions on the moral virtues. Two famous episodes, the Malopākhyāna and the Ramopākhyāna, occur in this Parva.

The Virāta Parva tells us about the Ajñātavāsa (exile incognito) of the Pāṇḍavas and Draupadī in the kingdom of king Virāta. It informs us that Yudhiṣṭhira disguised himself as the companion and counsellor of Virāta. Bhīma as a cook, Arjuna as a dance-master, Nakula as a horse-tamer, Sahadeva as an overseer of cattle and Draupadī as a sairandhri (the chambermaid) of the queen of Virāta.

From the Udyoga Parva we come to know that after the expiry of the thirteen years of banishment, Yudhiṣṭhira once more claimed the kingdom, but Duryodhana refused to give even an inch thereof to him. All attempts at negotiations proved futile and ultimately war was declared. Both the parties, that of the Kauravas and that of the Pāṇḍavas, began making preparations for the war.

The next four Parvas, namely, the Bhīṣma, the Droṇa, the Karṇa and the Śalya have been devoted to a detailed description of the sanguinary war of Kurukṣetra, which resulted in the entire annihilation of the Kaurava host with the exception of three survivors, namely, Aśvatthāmā, Kṛpācārya and Kṛtavarmā.

The Strī Parva has been devoted to the vilāpa (lament) of the ladies, who lost their near and dear ones in the war of Kurukṣetra, This is followed by a description of the performance of the funeral rites, viz. dāha and śrāddha of the deceased warriors.

Then comes the Śānti Parva, which comprises a sixth part of the total extent of the *Mahābhārata* and which is divided into three sections, namely, Rājadharmānuśāsana, Mokṣadharma and Āpaddharma. The first of these deals with politics, the second with ethics, and the third with Dharma in times of distress.

The Anuśāsana Parva is concerned mainly with ethical problems.

The Aśvamedhika Parva describes the performance of the Aśwamedha Yajña (horse-sacrifice) by Yudhiṣṭhira.

The Āśramavāsika Parva deals with Dhṛtarāṣṭra's departure to the forest as a hermit.

The Mausala Parva gives an account of the destruction of the Yadavas with the Musala (pestle) in accordance with the curse of Vālmīki.

The Mahāprasthānika Parva informs us that after ruling for thirty-six years, Yudhiṣṭhira entrusted the charge of his kingdom to Parīkṣita, the grandson of Arjuna, and proceeded to heaven in the company of his four brothers, wife and a dog (Dharmarāja in disguise).

As is indicated by its name Svargarohana, the eighteenth and the last Parva, describes the attainment of Svarga (heaven) by the leading characters of the *Mahābhārata* the Great Epic of India.

Besides this main narrative, the *Mahābhārata* contains many episodes, dialogues and discourses, which in fact make it a mine of information all the more. Taken together they are highly valuable for getting an insight into the different phases of India's ancient culture.

2

Dharma

Ancient Indian thinkers did not mark off the sphere of law, religion and ethics. In the *Mahābhārata* the same tendency is noticeable. In spite of this, there are many discussions about the rules of moral conduct and their applicability to the various stations in life, in the *Mahābhārata* and in ancient Indian literature. In conformity with the tendency of the ancient Indian thinkers of not dealing with ethics as a separate branch of knowledge, the ancient Indian literature lacks a precise and specific terminology for ethics. The following words, used in the *Mahābhārata* can, however, be interpreted to denote what we call ethics today. We have already seen above that these words have been used generally for politics in the *Mahābhārata* and other ancient works.[1] They have been used in the sense of ethics also. Vidura-niti, i.e. the ethical discourses of Vidura, is an example of its latter meaning.

Ācāra or Sadācāra means good conduct, which is the concern of ethics. Hence these words too can be taken to stand for ethics. According to the *Mahābhārata* Ācāra is a

1. Vide Supra, Chap. II, *Conception of Dandaniti*, pp. 43-5.

characteristic or sign of Dharma.[2] It is also the foundation of the latter.[3] According to the Udyoga Parva, Dharma results from Ācāra.[4] This view leads us to follow that in the *Mahābhārata* Dharma and Ācara are deemed to be mutually complementary and interdependent. Hence, Ācāra or Sadācāra also can be taken in the sense of ethics. Manu goes to the extent of identifying the two.[5]

Dharma: Dharma is a word with a very comprehensive import. It can be traced back to the Vedic literature, wherein it denotes law and custom.[6] In the *Mahābhārata* it has been used in different senses. When it is said that a particular person should do a particular act because it is his Dharma, the word means duty. Raja dharma (duties of the rulers), Praja dharma (duties of the subjects) and Mittra dharma (duties of a friend) are examples of this use of the term. It stands for the code of conduct in the case of Desi dharma, Kula dharma, Jati dharma, Varna dharma and Āsrama dharma. It denotes virtue and righteousness when used with reference to the Trvarga. Whatever be the meaning of the term in a particular context, it always imposes within limitations of the term in a particular context, it always imposes within limitations of human conduct. Ethics does the same thing. We can, therefore, conclude that in the *Mahābhārata* ethics has been given the name of Dharma as pointed out by Sukthankar, it has, at its basis, a "belief in the conservation of moral values"[7] and it "presupposes an eternal moral order."[8] Hence, says the Epic, "that is Dharma which maintains (order in) the Society."[9]

2. *Mbh.* Anuśāsana, CIV. 9.
3. *Ibid.*, Śānti, CIIX, 6; *Ibid.*, Udyoga, CXI, 15.
4. *Ibid.*, Śānti, C, 2.
5. Manu, I, 108 and 1:0.
6. *Ṛg Veda*, I, 22, 18; 164, 43, 50; III, 3, I, 17, I, 60, 6; V. 26, 6; 63, 7, 72, 2.
7. Sukthankar, *On the Meaning of the Mahābhārata*, p. 80.
8. *Ibid.*
9. *Mbh.* Karṇa, LXIX, 58.

There is no word in English language which conveys exactly the same sense as the word Dharma. Due to its untranslatability and comprehensive import, it has been interpreted by various modern scholars. Some of the views are being quoted below.

Giving an ethical interpretation of Dharma, B.G. Tilak says that it implies the "path leading to next-worldly happiness. Ethics may be given the name of Dharma.[9a] E.W. Hopkins says that it means "ethical Good Usage" and "implies in itself a code of conduct to avoid all crimes, murder, adultery, theft etc. to avoid no less spiritual sins, arrogance, envy, jealousy and so on to avoid all injury to others."[10] In the words of J.S. Mekenzie "the term Dharma covers not only conduct but the whole conglomeration of forms of conduct that were settled or established.[10a]

Dr. Bhagawan Das thinks it to be an ethico-religious conception and says that it includes "religious rites, piety, specific property, function etc. but above all the Duty, incumbent on a man in the situation he may be in."[11] He further says that "Dharma is characteristic property, scientifically; duty morally and legally; religion with all its implications psycho-physically and spiritually and righteousness and law generally, but duty above all."[12] According to A.K. Sen, it implies "an admixture of socio-ethical religious ideas, not a purely religious concept."[13] Radhakrishnan opines that:

> "Dharma is the stable condition, which is capable of giving perfect satisfaction to man and/or helping him in the attainment of happiness and salvation. Its end, according to him, is the welfare of all creation."[14]

9a. Sukthankara, B.S. (trans.), *Sri Bhagavadgita Rahasya*, Vol. I, p. 88.

10. Hopkins, E.W., *Ethics of India*, p. 92.

10a. Mekenzie, J.S., *Hindu Ethics*, p. 51.

11. *The Science of Social Organisation* (1910), 7.

12. *Ibid.*, pp. 49-50.

13. *Hindu Political Thought*, p. 4.

14. Radhakrishnan, S., *Indian Philosophy* (1929), pp. 505-6.

P.V. Kane interprets it as the "mode of life or a code of conduct."[15] To quote H.N. Sinha, "Dharma may bear the interpretation of customs and usage, both sacred and secular in society."[16] "Believing in the social interpretation of Dharma, J.J. Anjaria says that it stands for social law, duty, custom, religion or religious merit."[17] It is the "principle that holds together the whole universe, physical as well as moral. Hence, the word Dharma comes to mean firstly, the cosmic order and secondly, the law, governing human society."[18] To quote H.D. Bhattacharya, it is the "ideal in conduct towards which we must move in order to perfect ourselves spiritually."[19] Chandravarkar regards it as standing for "right thought, right word and right deed."[20] V. Raghavan remarks that the word has a comprehensive import. In his words:

> "The scope of the concept of Dharma is universal and comprehends even the personal habits of hygiene, details of courteous behaviour and moral endowments, duties of kings and the administration of justice and the seeking of summum bonum, spiritual realisation."[21]

To quote G.H. Mees, Dharma is the "fundamental motive force in the life of man as a social being."[22] It is the "underlying motive principle in the social evolution of humanity towards the manifestation and demonstration of the soul or in other words, of the basic oneness of Mankind."[23]It signified Vedic Ṛta, the ethical duty, virtue, good works, religious duty

15. *History of Dharma Śāstra*, Vol. II, p. 2.
16. *Sovereignty in Ancient India*, p. 27.
17. *Nature and Ground of Political Obligation ia the Hindu State*, p. 147.
18. *Ibid.*, p. 150.
19. The Meaning of Dharma, in the *Proceedings and Transactions of the Ninth All India Oriental Conference*, 1937, p. 653.
20. *A Manual of Hindu Ethics*, Introduction, p. viii.
21. *The Indian Heritage*, Introduction, p. xxxix.
22. *Dharma and Society*, Preface, p. xii.
23. *Ibid.*, p. 22.

and justice, the ideal, the God or the Absolute truth. Divine Justice, convention, a code of customs and traditions, common law, international or inter-tribal law and a compromise between the actual and the ideal condition."[24] B.K. Sarkar, however, explains it as "law, justice, duty, culture and what not."[25]

These quotations are enough to give us an idea of the comprehensive import of the word Dharma, on account of which it is well nigh untranslatable. Hence, to avoid confusion, we have used the word Dharma itself in whole of our work. To run any human activity smoothly, discipline and certain rules to guide that discipline, are necessary. The conception of Dharma meets this fundamental requirement in the Vedas, there is ample and adequate evidence to prove the existence of general ethical conceptions and an accepted standard of morality."[26] The *Mahābhārata* does the same thing. It recognizes the need of self-discipline in the formation of character.

Hence, it prescribes the observance of certain moral virtues, we will discuss them a little later in this chapter.

Classification of Dharma

A study of our Ancient Dharmaśāstric literature shows that the Ancient Indians classified Dharma in more than one way. Thus, on the basis of its sources,[27] it has been classified under the heads of Srauta, i.e., Vedic and Samṛta, i.e., Dharma based on Smṛtis and Sistācarana or the conduct of the noble men (nobleman).[28] In the *Mahābhārata* the classification of

24. *Ibid.*, p. 8.
25. Theory of Constitution in Hindu Political Philosophy, *Sir Asutosh Mukherjee Silver Jubilee*, Pt. II, p. 502.
26. *Ṛgveda*, X, 71; *Ibid.*, VII, 104, 12; *Ibid.*, VI, 28, 2.
27. *Mbh.* Vana, CCVII, 83; *Ibid.* Anuśāsana, C-XLI, 65. *Ibid.*, Śānti, CCC.LIII, 6. *Ibid.*, Anuśāsana, CLXII, 18. *Ibid.*, Vana, CCCXII, 117. *Manu*, II, 689. *Ibid.* II, 12, *Sukra*, III,38.
28. *Mahābhārata*, Śānti, CIX, 13.
Baudhayana Dharmasūtra, I, 1, 1-4.
Matsya Purana, 145-80-1. See also *Vayu Purana*, 59, 31-2 and 39; *Vasistha*, I, 4-5.

Dharma is three fold namely Desa-dharma (dharma for a particular country or place), Jati-dharma (dharma for a particular caste or class) and Kula-dharma (dharma or the Tradition belonging to one's own family).[29]

Another and a more comprehensive classification of Dharma is given by Mitāksara in his commentary on Yājñavalkya Smṛti. To him, Dharma is six fold and consists of Varna-Dharma (dharma for the different varnas), Āsrama-Dharma (dharma for the different āsrama), Varnāsrama Dharma (dharma of the different Varnas and Āsramas), Guna-Dharma (dharma for particular office), Nimitta-Dharma (occasional and expiatory dharma) and Sādhārana Dharma (universal dharma).[30]

It is obvious from the above mentioned account that according to the ancient Dharmaśāstra writers, the moral standard varies in accordance with the circumstances, place and time; social status, Varna, āsrama of the individual or of the group. Dharma, as conceived by them can be classified under the following heads:

1. Sādhārana Dharma or Nitya Dharma, i.e., the universal code of morality.
2. Visista Dharma, i.e. specific moral code.
   - (i) Varna Dharma i.e., the code of conduct for the different varnas.
   - (ii) Āsrama Dharma, i.e. the code of conduct for different āsramas.
3. Guna Dharma, the code meant for a particular office or circumstances.
4. Naimittika Dharma, i.e., occasional duties.
5. Āpad Dharma, i.e., code for the times of distress, and
6. Yuga Dharma, i.e., Code for the different ages.

29. *Mbh.* Śānti, LIV, 20. See also *ibid.* Bhīsma, III, 55.
30. Mitaksara on Yājñavalkya, (Ed. S.S. Setlur, Madras, 1912).

Sādhārana Dharma: The Sādhārana Dharma or the Nitya Dharma means the moral code, prescribed for all alike, i.e., the moral code, common to all humanity. This universal code consists of the moral virtues, to be observed by everybody, to whatever caste or creed, he or she may belong.

The *Mahābhārata* with its ethical back-ground has discourses on the moral virtues scattered throughout its whole body. The value of these qualities is recognised and emphasized by all religions. Some important moral virtues are given below:

Satya: Truthfulness is one of the fundamental essentials of moral life, as pictured in the *Mahābhārata*. According to it, Satya is the highest duty and there is nothing higher than this.[31] The *Mahābhārata* seems to give a metaphysical meaning of Satya and to identify it with Sat (reality) by saying that it is at the basis of everything.[32] It leads to prosperity, ultimately.[33] Its importance lies in the belief that it purifies the heart.[34] Hence one should win over untruth by truth.[35] In the Śānti Parva, Bhṛgu gives in detail, the merits of Satya and condemns asatya,[35a] side by side with this emphasis on Satya, the *Mahābhārata* mentions such occasions also, when untruth is to be given preference over truth. Thus one is allowed to speak a lie, where truth assumes the aspect of falsehood. The truth dissociated from righteousness is to be avoided.[36] Resort to falsehood is allowed when one's life is in risk, or on the occasion of marriage, or for the protection of wealth for the cause of Dharma, or when wealth has been taken away, or with ladies or for the sake of the preceptor.[37] Gautama allows

31. *Mbh.* Ādi Parva, LXXIV, 105; *Ibid.* Śānti, CIX, 4; *Ibid.* CCCXLII, 18. See also *ibid.* Vana, XXXIV, 22.
32. *Ibid.*, Śānti, CCLIX, 10; *Ibid.* CXCIX, 65.
33. *Mbh.* Śānti Parva, CXCIX, 70. See also *Ibid.* CIX, 1ff. *Ibid.* CXCIX, 64-70.
34. *Manu*, V, 109.
35. *Mbh.* Vana, CXCIV, 6.

35a. *Ibid.*, Śānti, CXC,1-5.

36. *Ibid.*, CIX, 5-8: *Manu*, IV, 138.
37. *Mbh.* Śānti Parva, C(XV, 30; *Ibid.* Ādi. LXXXII, 16-17; *Ibid.* Śānti, CIX, 19-20.

falsehood for the sake of saving a good man's life and prohibits employment for the sake of a wicked person.[38] In his opinion an infant, old man, idiot, intoxicated, insane, angry and frightened persons are not associated with sin even if they speak a lie.[39] To be brief, truth under all circumstances is preferable to falsehood, but it is permissible to indulge in falsehood for the sake of some important ends.

Ahimsa: Ahimsa, as understood by the ancient Indians, meant the practice of love, which consisted to not hurting others by thought, word or act (Mansa, Vācā and Karmana), having good feelings for others also come under its connotation. The *Mahābhārata* emphasizes it at several places.[40] According to Kautilya, Non-violence is a characteristic (Laksana) of Dharma.[41]

Brahmacarya: The ancient Hindus explained Brahmacarya as discipline and the control over all the sense organs. They believed that by leading the life of celibacy, i.e., the life of self-discipline and continence, dedicated to higher pursuits, one overcomes all difficulties.[42] Hence, there is the importance of Brahmacarya.

Dama: Like all the religions and all ethical systems of the Indian Philosophy, the *Mahābhārata* emphasizes the importance of dama, i.e., restraint of the sense-organs. The importance of the *Bhagavad-gita*, a section of the *Mahābhārata* can hardly be exaggerated so far as this moral virtue is concerned, because it presents one of the best discussions thereon. The *Gita* believes in complete self-restraint. Lord Kṛṣṇa tells Arjuna that the sensory organs should be completely checked.[43] Even attachment towards their objects should be shunned. One, who controls his acts, yet continually

38. *Gautama*, XIII.
39. *Ibid*., V.
40. *Mbh.* Ādi, XI, 13; *Ibid.* Śānti CCLXII, 2. See Buch : *Principles of Hindu Ethics*, pp. 443-67.
41. *Arthaśāstra* : Cānakya-Pranita Sutram.
42. *Mbh.* Śānti, CX, 14.
43. *Mbh.* Bhisma XXVI, 14.

thinks of the sensory objects, is a hypocrite (mithyācāra) and one having control in every respect, deserves praise.[44] While describing the attributes of Sthita prajña and Gunatīta, the ideal man of the Gita, this moral quality has always been referred to.[45] One should draw in the sense-organs from their objects like a tortoise that draws in its limbs.[46] Vidura compares the human body with a chariot (ratha), Sattva (the living principle) with its charioteer, sensory organs with horses and buddhi with the reins. He says that one, who does not control these horses, i.e., sense-organs cannot be free from the bondage of birth and death.[46a] Thus, the *Mahābhārata* attaches great importance of dama.

Ksama: According to the *Mahābhārata* forgiveness, specially in the persons possessing power, is praiseworthy.[47] But at the same time the Epic says that before forgiving anyone, it should be borne in mind whether that person really deserves it or not, i.e., good man only should be forgiven and never are the wicked one.[48] Thus, the *Mahābhārata* vindicates forgiveness, accompanied by discrimination.

In the Vana Parva, Yudhihiṣṭra speaks very highly of Ksama. According to him, everybody should have this virtue because victory favours him, who is possessed of Ksama. Referring to the view of Ksyapa he says:

> "Forgiveness is Dharma, sacrifice (Yajña), the Vedas, knowledge the Brahman, truth (Satya), penance (tapas) and purity (Sauca). The Universe is held together because of forgiveness. He is indeed a wise man, who forgives even those, who insult, rebuke and beat him. One possessed of Ksamā attains Brahman. He receives honour here and acquires a state of blessedness hereafter. Hence, it is the highest virtue."[49]

44. *Ibid.*, XXVII, 6-7.
45. *Ibid.*, XXVI, 55, 58-61; *Ibid.* XXXVIII, 25.
46. *Ibid.*, XXVI, 58. See also *ibid.* Śānti, CCXX, 2-17.
46a. *Ibid.* Stri, VII, 13-4. Cf. *Kathopanisad*, I, III, 3.
47. *Mbh.* Śānti, CXI, 68.
48. *Ibid.*, CII, 29
49. *Ibid.*, Vana, XXIX, 13-4, 31-3, 36-44.

Regard for mother, father and preceptor: The worship of, and regard for mother, father and preceptor has been regarded as the most important duty of everyone. By disregarding these persons one is called the greatest sinner.[50] Their worship, it is believed, helps one in gaining fame here, and the desired lokas, hereafter.[51] These three should not be killed even if they be harmful.[52] The *Mahābhārata* is in favour of respecting all the elders, because by insulting their elders even very powerful kings are ruined.[53] That the *Mahābhārata* attaches great importance to the respect of elders is evidenced also from the fact that two whole chapters are devoted to this topic.[54]

Śīla: According to the *Mahābhārata* one should possess the constituents of good behaviour (Śīla), which consists of absentention from animosity (adroha) in thought, word and deed, compassion (anugraha) and donation (dāna).[55] The importance of Śīla lies in the belief that Dharma, Satya (truth) and vṛtta (conduct) are dependent upon it.[56] This is illustrated in the legend of Prahlada, who was deprived of all the moral virtues, because he gave way his Śīla to Indra in the disguise of a Brāhmana.[57] Dhṛtarāṭṣra stresses the importance of Śīla for becoming successful in life.[58] Bhartṛhari holds it in a very high esteem by describing it as the best ornament.[59]

Madhura Vacana: The *Māhabhārata* says that one should always speak agreeable speech, because it helps one to be respectable. It lays down that even while making a gift, one

50. *Ibid.*, CVIII, 30.
51. *Ibid.* CVIII, 3; *Ibid.* III, 28.
52. *Mbh.* Śānti, CVIII, 20.
53. *Ibid.*, XXII, 24.
54. *Mbh.* Śānti, Chap. CVIII; *Ibid.* Anuśāsana, Chap. XXXI.
55 *Ibid.*, Śānti, CXXIV, 66.
56 *Ibid.*, CXXIV, 62.
57. Vide *ibid.* Chap. CXXIV.
58. *Ibid.* CXXIV, 15-6.
59. *Nitīsataka*, 83.

should utter sweet words. The fact that one complete chapter[60] has been devoted to it, shows clearly the importance, attached to it.

Saranāgata-raksā: The *Mahābhārata* speaks highly of this moral virtue. The kings as well as commoners have been equally and repeatedly asked to help and protect the suppliants. The householders are specially asked to do so.[61] Its importance was due to the belief that by its non-observance one could not attain salvation.[62] Transgressing it was supposed to associate kings and princes with a great sin like embryocide[63] whereas giving shelter to frightened person even for a moment, led to heaven.[64] Hence the suppliants should always be protected.[65] The story of Sibi attracts our attraction in this connection. Sibi cut away flesh from his body, but did not set free the pigeon that had come to the king for shelter. Sibi did so, because he had firmly promised to cherish the suppliants.[66] Due to this virtue, we are informed by the *Mahābhārata*, Sibi attained the Great Good (Samsiddhi).[67] The Epic attaches so much importance to it that it goes to the extent of saying that one should be hospitable even towards an enemy if the latter or later asks for shelter. To illustrate this, the *Mahabharata* gives the story of a hunter and a pair of pigeons.[68]

Atithī-Sevā: Atithīpuja (regard for a guest) being one of the Panca Maḥayajñas (five great sacrifices), the *Mahābhārata* lays down that it is a sacred duty of everyone.[69] It attaches so much importance to it that it goes to the extent of

60. *Mbh.* Śānti, Chap. LXXXIV.
61. *Ibid.*, CXLVI, 6.
62. *Ibid.*, CXLIX, 18.
63. *Mbh.* Śānti, CCCLX, 9.
64. *Ibid.*, LXXV, 34.
65. *Ibid.*, CXLIII, 2; *ibid.* Vana, CCXLIII, 6.
66. *Ibid.*, Anuśāsana, XXXII, 19.
67. *Ibid.* Śānti, CXLIII, 3.
68. *Ibid.*, Chaps. CXLIII ff.
69. *Ibid.* Anuśāsana, VII, 12; Cf. *Manu*, III, 106.

saying that even if an enemy happens to go to one's place, he should be received cordially and respected.[70]

Besides these moral virtues, the moral code of the *Mahābhārata* enjoins that one should practise Santosa (contentment)[71] and should live in the company of good man (Satsangati).[72] These moral virtues should be strictly observed, because they lead to salvation ultimately.[73]

The whole Epic being written with an ethical background, such slokas occur frequently in the work wherein it has been laid down that the above mentioned virtues should be followed and the vices should be avoided.

The slokas given in the footnote, clearly illustrate this point.[74]

The Gautama Dharmasūtra,[75] the Manu smṛti[76], the Arthaśāstra of Kautilya,[77] the Sukra Nītisāra[78] and the Bhāgavata Purāna[79] also mention these virtues. For a study of the moral virtues, the Durgātitarana adhyāya of the Śānti Parva[80] is of great importance. Therein Yudhiṣṭhira requests Bhīsma to enumerate the ways to overcome difficulties and adversities. In reply, Bhīsma refers to some moral virtues and says that those persons free themselves from difficulties and calamities (durgā) who are self-controlled (Samayatātmano), who do not indulge (extremely) in the objects of sense-organs (Visayān Nigṛhnanti), who are not proud (dambhaandcaranti), who are not jealous of other's prosperity, who accommodate and accord welcome to guests, who respect and follow their parents, who do not commit sins, who are attached to their

70. *Mbh.* Śānti, CXLVI.
71. *Mbh.* Santi, XXI, 2.
72. *Ibid.* Vana, I, 24-30; *Ibid.* Śānti, CLII, 2? ff.
73. *Ibid.*, Śānti, CCLXX, 39-40.
74. *Mbh.* Śānti, LX, 7-8.
75. *Gautama Dharmasūtra*, VIII, 20-21.
76. *Manu*, X, 63; *Ibid* VI, 92.
77. *Ibid.*, p. 10.
78. *Sukra*, III, 1 cf.
79. *Bhāgavata Purāna*, XI, 17, 21.
80. *Mbh.* Śānti, Chap. CX.

own wives, who indulge in sexual intercourse only for having children (and for the sake of enjoyment), who perform sacrifices, who speak truth, who shun anger, who avoid sweets, meat and wine, who speak sweet words, who do not do to others what is disagreeable to themselves, i.e., who treat others in the way they want themselves to be treated,[81] and in whom the Sattva Guna is prominent.

Viśista Dharma: Sādhārana Dharma, as we have already seen, was common to all, irrespective of caste and creed. Viśista Dharma, however, as is clear from the word Viśista itself, stood for the Dharma specifically laid down for different persons or groups of persons. It can be clarified under the heads of varna dharma (dharma of the different classes or castes) and Āsrama dharma (code for the different orders or stages of life).

Varna Dharma: Injunctions, based on the scheme of four varnas and laid down for the members of the different varnas come under the category of varna dharma.

The Hindu society consisted of four classes or castes, known as Varna, down from the Vedic times, as is evidenced by the Purusasūkta of the Ṛg Veda.[82] The four varnas are the Brāhmana, Ksatriya, Vaisya and Sūdra. The ancient Indian thinkers laid down specific and different codes for their conduct.

According to the *Bhagavadgītā* this is their inherently natural duty.[83] Besides, the moral virtues like truthfulness, control over the sense-organs, hospitality towards others and righteous conduct are prescribed for them.[84] The *Mahābhārata* enjoins that they should perform sacrifices, but without reciting the mantras.[85] These were in brief, the specific duties of the four Varnas.[86]

81. Cf. *Mbh*. Śānti, CCLIX, 20.
82. Ṛg Veda, X, 90, 12. Also *Mbh*. Santi, LXXII, 4-5, *Ibid.*, CCXCVI.
83. *Mbh*. Bhīsma, XLII, 44.
84. *Ibid*. Anuśāsana, CXLI, 57-9; *Ibid*, Śānti, CLXXXIX, 7.
85. *Ibid*. LX, 37; *Ibid*. Anuśāsana, XIV, *Ibid* Śānti, CLXXXIX.
86. See Kane : *History of Dharmaśāstra*, Vol. II, pp. 105-65.

The *Mahābhārata* emphatically says that one should do his ordained duties properly and sincerely, because it earns glory[87] and leads to heaven.[88] To illustrate the importance of observing Svadharma (one's own dharma) Ṛsi Markandeya narrates the story of the dutiful hunter (dharma-Vyādha) of Mithila, who discoursed on the principles of Dharma to a Brāhmana named Kausika. Therein the hunter says that glory can be earned by sticking to the code prescribed specifically for different varnas.[89] Maintaining the same opinion Kṛṣṇa saya in the *Bhagavatgītā*:

> "One's own dharma, even if defective is better than the dharma of others. Death while doing one's dharma is better than adopting the dharma of others."[90]

Manu also holds the same view. He says:

> "It is better that one should live by doing the vile works allotted to his own caste than embrace the vocation of superior caste for livelihood; livirg by adopting the vocation of another caste, one becomes degraded the very day."[91]

Āsrama Dharma: To the ancient Indian thinkers, man's life was "a kind of schooling or self-discipline."[92] They enumerated four stages thereof, known by the term, 'Āsrama'. The Hindu scheme of the four fold āsramas or the stages of life is a unique contribution to the thought of the ancient world. These four stages of life are:

87. *Mbh.* Vana, CCVIII, 39.
88. *Ibid.* Śānti CXCI, 6. cf. Arthaśāstra, 1.3.14.
89. *Mbh.* Vana, Chaps, CCVIIff.
90. *Ibid.* Bhīsma, XXVII, 35; *Ibid.* XLII 48. cf. *Ibid* Śānti, XXXII, 23.
91. *Manu*, X, 97.
92. P.N. Prabhu : *Hindu Social Organisation*, p. 78.

(i) Brahmacarya Āsrama;

(ii) Gṛhastha Āsrama;

(iii) Vanaprastha Āsrama; and

(iv) Sanyas Āsrama.[93]

They are connected with the Hindu conception of the four fold purusarthas or the goals of life, viz., Dharma, Kama and Moksa.[94] According to the *Mahābhārata*, the āsramas are ladders to reach the Brahma-Loka, the ultimate goal of life.[95] The proper observance of āsrama-dharma helps one to overcome all sorts of calamities and difficulties[96] and to attain salvation.[97] We shall now take up the code of conduct, specifically prescribed for the persons, belonging to different stages.

Order of these Āsramas: According to the *Mahābhārata* one should first of all undergo the duties of the Brahmacarya Āsrama, i.e., the state of studenthood, wherein self-discipline should be practised. Thereafter one should enter into the Grihasthāsrama, i.e., the stage wherein one should lead the life of a house-holder. Third was the Vānaprasthāsrama which enjoined living in a forest. The fourth and the last Āsrama, viz , Sanyas Āsrama or Bhaiksatvan was the life of complete renunciation.[98] This order was to be strictly followed, because if observed properly, it was supposed to produce good results.[99] Indra told the same thing to a group of young boys, who had become forest-dwellers.[100] A Brāhmana, however, could enter the Vānaprastha āsrama immediately after the Brahmacarya Āsrama, i.e., he was allowed to leave

93. *Mbh.* Śānti, LXI, 2.
94. Vide Mees : *Dharma and Society*, p. 27.
95. *Mbh.* Śānti, CCXLII, 15.
96. *Ibid* CX, 2.
97. *Ibid.*, Śānti Chap. CCLXX.
98. *Mbh.* Śānti, LXI, 3-4.
99. *Mbh.* Śānti, CX, 2.
100. Vide Supra, Chap. II.

behind the Grihastha Āsrama, if he was very anxious to do so.[101]

Guna Dharma: By Guna Dharma is implied the code, prescribed for a person by virtue of his holding a particular office. Rāja-dharma (code for the rulers) is an example of Guna Dharma, because it deals with the duties and rules of conduct, prescribed for the rulers only. According to the *Mahābhārata* a king, though he is vested with power and authority, should work within proper limits. He should be guided by dharma and should be well-versed in Niti. The very importance of a king lies in his capacity and functions of maintaining Dharma and not for furthering his own ambition (Kama) and selfish interests. A king who maintains Dharma is taken as a God (deva) and he who follows the path of Adharma is sure to go to hell. He is to wield the rod of chastisement and to exert actively with a view to preserve the fundamental principles of social morality. Rājadharma, as presbribed in the *Mahābhārata* shows that all the problems connected with the State have been included therein and a high political morality is prescribed.[102]

Naimittika Dharma: Naimittika Dharma implied the duties, to be done with a special purpose, such as the expiatory rites, to be performed after behaving in some prohibited way. The *Mahābhārata* gives a very long list of the acts, after doing which one becomes liable to adopt the expiatory methods. The list consists of the following not doing the prescribed acts, doing the prohibited acts, behaving deceitfully, against the precepts, laid down in the Dharmaśāstras, non-observance of the Varnāsrama Dharma, i.e., code specifically prescribed for the different Varnas, and Āsrama, falling from a vow, abandoning the sacred fire, slaying the preceptor or a woman, opposing the preceptor and setting fire to a dwelling house.[103]

The Epic gives a list of the expiatory rites, some of which are begging alms, practising penance and religious rites,

101. *Mbh.* Śānti, LXI, 7.

102. See supra, *Monarchy and Morals*, pp. 192ff.

103. *Mbh.* Śānti. Chap. XXXIV.

subsisting upon only one mean, becoming a Brahmacārin, sleeping on bare ground, walking long distances, reciting the Vedas, observing hard vows and fasts and performing the sacrifices.[104] The view of Manu on the prohibited acts and the expiatory rites also have been given in the *Mahābhārata*.[105]

Āpaddharma: The moral code of the *Mahābhārata* does not recognise a universal standard. The standard varies with different persons, places, circumstances and other factors. The code of behaviour, prescribed for times of danger differs from that of the ordinary peaceful times and has been styled as Āpaddharma.[106] According to the *Mahābhārata* the abnormal times have an ethics of their own, and of dangerous circumsstances, social and political morality and customs can be suspended. The members of a Varna can adopt the duties and functions of another,[107] for instance, Brāhmanas as well as other Varnas can take up arms and fight.[108]

The political behaviour of such times was also different for example the rates of taxation could be raised and even some extra-taxes could be imposed. Even the Brâhmanas were not to be exempted from being taxed.[109] When war was going on, the victorious side was to follow the ethics of war, but for the defeated party it was the āpattikāta and the Āpaddharma and it permitted the suspension of the rules of morality. Thus in the times of distress, self-preservation became the highest law and justified all means.

Bhīsma on the basis of experience and practice told Yudhiṣṭhira that one should not always stick to the letters or scriptures. It was possible to imagine circumstances of the fall of man and in such time extra-ordinary maxims had to be applied to the conduct of affairs. Needless to say that the

104. *Mbh.* Śānti, Chap. XXXV.
105. *Ibid.* Chap. XXXVI.
106. See Infra, Chap. X. Āpaddharma, pp. ff.
107. *Mbh.* Śānti, LXXVIII, 2.
108. *Ibid.*, LXXVIII, 34.
109. *Ibid* , LXXVI, 5.

moral standard of the Āpaddharma is different from that of the Sāmānya or Sādhāran Dharma.

Yuga Dharma: Ancient Indian thinkers believed in the existence of four ages, viz., Satya Yuga or Kṛta Yuga, Tretā Yuga, Dvāpara Yuga and Kali Yuga.

The moral code varied in accordance with the Yuga. In the Śānti Parva, Bhīsma tells Yudhiṣṭhira, "of one kind is the Dharma in the Kṛta age, different is it in the Tretā age. Of one kind is it in the Dvāpara age and different is it in the Kali age. Dharma, in the different Yugas, is laid down according to the powers of human beings in the respective ages."[110] Manu holds the same view.[111] In the Vāna Parva Hanumāna describes the respective duties, to be done in the four ages.[112]

The End of Ethics: Besides social, moral and religious development, ethics, as conceived in the *Mahābhārata*, aims at salvation, which consists in the purification and uplift of the individual soul for realising its true nature as the essence of the Universal Soul variously known as the Brāhman, Isvara, Parmātmā or the Absolute. The goal of liberation is the Absolute in which the liberated souls merge. Thus, according to the *Mahābhārata* a super-moral state is variously described as Gunatitava.[113]

Yagatva,[114] Sthitaprajñatva,[115] Moksa or Mukti[116] is the ultimate goal of human life. At some places, it regards the attainment of heaven (Svarga-prāpti) as the final goal of human life and as the end of Ethics. According to Kanāda, it is Dharma, which leads to worldly prosperity as well as emancipation.[117] The same is the view of Somdeva Sūri also.[118]

110. *Mbh.* Santi, CCLX, 8.
111. *Manu*, I, 85.
112. *Mbh.* Vana, Chap. CXLIX.
113. *Ibid.*, Bhīsma, XXXVIII, 25.
114. *Ibid.*, XXX, 3-32.
115. *Ibid* , XXVI, 54-71.
116. *Ibid.*, LXIX, 28.
117. Kane, *Vaisesika Sūtra*, Vol. I, p. 3.
118. *Nitivakyamṛta* 1.1.

The *Mahābhārata* repeatedly says that one can realise the ultimate goal by following the above mentioned moral code, by properly performing one's ordained duties without thinking of, and caring for, the fruits derived therefrom. It advocates renunciation in action and not the renunciation of action. This is known as Niskāma Karma or as Asanga Karma (detached actions),[119] and is the bedrock of Ethics, as conceived in the *Mahābhārata*.[120]

Like the Ethics of the *Mahābhārata* the ethical systems of the different schools of Indian Philosophy also have the same end and they lay a similar emphasis on ethical discipline for the realisation of this ultimate goal. The Yoga system of Fātanjali, which regards human body as the instrument (of the expression of spiritual life), prescribes the eightfold path, consisting of Yama, Niyama, Āsana, Nididhyāsana, Pratyāhāra, Dharanā, Dhyāna, and Samādhi.[121] According to Kapila the founder of Sānkhya Philosophy, one should shun and avoid the vices like asmitā (egoism), rāga (attachment), dvesa (contempt) and abhinivesa (fear). By doing so and by having a correct knowledge of the relation between Purusa and Prakṛti, one attains Moksa.[122]

According to Knāda righteousness and virtuous activities are important in as much as the help one have the true knowledge, which make it possible for one to distinguish between soul, body and senses.[123] The Vaisesikas believe that the realisation of emancipation is possible by having a selfless insight into truth of things and after realising that all souls are alike.[124]

In the Jain Philosophy also the moral virtues like non-violence, charity, truth, hospitable conduct, non-stealing and renunciation of worldly interests have been laid down and

119. *Mbh.* Bhisma, XXVI, 47-8.
120. Hiriyanna, M., *Outlines of Indian Philosophy*, p. 125.
121. Radhakrishnan, S., *Indian Philosophy*, Vol. II, pp. 352.
122. Radhakrishnan, *op. cit.*, Vol. II, p. 307. Hiriyanna, *op. cit.*, p. 267.
123. Radhakrishnan, *op. cit.*, Vol. II, p. 161.
124. *Ibid.*, p. 222.

it is said that their observance leads to Nirvana, the final deliverance.[125] The importance of ethical discipline has been recognised in the Buddhist school of Indian Philosophy also. It lays down an eight-fold path consisting of Sammaditthi (Samyak dṛṣṭi), Sammasamkappa (Samyak Samkalpa), Sammāvāca (Samyakvak), Sammā Kammānta (Samyak Karmanta), Sammā ājīva (Samyagajiva,Samma Vyayama, Samyak Vyayam) Sammā Sati (Samyak Smṛti) and Sammā Samādhi (Samyak Samadhi). It further says that one should keep one's mind free from attachment (Raga) and hatred (dvesa) while doing some action.[126]

The primary end of ethics as conceived in the *Mahābhārata* and the different schools of Indian Philosophy is salvation, which means freedom from the bondage of birth and death and its secondary aim is the worldly prosperity.

We shall now deal with the responsibility of the State towards social morality. In the *Mahābhārata* the establishment of Dharma has been proclaimed to be an important function of the State. The Epic goes to the extent of saying that it was for the cause of Dharma that sovereignty existed.[127] For the realisation of this function, the State was given the right of exercising Danda.

The king's great privilege was his power of punishment or, as the *Mahābhārata* calls it, Danda. Danda was regarded capable of restraining[128] the natural turbulence and depravity of man, which led them to violate different rules and regulations. It was Danda which made them follow Dharma.[129] In its absence, chaos prevailed[130] and people did not do their duties.[131]

125. *Ibid.*, Vol. I, p. 325.
126. *Ibid.*, Vol. I.
127. *Mbh.* Śānti, XC, 3.
128. *Mbh.* Śānti, CXXI, 56.
129. *Ibid.* CXXI, 36.
130. *Ibid.*, Ādi, XLI, 27-31.
131. *Ibid.*, Śānti, XV, 41-5. See also, *Ibid.* CXXI, 37-9.

To Manu people become righteous, only due to the fear of Danda[132], in its absence vices creep in.[133] Hence, Danda is Dharma.[134] In the opinion of Sukra, Danda means the absence of bad conduct and Danda is the means, which makes people restrained.[135] Not to speak of men, even gods stick to Dharma, due to the fear of Danda.[136] Kāmandaka also feels the necessity of Danda for the establishment of Dharma.[137] Since Danda played such an important part in the enforcement of Dharma, the king had been given the right of exercising Danda for the cause of morality.[138] It was the duty of a king to punish the wicked and the unrighteous people,[139] and to establish Dharma thereby. If he daes not punish such persons, he earns infamy (ayasa) and goes to hell.[140] Put briefly, it was the responsibility of the State to enforce and establish Dharma.

The *Mahābhārata* does not believe in the universality or uniformity of moral standard, which according to it, varies in conformity with the changes of time, place, circumstances and other factors [141] According to it every situation carries its own morals. Abnormal circumstances justify resort to abnormal expedients. The code of conduct, prescribed for times of distress (Āpattikāla) has been styled Āpaddharma in the *Mahābharata*. In clearcut terms, Bhīsma tells Yudhiṣṭhira that the duties of those men, who are able and competent (i.e. who are under ordinary circumstances) are different from those, who have fallen in distress.[142] This is quite in the fitness of things, because what is true of a healthy man is not

132. *Manu*, VII, 22.
133. *Ibid.*, VII, 24.
134. *Ibid.*, VII, 18.
135. *Sukra*, IV, 40. See also *Ibid.* I, 156.
136. *Sukra*, I, 23, 25.
137. *Kamandaka*, II, 41-3.
138. *Sukra*. I, 60. See also *Arthaśāstra*, 3, 54.
139. *Mbh.* Śānti, CXXI, 8.
140. *Manu*, VIII, 128.
141. Supra, *Conception of Ethics*, pp. 145-6.
142. *Mbh.* Śānti, CXXX, 14.

true of a patient. In the same way what is true of a man in famine is not true of a man in a good season. In accordance with place and time Adharma becomes Dharma and vice-versa.[143] A staunch supporter of the changing morality, the Epic advises one to neglect Svadharma and adopt others' professions, if unable to maintain oneself by the former. Hence it condemns that person, who does not follow svadharma in ordinary times as well as that person, who sticks to svadharma even in times of distress.[144] It lacks consistency as regards the place of Dharma under abnormal circumstances. At some places it says that one is not censured by taking recourse to the otherwise prohibited deeds[145] and at others it lays down that the prohibited (nindita) acts should not be done.[146] According to it that person, who follows Dharma even in the āpattikala is the foremost among those, who are conversant with Dharma.[147] These contradictory statements can be reconciled by saying that although the *Mahābhārata* prescribes a different moral standard for the season (time) of distress, yet it says that one should violate Dharma only as the last resort.

Āpaddharma for different Varnas

As it strongly upholds the observance of Svadharma the *Mahābhārata* says that one should not give up the code of conduct, specifically prescribed for one's varna.[148] This injunction, however, was meant for ordinary times only. The Epic believes that abnormal times have their own ethics. It, therefore, permits alterations in the Varna Dharma under abnormal circumstances. In the Udyoga Parva, Yudhiṣṭhira says to Vidura:

143. *Ibid.*, LXXXVIII, 32.
144. *Ibid.*, Udyoga, XXVIII, 4.
145. *Ibid*, Śānti, CXXXII, 6.
146. *Ibid.*, Ādi, CLXL: 1. Cf. *Ibid.* XXXVII, 20.
147. *Ibid.* CLIV, 14.
148. See Supra, *op. cit.*, p. 132.

"Virtue and vice, which are both eternal and absolute, exchange their aspects during seasons of distress. One should follow without deviation the duties prescribed for the order to which one (he?) belongs by birth. Know O Sanjaya, that duties in season of distress are otherwise. When his means of living are totally gone, the man, who (that?) is destitude should certainly desire those other means by which he may be able to discharge the sanctioned duties of his order. One that is not destitute of his means of living, as also one that is in distress, are, O Sanjaya, both to be blamed if they act as if the state of each were otherwise. When the creator hath ordained expiation for those Brāhmanas, who without wishing for self-destruction, betake themselves to acts not sanctioned for them, this proves that people may, in seasons of distress, betake to acts not ordained for the orders to which they belong. And O Sanjaya, thou shouldest regard as worthy those (them?) that censure to the practices of their own order in usual times as also those that do not adhere to them in seasons of distress, though thou shouldest censure them that act otherwise in usual times while adhering to their ordained practices during times of distress."[149]

Similar is the view of Bhīsma, who says:

"For one, afflicted, what can be an improper outlet? For a person immured (within a dungeon and seeking escape) what can be an improper path? When a person becomes inflicted, he escapes by even an improper path."[150]

For these reasons, the *Mahābhārata* and some other ancient Indian works say that the Varna Dharma can be relaxed under abnormal circumstances and hence, they allow the members

149. *Mbh.* Udyoga, XXVIII, 2-5.

150. *Ibid.*, Śānti, CXXX, 22.

of a Varna to adopt the professions of the other varnas, under extra-ordinary circumstances.

As regards the āpaddharma for a Brāhmana, the *Mahābhārata* says that a Brhāmana, who does not want to give up his children and compassion, should take recourse to āpaddharma under the following circumstances. "When righteousness suffers decay and is transgressed by all, when unrighteousness becomes righteousness and righteousness assumes the form of its reverse, when all wholesome restraints disappear, and all traits in respect of righteousness are disturbed and confounded, when people are oppressed by kings and robbers, when men of all the four modes of life become stupefied in respect of their duties and all acts lose their merit, when men are cause of fear in every direction in consequences of lust and coveteousness and folly, when all creatures chose to crush one another, when they slay one another by deceitful means and deceive one another in their mutual dealings, when houses are burnt down throughout the country, when the Brāhāmanas become exceedingly afflicted, when the clouds do not pour a drop of rain, when every one's hand is turned against every one's neighbour, when all the necessities of life fall under the power of robbers, when traced such a season of terrible distress sets in."[151]

In ancient India it were generally the Ksatriyas, who formed the military class. Fighting was laid down as their foremost duty,[152] because they were created for fighting battles and for attaining victory.[153] An Army consisting of Ksatriyas was given preference over that, consisting of other Varnas.[154] But the members of the remaining three Varnas, viz. Brahmana, Vaisya and Sudra also were allowed to take up arms under certain circumstances, for example, when ordered by a king[155], when the rules for holding society were neglected, when Varna-Sankara (mixture of caste) was taking place, when

151. *Mbh.*, Śānti, CXLI, 1-8.
152. See Supra, *op. cit.*, pp. 128-9.
153. *Mbh.* Udyoga, CXXXV, 13.
154. *Arthaśāstra*, Bk. IX, 2, 43-7.
155. *Mbh.* Salya, LXV, 42.

dasyus were causing confusion[156] and when Ksatriyas were used for fight, unable to protect (themselves and others) and were making too much of the enemy.[157] The *Mahābhārata* further says that a Brāhmana should take up arms for protecting the remaining three varnas, for saving his life, for preventing defects of the varnas (varna dosa, i.e., mixture of caste) and for checking and bringing under control the wicked persons.[158] According to the Epic he does not incur sin by doing so. Gautama,[159] Manu,[160] Vasistha,[161] Yajnavalkya,[162] Sukra[163] and Bauhāyana[164] also permit him to adopt the Ksatriya-dharma under abnormal circumstances. The *Mahābhārata* mentions some non-Ksatriya warriors who adopted Ksatriya-dharma willingly and not as their āpaddharma. The great warrior Dronācārya, who was a Brāhmana by birth and who was one of the Senapatis of the Kauravas during the war of Kuruksetra, Asvatthama, the son of Dronācārya and Yuyutsu, who was the son of a Vaisya woman, are some illustrations of such warriors in the Epic. Pusyamitra, a Brāhmana and the senāpati of the last Mauryan king Bṛhadratha may be referred to as historical example of the Brāhmana warriors.

In the Śānti Parva, Yudhihṣiṭra asks Bhīsma whether a non-Ksatriya was justified in wielding tha rod of chastisement with a view to protecting the people when the robbers were troubling them, an inter-mixture of varnas (varna samkar) was taking place, confusion was creeping in and the Ksatriyas had become incompetent (to rule).[165] In reply Bhīsma said:

156. *Ibid.* Śānti, LXXVIII, 18.
157. *Ibid.*, CXV, 5.
158. *Mbh.* Śānti, LXXVIII, 29, 34.
159. *Gautama*, VII, 25. See also *Ibid.* VII, 6.
160. *Manu*, VIII, 318.
161. *Vasistha*, III, 24.
162. *Yajnavalkya*, sss, 35.
163. *Sukra*, IV, 11, 35-6.
164. *Baudhāyana Dharmaśāstra*, 11, 2, 80.
165. *Mbh.* Śānti, LXXVIII, 35-7.

"Be he a Sūdra or be he the member of any order, he who (that?) becomes a raft on a raftless current, or a means of crossing where means there are none, certainly deserves respect in every way. That person, O king, relying upon whom helpless men, oppressed and made miserable by robbers, live happily, deserves to be lovingly worshipped by all as if he were a near kinsman. The person, O thou of Kuru's race, that dispels the fear of others, always deserves respect. What use is there of bulls that would not bear burdens, or of king that would not yield milk, or of a wife that is barren? Similarly what need is there for a king that is not competent to grant protection? As an elephant made of wood, or a dear made of leather, or a person without wealth, or one that is as much, or a field that is sterile, even so is a Brāhmana that is void of Vedic lore and a king incapable of granting protection. Both of them are like a cloud that does not pour rain. That person who always protects the good and restrains the wicked, deserves to become a king and to govern the world."[166]

Manu says that a Brāhmana should not live in the kingdom ruled by a Sūdra.[167] This clearly indicates that Manu was not unaware of the Sūdra rulers. There are many historical examples of non-Ksatriya rulers in ancient India. Mahapadmananda, the founder of Handa dynasty was a Sūdra and has been referred to as "Sudragarbhodbhava."[168] Pusyamitra Sunga, a Brāhmana and the Senapati of Bṛhadraths, the last Mauryan King killed the latter, and founded the Sunga dynasty of rulers. Kanvas and Kadambas also were Brāhmanas. This shows that the rule of the members of the Varnas, other than Ksatriya, was actually practised in ancient India.

In the Śānti Parva, Bhīsma says to Yudhiṣṭhra :

166. *Ibid.* Śānti, LXXVIII, 38-44.

167. *Manu*, VI, 61.

168. *Visnu Purana*, IV, 24, 20-21.

> "When a Ksatriya's means of support are gone, what should he not take excepting what belongs to ascetics and what is owned by Brāhmanas .... Even as a Brāhmana in a season of distress may officiate at the sacrifice of a person for whom he should never officiate (at other and ordinary times) and eat forbidden food, so there is no doubt that Ksatriya in distress may take wealth from every one except ascetics and Brāhmanas.... In a season of distress, when ordinary practices cannot be followed, a Ksatriya may live by even unjust and improper means. The very Brāhmanas, it is seen, do the same when their means of living are destroyed."[169]

A Ksatriya was allowed to lead the life of complete renunciation (sanyāsa) in the āpattikāla. In the same way, a Sūdra, who could not earn his livelihood by following the code of conduct, prescribed for him, could maintain himself by taking recourse to the professions of a Vaisya, viz. trade and commerce (vanijya), cattle rearing (pasupalyam) and crafts (silpopajivanam). Similar is the view of Yājñavalkya also.

Manu also lays down the duties and profession that the members of the four varnas should do in āpattikāla. According to him a Brāhmana, failing to earn his living by following Svadharma was neither degraded nor associated with sin even if he accepted from all men, taught the Vedas to an unworthy person, officiated as priest at the sacrifice of a degraded institutor or accepted gifts of vile. He further lays down that "by taking his food at a place (however sinful or unholy), a Brāhmana on the point of death, like unto the ether purging off all dust, shall not be associated with sin."[170]

Another alternative before a Brāhmana was to follow the code of conduct prescribed for the Ksatriyas. Not able to maintain himself even by the Ksatriya dharma he should take recourse to the Vaisya-dharma. But he should avoid violence by not indulging in cultivation, which is not free from violence, because many creatures are destroyed wittingly or

169. *Mbh.* Śānti, CXXX, 20-21, 25.

170. *Manu*, X, 104.

unwittingly by the iron-bound plough when it penetrates into the earth. Under extra-ordinary circumstances, a Brāhmana or a Ksatriya should maintain himself by "selling the uncondemnable and wealth-augmenting articles of trade out of those which are (ordinarily) sold by a Vaisya. Manu gives a list of these articles, by selling which a Brāhmana or a Ksatriya is degraded to the Vaisya or Sūdra Varnas.[171] Under similar circumstances, i.e., in the season of calamity a Vaisya should do the vocation of the Sūdras. But even at that time he should not do the condemnable works prescribed for the Sūdras.[172] According to the commentator Kulluka these works include eating of (ucohista food), attending on the members of the Brāhmana, Ksatriya and Vaisya Varnas. Like the *Mahābhārata* the Manu Smṛti also permits a Sūdra to become an artisan to save the life of his wife and children from starvation.

It is noteworthy in this connection that according to this view the member of a Varna should take recourse to the duties and profession of the Varna, immediately below their own and another to that of a higher one. He says that a king should take away his belongings and banish him from his kingdom. A Sūdra, however, was allowed to adopt Vaisya-dharma, probably because he belonged to the lowest person and there was no Varna, lower than that of his own, the avocations whereof he would adopt.

Speaking about the Āpaddharma of a Brāhmana, Yājñavalkya says that a Brāhmana, failing to earn his livelihood by his Svadharma should follow the duties and professions of the Ksatriyas or Vaisyas. He should revert to his Dharma, after the calamity was over. Like Manu, Yājñavalkya also gives a list of the things which he should sell as well as those which he should not. He allows a Brāhmana, fallen in the distress, to eat everywhere and to accept gift from everyone and says that he does not incur sin thereby like the burning fire.

171. *Manu*, X, 85-94.

172. *Ibid.* X. 98. See also Kane, *op. cit.*, Vol. II, pp. 126-9.

Stealing which was highly condemned otherwise also has been permitted by the *Mahābhārata* in the āpattikāla. According to it even a Brāhmana could take recourse to theft, with a view to saving his life and by so doing he was not associated with sin. It further says that "in the first place, one should steal from a lower person. Failing such a person one may steal from one's equal. Failing an equal, one may steal from every eminent and a righteous person."[173]

In extra-ordinary times, the members of the Brāhmana, Ksatriya and Vaisya varnas were allowed to eat the flesh of some animals. Thus it is said in the Śānti Parva, only the five kinds of five-clawed animals are clean food for Brāhmanas, Ksatriyas and Vaisyas, as laid down in the scriptures.

In this connection the dialogue, once held between a Cāndāla and sage Visvāmitra attracts our attention. It is said in the Śānti Parva that once upon a time, at the end of the Tretā Yuga and before the beginning of the Dvāpara Yuga, rains did not pour for twelve consecutive years. Rivers, lakes, streams and other water reservoirs dried up. Consequently crops were destroyed and famine took place. Many people got starved to death. Population decayed. Robbers raised up their heads and began looting the people. Thus complete disorder and chaos crept in. Under these circumstances, Visvāmitra and his family members also could not get anything to eat and live upon. Leaving his wife and children, Visvāmitra went to a colony of cāndālas in search of food. In one house, he saw a piece of a recently slain dog's thigh and decided to steal it in order to appease his hunger. The Cāndāla, whom the sage had taken to be sleeping was in fact awake and he caught him red-handed. After knowing that the thief was no other than the famous sage Visvāmitra, the Cāndāla repeatedly told him not to commit a great sin by eating the flesh and that too of a dog's thigh. But the sage would not listen to him by arguing that āpaddharma permitted it. In āpattikāla, self-preservation was the highest law and it justified recourse to all sorts of means, fair and foul, commended or condemned, with a view to saving one's life. Afterwards, he took away

173. *Mbh.* Śānti, CXLI, 39.

the meat and offered the same to gods. After doing all these things he actually ate up the meat.

Manu also sites examples of some important personalities who took recourse to such things as their āpaddharma. We are informed that "the hungry (sage) Ajigarta for having attempted to kill his son (Sunahsesa) in order to appease his hunger (with his flesh), was not associated with the sin (of child killing). The famishad Vāmadeva, the knower of sin and virtue for having wished to eat dog's flesh in order to avoid death from starvation was not associated with the sin (of eating dog's flesh). Oppressed by hunger in a lonely forest, the (holy) Bhāradvāja of great austerity, together with his son was not associated with the sin (of taking vile gifts) for having accepted the gift of a large number of kins from Prahu who was a carpenter. Oppressed by hunger, the holy Visvāmitra, the knower of merits and demerits, for having accepted the gift of the flesh of a dog's thigh from the hands of Cāndāla, was not associated with sin.

From the foregoing paragraphs it is easy to infer that in extra-ordinary times, the ordinary rules of morality were held in abeyance or sometimes thrown to winds and recourse could be had even to those acts, which were strictly prohibited as great sins and heinous crimes in ordinary time.

The *Mahābhārata* does not believe in the universality and uniformity of moral standard (Dharma). According to it, every situation carries its own Morals. Dharma varies in accordance with desa (place) and kāla (time). The same is the case with the āpattikāla. Morality, prescribed for such time has been called Āpaddharma in the *Mahābhārata* as well as in other ancient Indian works.

As regards political morality in the Āpattikāla, we find that sometimes the same moral code, which is prescribed for ordinary times has been prescribed for extra-ordinary times also, but sometimes it is completely contradictory. Behaviour towards Brāhmanas, attitude towards the conduct of foreign affairs, possession of wisdom, lack of lethargic habits, presence of mind, procrastination and strength may be cited as the examples of the former taxation, behaviour towards the members of family and Prajapidama, as those of the latter.

The foremost duties of a king in āpattikāla is to defend his kingdom, to escape defeat at the hands of his enemy and to save his life. For the latter, he has been allowed and advised to take recourse to all sorts of means, righteous or unrighteous, fair and foul and noble or ignoble. If alive he can restore his lost kingdom and other possessions whereas one who is dead, stands no chance to do all these things. But so far as possible he should not transgress Dharma. In other words, the least possible violation of Dharma is desired by the *Mahābhārata*. After āpattikāla is over he is to undergo expatriation. The same is the case with regard to enriching the treasury by doubtful methods in Āpattikāla. Thus, the ordinary fiscal rules were to be suspended in accordance with the demand of the situation.

Coming to the social morality we find the same tendency. In ordinary times one should never give up Svadharma, i.e., the code of conduct, specifically prescribed for one's own Varna. In āpattikāla, however, these rules should be relaxed. Failing to earn their livelihood by following Svadharma the members of one Varna could adopt the avocations and do the duties of other Varnas. In doing so, they should bear this in mind, that they adopt the avocations of varnas lower than their own, and never that of the higher varnas. According to Manu, those who violate this rule should be punished. Thus a Brāhmana should do the duties of the Ksatriyas and failing to maintain himself by the Ksatriya Dharma, he should adopt the Vaisya Dharma. A Ksatriya should resort to the Vaisya Dharma. But the Brahmnas and the Ksatriyas, who have adopted the Vaisya Dharma should not do cultivation, because that is not free from violence. They should sell only certain things, otherwise they are degraded. Similarly a Vaisya was free to follow the Sūdra Dharma but should not do the undignified works, done by the Sūdras. Sometimes the Vaisyas were allowed to take up arms, which is evidently the Ksatriya-Dharma and hence the Dharma of a higher Varna. But there is no instance of their being punished. This is in contradiction with the rule that in no case should the members of one varna adopt the avocation of a higher varna. Since there was no Varna, lower than the Sūdra the duties whereof a Sūdra should adopt, the *Mahābhārata* lays down that he should take recourse to fine arts such as painting and sculpture.

In brief, the *Mahābhārata* holds the view that the social morality as well as the political morality is bound to change in accordance with the changing times and circumstances. And this is quite in the fitness of things, because what is true of a sick man could not be and should be true of a healthy man, what is applicable to a competent person should not be so in case of one, who is famine-stricken. This according to the *Mahābhārata* and other ancient Indian works, is the idea that underlies Āpaddharma, i.e., the morality of the season of distress and extra-ordinary circumstances. The state, according to the *Mahābhārata*, recognized the code of exceptional morality under special circumstances for maintaining the social order, which was its main duty.

3

Purusharthas

In the present chapter we propose to elucidate the various meanings and kinds of Purushartha. The term 'Purushartha' has been used as 'the values of life'. But 'the values of life' have always meant to thinkers of the west those ultimate values which are referred to as Truth, Goodness and Beauty. They can exist apart from the objects possessing them. They are not subjective, but are entirely objective and absolute to them. But 'Purushartha' means and connotes the aims and purposes of life or the fundamental aspirations of man. The term "Purushartha" not only denotes what the objectives of life should be, but it also comprehends what the objectives of life are as the result of the psychological tendencies of the individual. These Purusharthas are said to be fourfold. The Agni Purana states expressly that Dharma, Artha, Kama and Moksha are the four Purusharthas. All Indian thinkers are agreed that the Purusharthas can be classified into these four categories and that all the aims and aspirations of man are comprised in these four words or categories. This fourfold Purushartha classification is so well-established that it forms part of the Sankalpa that is pronounced by every Hindu before any ritual, ceremony or other religious or charitable act is begun.

It is well-recognized principle that every ritual ceremony, or other religious act is performed for the purpose of enabling the individual who performs it to realise these four Purusharthas of life. Whenever these are mentioned the order has always been that dharma was the first, artha was the second, kama was the third, and the fourth and last moksha. No Hindu has ever thought even in the fun or for love of change, to mention these four in any different order. Hence we see the order in which they are referred to has great significance and there is meaning behind it. A change in the order may alter the scope, content and relative importance of these four objects of life. We shall now consider the exact significance and connotation of these four Purusharthas, dharma, artha, kama and moksha. In Tamil classics they are mentioned as "Aram, Porul, Inbam and Veedu."

Vyasa, Valmiki and Valluvar are the greatest exponents of the fourfold Purusharthas. Vyasa confidently claims in the *Mahābhārata* that 'as regards dharma, artha, kama and moksha, what is found here may be elsewhere and what is not here will be found nowhere else'. His Epic is a completely exhaustive treatise on this great topic. The *Rāmāyana* also subscribes to this view. It deals with the worth of kama and artha and treats in extenso of dharma and moksha. The *Mahābhārata* in the Śānti Parva gives the caption "moksha dharma", moksha as part of Dharma. Now of the four Purusharthas, Indian thinkers consider that the first two stand in relation to the next two as Sadhana and Sadhya as means and ends. Thus we come to the conclusion that dharma and moksha are of primary importance while artha and kama secondary because dharma is the ruling principle of life while moksha is the ultimate goal. In between are artha and kama which are natural aspirations of every man in life. They refer to acquiring the means for material prosperity and to enjoying the innocent pleasures of life. Dharma being placed first as the ruling principle, both artha and kama must be subject to dharma There must be no acquisition of wealth which violates the principles of Dharma. Similarly also no enjoyment is to be desired which is opposed to dharma. The Lord has said in the *Gītā*: "I am Kama which is not opposed to dharma."[1] As artha enables man to enjoy the comforts and pleasures of life, it is placed before kama and it is one of the fundamental ideas in relation to these Purusharthas that dharma is the legitimate source of artha and kama. All these three must be pursued with the ultimate goal of moksha ever present to the mind. There may be exceptions in the case of those who renounce both arth and kama with a view to realise moksha. When a person seeks refuge in the Lord, even dharma may be abandoned. The last verse of the *Gitā* says: "Renounce all dharmas and take refuge in Me alone."[2] These are only for specially gifted persons. But, to the ordinary run of mankind, all the four are legitimate ideals and objectives of life in their sequence.

Now, being the primary importance of dharma and moksha we should explain their importance clearly. We find that all thinkers, Eastern and Western, are agreed that every effort or activity in life is directed towards the attainment of happiness. Rama has affirmed it in the Ayodhya Kand.[3] But the painful Truth remains, that the happiness which we enjoy is transitory, fleeting and illusory and is often mingled with misery and suffering. Also it is not the lot of all to be happy. Even those who enjoy moments of happiness are not fortunate to be happy till the end.

Man longs, therefore, for pure joy, unalloyed, everlasting happiness, free from the least trace of misery and pain. Here on earth "We look before and after and pine for what is not; our sincerest laughter is fraught with pain, and our sweetest songs are those that tell of saddest thoughts." Death, disease, old age, poverty and want bring in their train untold misery. The human heart is sick with hope deferred, expectations blasted, ambition wrecked and desire unfulfilled.[4]

Hence, man anxiously looks forward to a state of supreme bliss beyond earthly existence. "To whom has been

1. *Gitā*.
2. *Gitā*, Chapter 18; Sloka 66.
3. *Rāmāyana*, Ayodhya Kand.
4. *Ibid*.

the lot to be happy till the end ?"[5] Hence, our great sages and philosophers recognize both kama or worldly happiness and moksha. Both have been considered happiness and of the two, moksha has been considered as the Supreme Purushartha.

In his Nyaya Sutra, Gautama clearly enunciates the nature of moksha and the means of attaining it. "Moksha results from the extinction of dosha, lust and hate, which extinguish all karmas, which again results in the cessation of all birth, which again results in the annulment of sorrow."[6] All Indian thinkers are agreed that the highest aspiration of the human soul should be to attain moksha, that human life should be one continuous preparation for it and that the longing for mukti should permeate man's whole being.

Thus, this acceptance by all Schools of Indian thought of moksha as the Supreme goal of human aspiration and as the lode-star of all human effort has given a unique direction to Hindu Ethics. It has led the aspirants to insist upon a life of unselfish, disinterested service and duty, and of annihilation of the ego, in short to emphasize karmayoga, or Nishkama karma. It is the firm conviction of our great sages and seers that the highest interests of life are served best by the practice of unselfishness and disinterested devotion to duty. The man whose highest aspiration is to attain moksha comes to the conviction, as a corollary to this belief, that man is more than anything else, essentially, a spirit and that it is the life of the spirit even on the earth, or as Aldous Huxley pithily puts it is "the dying to self" that will enable him to attain moksha either here or hereafter. In fact, as Rev. Homes states of Mahatma Gandhi "His confidence in eternity makes possible his happiness in time."

Thus we realise that the enunciation and acceptance of moksha as the Supreme goal of life by Indian thinkers has given a unique direction to the whole philosophy of life unparalleled in the history of thought in any other country.

Among the four Purusharthas, moksha is mentioned as the last as it is the supreme, or Parama-Purushartha. Next in

5. *Ibid.*
6. See Gautama Nyaya Sutra.

order comes kama. There is one feature common to both of them. Moksha is Supreme, unalloyed, eternal happiness while kama denotes the happiness or joy enjoyed by ordinary mortals in life. They both have as already mentioned the element of happiness. That is why in Tamil religious literature, kama is called "Chitrinba" while moksha is called "Perinba". Thus "Chitrinba" means the small transient joys of life on earth while "Perinba" denotes supreme happiness. In this way, kama and moksha may be called "Sadhya purushartha" while dharma and artha can be called "Sadhana Purusharthas". Through the medium of dharma and artha, one is enabled to attain kama and moksha.

The happiness that is derived from the performance of duty and from leading a pure and noble life is commended. Kama is not merely confined to the low pleasures of the senses. Hence it is that the Lord in the *Gītā* says when enumerating his various Vibhutis that He is the embodiment of kama which is not opposed to or inconsistent with the pursuit and performance of dharma. It is that kama which is sinful and which is contrary to the dictates of one's conscience or of dharma that is condemned by Indian thinkers. Hence they have viewed kama or the joy of life as one of the legitimate aspirations of man.

Now, we come to know about the artha. By artha is meant wealth. In its general connote it may include all material comforts, economic welfare and security. This wealth is regarded as the primary purpose of life. Without it, human existence is impossible. Artha is the foundation upon which the whole structure of life has been built and all the other Purusharthas can be achieved only by the fulfilment of this primary purpose in life. The word artha has a very wide significance as in the 'Artha Sastra'. But the meaning of this word in the context of the Purushartha is the acquisition of wealth for livelihood and material comforts. According to Indian thinkers, the economic factor is an essential element of human life. There is no sin in the acquisition of wealth nor is there any virtue in poverty. Wealth does not contemplate asceticism as part of the normal good life. Our seers do not look down upon the efforts to increase a man's wealth. Avvai the great talented lady—moralist of the Tamil land, said, "Go even across the billowy ocean and acquire wealth. In the *Bhagvadgītā* the Lord characterises the artharthi who worships God for the sake of wealth as a noble person. Valmiki puts in the mouth of Lakshmana a panegyric on Artha as a primary and praiseworthy goal of life. He says :

> "From wealth amassed and increased all actions proceed as rivers from mountains. If a person abandons wealth, seeking happiness he begins to commit sin and wrong and to lead a sinful life with increased longing for enjoyment. To the wealthy exist friends and relations. A wealthy man is regarded by people. He is considered a learned, lucky and an intelligent man."[7]

Nilakantha Dikshita points out the importance of artha thus :

> "Dharma is earned by artha and by dharma, artha is earned. The one is the means and support of the other and vice versa. Artha is the source of the whole world. The loss of wealth spells ruin. The knowledge of karma leads to moksha. Artha is the authoriser of karma. Therefore by artha alone there is moksha; Kaivalya cannot be attained by poverty."[8]

Arjuna establishes that "dharma and kama are the limbs of artha. Agriculture, trade, cattle-rearing and all crafts are all done for acquisition of wealth alone."[9] Manu says "wealth should be acquired for livelihood." According to Indian thinkers, the enjoyment of wealth should not be opposed to the principles of Dharma. If this pursuit of wealth means loss and harm to others, then it is not right. Kalidasa praises the acquiring of wealth for the sake of giving to others :

7. Valmiki, Yuddha Kanda, Sarga 13, Slokas 32-58.
8. Dikshita Nilakantha, Sabharanjana Sataka, Sloka 78.
9. *Mbh.*, Śānti Parva, Chap. 80.

"Certainly wealth and enjoyment of it are not in any sense opposed to righteous conduct, or perfect morals. Acquisition is purified by giving and service."[10]

Among the four Purusharthas, dharms is always mentioned first. This order is never changed. The four Purusharthas are also referred to as *Chaturvarga* and the first three, dharma, artha and kama frequently go together and are referred to as *trivarga.* Science fully developed by culture and suffused with love of all beings.

Relation between the Purusharthas

We shall now proceed to consider the inter-relation of the four Purusharthas and their relative importance according to Indian thought. Dharma, Artha and Kama go together. They are known as trivarga and moksha stands by itself. As moksha is the ideal mostly to be attained in after-life, though as already pointed out the possibility of jivanmukti is recognized by some schools of thought as the Advaita, it is left alone and dealt with apart from the other three which pertain to life on earth. That is why the saint Tiruvalluvar, in the immortal Kural, dealt with the objects of life under the three captions of Aram, Porula and Inbam though he comprehended the ideal of Moksha under the subheading of Aram, Turavaram, Meyunarthal, even as the *Mahābhārata* speaks of Moksha as a Dharma.

Though they deal with Dharma, Artha, Kama and Moksha, the Smritis have come to be known as Dharma Sastra, because they deal with the four Purusharthas. Dharma is the primary objective for man and Artha and Kama are secondary, to be controlled by Dharma and are properly the fruit of the pursuit of Dharma. Mitakshara has thrown light on the essential features of Dharma.[11] He further elucidates that the source of Artha is Dharma, but not vice versa; for, Dharma can be performed without the help of Artha, for

10. Kalidasa, *Raghuvamsa*, 1-7. 4-86.

11. See Mitakshara, *Commentary on Yajnavalkya Smriti.*

instance by Japa and Tapas. But without Dharma there will be no bit of Artha. Similarly Kama and Moksha. Nilkantha Dikshita echoes the same idea in a fine verse thus :

> "If I have not sufficient wealth I shall abandon the Dharma which requires wealth for its performance. There are many that can be performed by bodily activities. Even if the body is weary, there can be no loss of Dharma by that. We shall fix our thoughts once at least on Siva and realise our objective."

Their Relative Importance

Manu discusses the question, which of the three or whether all the three should be the objectives of life. After referring to the opinion of some that Dharma and Artha are the only good in life and to that of others that Artha and Kama are the highest good and of some others that Artha is the sole aim of life and of still others that Dharma is the only good, he concludes that virtue, wealth and desire form combinedly the good in life.[12]

In the *Rāmāyana*, one of the questions put by Rama to Bharata is as follows :

> "Do you work for all the three, Artha, Dharma and Kama, after dividing your time among the three appropriately ?"[13]

This idea proceeds on the principle that all the three Purusharthas are essential and they together comprehend the aspiration of the integrated personality of man. In the *Mahābhārata*, Vyasa gives a very interesting account of a discussion between the five Pandava brothers and Vidura as regards the relative importance of the four Purusharthas. Vidura stresses the supremacy of Dharma and next only are Artha and Kama as Dharma is the foundation for Artha and

12. Manu, 2, Sloka 224.
13. Ayodhya Kand, Kacchit Sarga.

Kama. While Arjuna emphasizes the need for Artha without which both Dharma and Kama cannot be achieved, Bhimasena stresses the importance of Kama. The twins Nakula and Sahadeva clearly lay down that all the three must be pursued by man and are equally important.[14] The last words of this verse are similar to the words already referred to in the *Rāmāyana*. The same idea of the equal importance for man of all the four Purusharthas is beautifully expressed in a poetic simile by Kalidasa. He likens the four sons of Dasaratha to the four Purusharthas, Dharma, Artha, Kama and Moksha and says that the four brothers together shine as the embodiments of the four Purusharthas.[15] He further says that Rama pursued Dharma, Artha and Kama equally as was his attitude towards his three brothers.[16]

Vyasa indicates the period of time every day for the pursuit of each one, Dharma, Artha and Kama and the period of the age of man for everyone of the three. Morning should be devoted to Dharma, daytime to Artha and the rest to Kama. The first part of a man's life may be devoted to Kama, the second part to Artha and the last to Dharma.[17] The division of the period should not be understood strictly in the sense that each should be devoted to a particular Dharma entirely to the exclusion of the others; it means only that it should be largely devoted to the Purusharthas indicated in the verse. The Vishnu Purana also lays down that the three Purusharthas should be pursued by every individual thus :

> "Rising up early morning with clear intellect, one should think of Dharma and of Artha not inconsistent with it and of Kama without violation of the two. Your attitude must be the same to all the three, lest both seen and unseen results should be destroyed. If Dharma is likely to be endangered, then both Artha and Kama should be abandoned. Even Dharma may be abandoned,

14. *Mbh.*, Śānti Parva, Āpad Dharma Portion, Chap. 146.
15. Kalidasa, *Raghuvamsa*, 10 Sarga, Sloka 85.
16. *Ibid.*, 14 Sarga, Sloka 21.
17. See *Mbh.*, Sabha Parva, Narada-Dharmaputra-Samvada.

> if it is opposed to public opinion and if it is not conducive to the happiness of society."[18]

Artha and Kama to be regulated by Dharma

While stressing the equal importance of Dharma, Artha and Kama for man, Indian thinkers have always advocated the principle that the pursuit of Artha and Kama should be regulated by the requirements and injunctions of Dharma. They condemn the unrestrained passionate pursuit of either Artha or Kama regardless of Dharma, which they regard as the substratum for the realisation of the aspiration by man of Artha and Kama.

Indian thinkers regard Dharma as the upholder and maintainer of society and the world order. The individual can never aspire for the enjoyment of wealth and happiness unless the world order and the stability of society are maintained. In the third of the four verses forming the Bharata Savitri mentioned towards the end of *Mahābhārata* as the essence of the teaching of that great work, Vyasa emphasizes passionately the Supreme importance of Dharma as follows :

> "With uplifted arm, I cry from the house tops, but none hears me. It is from Dharma that Artha and Kama result; why then is Dharma not followed."[19]

He recognises here that Artha and Kama satisfy the psychological tendencies of man and they form essentially the two fundamental aspirations of every individual. At the same time he firmly enunciates the principle that Dharma should regulate the pursuit of man for the realisation of the rational aspiration of Artha and Kama.

Saint Valluvar echoes the same sentiment in the following Kural :

> "Is there anything higher in life than Dharma ? It secures Moksha and Artha."

18. See Vishnu Purana.
19. See *Mbh*.

The Puranauuru also says the same thing :

> He who pursues Dharma secures Moksha, Artha and Kama. In the *Rāmāyana* Sita reminds her husband on his entering the Dandaka forest for fulfilling his vow of exterminating the Rakshasas, that from Dharma, Artha results and also Sukha or Kama. Dharma is the essence of the Universe."[20]

Nilakantha, the commentator of the *Mahābhārata* says in one of his introductory verses that when sublimated by Dharma, Artha and Kama take a loftier shape. Petty minded men pursue Artha and Kama for the satisfaction of sensual enjoyments and desires; and pursue even Dharma for the sake of material objects here and hereafter, for the pleasures of Svarga. But great men pursue Dharma so that their minds may be purified, and aspire for wealth so that religious sacrifices may be performed for the welfare of mankind and for the sustenance of their lives and they eagerly desire to attain moksha. He adds that the way of the petty-minded and of the great ones are illustrated by the story of the lives of the Dhratrashtra and of the Pandavas.[21] Let every individual avoid the acquisition of wealth and the gratification of his desires if they are opposed to Dharma and avoid also those acts of Dharma which are opposed to and hurt the feelings of the general public and lead not to joy even in afterlife.[22]

The poet Bhavabhuti describes the man of real Vedic culture thus : Wealth and material comforts are desired by him for the sake of service and charity to his fellow-beings and for fulfilment of his religious duties. Married life is desired only for the sake of progeny and long life is wished for the practice of spirituality. Similarly, Kalidasa in the Raghuvamsa, describing the greatness of the kings of Raghu line says, that they acquired wealth for the sake of giving and courted the pleasures of married life only for the sake of

20. *Rāmāyana*, Aranyakanda, 9 Sarga, Slaka 30.
21. See Nilakantha Introductory Verse.
22. Manu, Chap. IV, Sloka 176.

progeny.[23]

The great Indian lady moralist Auvvai says : Dharma consists in the making of gifts; wealth soul be acquired without doing evil. Kama is pure love and regard subsisting between the two life-partners who are of one mind; Moksha is the renunciation of all the preceding three purusharthas by thinking upon the Supreme.

In the fourth Adhyaya of the Manu Smriti, it is laid down that every individual may earn his livelihood only by acts which are not reprehensible and not opposed to Dharma, and which do not entail much suffering.[24] Again it is said in Manu Smriti that we must not earn money by acts which involve the pleasure of the senses nor by forbidden methods; whether one is in want or possessed of means, one must not try to acquire wealth from any and every source without discrimination.[25]

According to Indian thought, Dharma regulates both the acquisition of wealth and material comforts and satisfaction of our desire. Valmiki puts in the mouth of Rama the ideas contained in the above verses when he gave advice to Lakshmana on the eve of his banishment to the forest. Rama says that it is found by experience in the world that Dharma, Artha and Kama are attained as the fruit of the pursuit of Dharma alone and those acts which give rise to realisation of these three purusharthas are to be followed, much in the same manner as by marriage one is able to attain the three purusharthas on account of a beloved and obedient wife who has given birth to a good son.[26] But if all the three purusharthas cannot be attained by any act, then, at least that which is conducive to Dharma should be followed. If, on the other hand, one is bent upon the pursuit of wealth alone, he becomes the enemy of all and he who is determined to be a hedonist does not merit any praise.

23. Kalidasa, *Raghuvamsa*, Sarga 1, Sloka 7.
24. *Manu Smriti*, Chap. IV, Sloka 3.
25. *Ibid.*, Chap. IV, Sloka 15.
26. See Valmiki Ramayana.

The ideal of leading a life of Dharma alone, without caring for the pursuit of wealth and even at the sacrifice of material happiness is only for the chosen few who are worthy of the appellation of Rishis. That is why Rama boldly proclaimed to Kaikeyi that he was determined to lead a life of Dharma like the Rishis and that he was not intent upon Artha at all in his conduct through life.

In the *Mahābhārata*, Vana Parva Vyasa has put the same idea in an arresting manner thus. He classifies men into four kinds. Those who care for material happiness in the present life and do not care for after-life; secondly, those who do not care for material happiness at all during their life on earth but prepare themselves for eternal happiness after death; then those who care for material happiness here and for happiness hereafter; and lastly those who do not care for either happiness here or in the hereafter. For the first category he gives the illustration of the Rajaputra who leads a life of material happiness here only and does not care for the future. For the second category he gives the example of the Rishi. For the third he cites the illustration of the good man of the world and for the last category he gives the example of the cruel hunter. Thus Dharma gives coherence and direction to the different activities of life. It is a complete code of life, the harmony of the whole man, who finds the right way for the just law of living. But higher than Dharma is the great ideal of spiritual freedom which ennobles the whole life of the individual and the whole order of society. According to G.H. Mees, Moksha is the kingdom of God, while Dharma is the kingdom of God on earth. Hence, according to Indian thought the four purusharthas exhaust all the elements of the fundamental aspiration of an individual who wants to lead a good and well-ordered life on earth.[27]

The supreme aim of social order is to train human beings to attain a state of complete freedom from all bondage including the shackles of the human body, and of supreme everlasting happiness unmixed with any misery or sufferings. Yet, it is not divorced from temporal ends for a development of

27. See G.H. Mees, *Dharma and Society*.

social conditions which will enable every individual to attain a high standard of moral, material and intellectual life, which will be in harmony with the good and peace of all and will be consistent with the dignity and liberty of the human personality. The pursuit of these four purusharthas must be based on the fundamental principles of truth, ahimsa and compassion for all, self-sacrifice and self-control. The great message and the clarion call of the sages of the Upnishad to mankind is summed up in three words each beginning with the letter "Da", namely "Dana, Daya and Dama." A beautiful story is told in the Upnishad. Once upon a time the devas, manushyas and rakshasas approached Prajapati for advice. He vanished from their presence and there was only a peal of thunder, similar to the sound "Da, Da, Da."

Each group interpreted this as advice summed up in a word beginning with the letter "Da", in accordance with what it felt it lacked. The devas who lacked self-control interpreted it as "Dama", the rakshasas who were notorious for cruelty, interpreted it as "Daya" or compassion, and the men whose characteristic was the possessive instinct interpreted it as "Dana" or charity. All the three groups met and communicated to each other the three words denoting the message of Prajapati. Sankara very wisely observed in his commentary that all the three groups are found among men and the message contained in the three words, Dana, Daya and Dama is for all humanity. Thus the Vedic sage drew his profound inspiration from the sounds of pealing thunder which reverberated throughout the world. These three words are fit to be written in letters of gold not only on the portals of the United Nations Organisation working for world peace and for common humanity but also on the tablet of the heart of every individual in society. The nations composing humanity also should lay this message to their hearts. Otherwise there is no hope for humanity and no prospect for the peace of the world. We find that the same memorable message inscribed in enduring rock in the Heliodorus column erected at Besnagar, a place 30 miles north-east of Bhopal. This granite pillar was erected, as found in the inscription, by Heliodorus, a Greek, who calls himself a Bhagavata, sent as messenger by Antialkidas of

Syria. The last portion is in Prakrit. These three are the same as found in Sanatasujatiya of the *Mahābhārata* : self-control, renunciation and faultlessness, these three are the foundations of immortality. By their clear analysis of the fundamental aspirations of heart and by the enunciation of the high ideals which man should possess and for which he should work as a unit of society and as a citizen of the world, Indian thinkers have made a unique contribution to the thought of mankind.

Thus we find that Dharma has a great importance and supreme status in the *Mahābhārata.* There is no word in English, possessing exactly the same connotation as the word 'Dharma'. To the ancient Indians, this word had different meanings in different contexts and periods. It denoted law, virtue, righteousness, religion, innate propriety of a thing, justice, proper and specific duties, functions, moral precepts, and righteous course of conduct.[28] In the scheme of Tṛvarga, it denoted the last meaning, i.e. the righteous course of conduct or righteous and proper performance of one's duties.[29] According to the *Mahābhārata*, Dharma should be capable of helping others too. That, which troubles others is not Dharma at all. Then it becomes a vice and bad conduct. One who practises it for its own sake is, according to Bhimsena, like a blind man unable to perceive solar light.[30]

Artha : Artha is the next object of life in the scheme of Tṛvarga. Literally, the word means wealth. But this is a narrow meaning of the term. In this context, however, it implies material prosperity i e. worldly achievements. To Sri Aurobindo, Artha stands for "vital interests."[31]

28. For details on Dharma, see infra, Conception of Ethics in *Mahā bhārata*, pp. 101-7.

29. Sri Aurobindo renders the word *Dharma* as "ethics and religion," in *The Human Cycle* (Pondicherry, 1949) quoted by V P. Verma : *Studies in Hindu Political Thought and its Metaphysical Foundations*, p. 53, F.N. 1.

30 *Mbh.* Vana, XXXIII, 21-3.

31. Sri Aurobindo: *The Human Cycle*, quoted by V.P. Varma: *Studies in Hindu Political Thought and Metaphysical Foundations*, p. 53, f.n 1.

According to the *Mahābhārata*, Artha, for its own sake, has no meaning. It should be properly utilized in making donations etc. Otherwise the possessor does not understand its purpose and he is just like a servant, who is assigned the task of looking after the kine in the forest.[32] Thus, Artha implies honourable and legitimate earning of wealth with a view to practise Dharma

Kama : In its narrow sense, the term Kama stands for sexual desires. In its broader sense, however, it stands for desires as such. The *Mahābhārata* explains *Kama* as the pleasure derived from the possession of wealth.[33] Further it says that Kama is the joy, that results from the sense-organs, mind (Mana) and heart, when they are directed to their respective objects.[34] It is noteworthy in this connection that the ancient Indian thinkers did not condemn Kama altogether. They have due place to it, of course the lowest, in their scheme of Trvarga. Thus they sanctioned the satisfaction of all sorts of desires, but emphasized that the same should be within limits.

32. *Mbh.*, Vana XXXIII, 24.
33. *Ibid* , XXXIII, 30.
34. *Ibid.*, XXXIII, 37-8. See also *Ibid.* CXXIII, 6.

4

Varnashrama Dharma

In this chapter we propose to discuss the elements of individual and social ethics as envisaged in the *Mahābhārata*. Man leads two kinds of life, i.e., an individual life and a social life. An individual life is the self-centred life—a life which the individual lives for himself. A social life, on the other hand, is a life which an individual shares with other fellow creatures of the society. Consequently there are two kinds of ethics—individual and social—corresponding to two sorts of life.

The social and individual ethics can be traced in the scheme of Varnāsrama dharmas. The Varnadharmas are the duties relating to one's varna. The āsramadharmas are the duties relating to one's specific stage of life. These two kinds of dharmas constitute the very essence of two kinds of ethics, i.e., individual and social. The doctrine of varna lays stress on the special aspect and that of āsrama the individual aspect of ethics. These two aspects are inextricably related to each other. P.H. Valavalkar has aptly observed :

> "Of course, both the kinds of dharmas (Āsrama and Varnadharma) concern themselves with the organisation and management of the individual as well as the group or the society; but the difference may be said to

> be in the manner of approach and emphasis in the organisation of man and his activities in regard to the two kinds of dharmas. In the scheme of the *āsramas*, the problem is approached from the point of view of the training of the individual through specifically provided environments at different stages of his life; in the Varna-organization, on the other hand, the problem is considered from the point of view of the larger group, and the individual's position is defined in this group with reference to his innate nature."[1]

S.K. Maitra also observes :

> "The Varnāsrama-dharmas thus represent a code of relative duties and constitute the relativistic ethics of the Hindus. It comprises the ethics of sociality as well as the ethics of individual capacity and is thus fuller and more comprehensive than the Platonic Scheme which is the ethics of sociality only."[2]

The Original Concept of Dharma : the Ṛta

The ancient Indian thinkers believed that this world is not a chaos but a cosmos. The basic principle of Hindu ethics is the assumption of universe which is lawful to the core, and if this lawfulness of the world is understood properly, human conduct, activities, and institutions can be better organised and its destiny shall be better shaped. The Ṛg Vedic seers hold the belief that there is a divine cosmic order and regularity in the universel process. There is a Universal law of orderliness and correct behaviour of the things. They emphasized the cosmic view of the world with all its implications. The concept of Ṛta, the cosmic order, the forerunner of the later Indian concept of Dharma, is perhaps the highest and noblest flight of the Ṛg Vedic thought and imagination. It is the recognition of the cosmic order and law prevailing in

1. Valavalkar, P.H., *Hindu Social Institutions*, p. 281.
2. Maitra, S.K., *The Ethics of the Hindus*, p. 1.

nature. It is the regular 'course of things'. It stands for the immutable, transcendental and immanent law of nature by which the universe is governed and becomes systematised, organised and harmonised, and avoids chaos and confusion. This concept of Ṛta must have originated from the observance of regularity in nature—regular movements of the sun, the moon and the stars and the succession of days after nights and one season after another. In the physical sense the Ṛta "Like a wheel circumscribes the universe, regulates it and keeps it in its place, in varuna's pāsa and has for its physical basis the belt of zodiac from which no luminary (deva) may deviate and the penalty for transgression whereof is ensharement verify by the shackles of non-Ṛta or darkness of death."[3] This is why devas are said to be born in Ṛta and governed by it. Next, the Ṛta denotes the cosmic order or law working in nature. Further, in the moral sense, the word stands for 'order', 'truth' or 'right', and in the religious sense it means 'rite'.[4] Ṛta is, therefore, not only cosmic order or law working in the nature, but it has a moral aspect also. On the moral plane, Ṛta leads to the triumph of order over disorder, good over evil. There is thus a coordination between natural law and moral law, cosmic order and moral order. It is at once the organising principle of the universe and the divine ordering of earthly life. Ṛta is the unchanging principle that pervades and controls the succession of phenomena, both natural and human. Everything in the world is regulated by rhythm, periodity and cycles. This cosmic rhythm creates order and system in the universe. It brings about a cosmic orderliness and law in the universal process through whose operation this whole cosmos is sustained. This works in natural as well as in human sphere. In human sphere, it creates moral order which binds the society together.

Varuna is the upholder and administrator of this cosmic law which regulates all activities in this world. He is the embodiment of law and order,[5] and he obeys the universal

3. Apte, M.V., *The Vedic Age*, pp. 365-66.
4. *Ibid*, p. 379.
5. *Ṛg Veda* V. 66.1.68.1.

moral law which he himself has established. This upholder of cosmic order Varuna, is also regarded as the lord of human morality. It is the function of Varuna to see that there occurs no transgression of law cosmic or human.[6] Sin consists in the transgression of law, or ordinances, the Vrata of Varuna.[7] The sin or 'un-Ṛta' results from the violation of Ṛta or order in the moral sphere. "Morality is an expression of the divine law tenoted by the term Ṛta, sin is the opposition to that law and the sinner is one who is out of harmony with the higher spiritual environment which encompasses and controls the world."[8]

"Ṛta is the universal principle, the unchanging law, physical and moral, the real and eternal, on which the whole universe is founded. All objects, all creatures are subject to Ṛta."[9] The Ṛg Vedic Aryans had deep convictions in the existence of the natural and moral law, its power and importance and its undeviating operation and working. According to Max Muller, Ṛta was regarded in the Vedic days as "the straight lines." "It is applied to the straight line of the sun, in its daily course, to the straight line followed by day and night, to the straight line that regulates the seasons, to the straight line, which, in spite of many momentary deviations, was discovered to run through the whole realm of natu-e. We call that Ṛta, that straight, direct or right line, when we apply it in a more general sense, *The law of Nature* and when we apply it to the moral world, we try to express the same idea again by speaking of the *Moral law*, the law on which our life is founded, the eternal law of Right and Reason or it may be 'that which makes for righteousness'—both within us and without...A recognition of straight line in the world without, and the world within, was raised into the high faith, a faith is a law that underlines everything, a law in which we may trust, whatever befall, a law which speaks within us with the divine voice of conscience, and tells us 'This is Ṛta', 'This is

6. *Ṛg*. V. 85.
7. *Ṛg*. I.25.1; VII 89.5, VII. 86.6; VII.88.5.6.
8. Hopkins, *Ethics of India*, p. 2ff.
9. Mehta, P.D., *Early Indian Religious Thought*, p. 42.

right', 'This is true', whatever the statues of our ancestors or even the voices of our bright gods may say to the contrary."[10] According to Rudolf Otto, the word Ṛta comes from the root. 'Ar' to arrange, to order, to regulate (German orden). He says :

> "It really means the regulated, the ordered. And not so much the state of order and the process as the principle behind this state and the power that holds and regulates the process. Ṛta is a binding power constraining to order. It was to be found also in social life, in the life of the clan, of the tribe and the family, the binding order of morals, customs, laws and manners in the constitution of social classes and of the labour communities, in compacts and oaths, in marriage, in the relations of individuals, of clans, in public law and private conduct, was also Ṛta, based upon Ṛta. It appeared in social life as the continuation of cosmic binding order."[11]

The term Ṛta stands for the impersonal order or law, and is, in the Vedas, the sustaining principle of the higher end of the lower world. It signifies a cosmic order and also stands as much for a social as for a moral order. It allots everpthing, its sphere and status in the scheme of things, for instance, varuna, the guardian of Ṛta, has spread the earth and set the sun in motion and pours out the rain but sees to it that one ocean is not filled to overflowing by many rivers.[12] Thus it is the principle of limit which binds both gods and men and keeps them within their orbit. Any transgression of the limit set by Rta brings chaos and misery and its observance brings about prosperity and affluence.[13] It was conceived that the secret of the regular and planned working of the

10. Max Muller, *India, What Can It Teach Us* (Munshi Ram Manoharlal, Delhi, 1961), pp. 209-10.
11. Quoted by G.H. Mees, *Dharma and Society* (Luzac & Co., London, 1935), p 10.
12. *Ṛg*. V. 85.
13. *Ṛg*. IV.23.8-10.

various phenomena lay in the fact that everything in the cosmos was bound down and controlled by a great sovereign, Varuna who is supposed to enforce and maintain the cosmic law, the Ṛta.[14]

The Ṛta reduces chaos to cosmos, and provides order and integration to matter, and brings about unity in diversity and uniformity in the manifold phenomena of nature. It creates order summetry, rhythm and harmony in nature as well as in the moral world. The Ṛta, which holds together the cosmos through natural law establishes order and discipline in the social and individual life of men through moral law.

Along with Varuna, Mitra is also the keeper of the Ṛta. They both jointly sustain the Ṛta and punish its transgressor. They watch over the action of men, over their truth speaking and sincerity between man and man, their promises, contracts and treaties.[15] They do not harm those who honour and obey the laws of Ṛta, rather are bounteous to them.[16] Thus they are the upholder and protector of moral order and represent the ideal values of social life finding expression in the Ṛta.

Like the Greek conception of Fate, Ṛta too is inviolable and independent of the wills of gods. The gods too have to obey Ṛta. But the Greeks found in the Fate a power which can be inscrutable and to some extent arbitrary whose course could not be divined. It fore-ordained the course of mortal life beyond the power of anybody to alter it. This view of Fate led to the typical Greek conception of tragedy that man was a helpless victim of Fate. Ṛta, on the other hand, never became fore-ordained and arbitrary. It ever remained eternal law and eternal justice.[17]

The concept of Rta is perhaps the finest concept in the

14. Philologically the word 'Varuna' is derived from the root 'Vṛ' which means 'to bind, 'to cover' or 'to encompass'.

15. *Ṛg*. VIII.60.5.

16. *Ṛg*. VIII.22, 15-16

17. Bose A.C., *The Call of the Vedas* (Bhartiya Vidya Bhavan, Bombay, 1960), p. 50.

Ṛg Vedic thought.[18] It postulates the firm belief that the universe is an ordered cosmos not subject to whims, caprices, fancies, arbitrariness and chance, but to the eternal, unviolable and immutable laws which bind everyone, gods and men, and punish every transgressor.[19] Ṛta, the cosmic law, was all-pervading, omnipotent and inexorable, from which creation sprang and by which it was regulated and maintained. Everything existed in and through it. It controlled both natural and spiritual spheres. Gods were no more than its guardians. Moral and social orders too were regulated by it. Ṛta was one and indivisible operating in the material as well as moral and spiritual fields.

The Ṛta had a moral aspect also. According to it no wrong doer would go scotfree, rather would suffer the consequence of his wrong doing. The nemesis would take hold of him and punish him. The Ṛg Vedic Aryans looked to the ideal of translating the cosmic Ṛta into social order. They desired to make order prevail overdis order, cosmos over chaos, good over evil—the Ṛta over un-Ṛta. The existence of evil is recognised, but they hope and believe that the evil can be fought and suppressed both within us and without us. Indra's victory over vratra—the power of darkness and evil as opposed to Ṛta—is he symbol of the ultimate triumph of goodness. virtue and law over evil, view and disorder. Everyone has his own Vṛtra—the counterpart of the cosmic Vṛtra—to fight and suppress. It can be fought successfully and suppressed only when one is valiant and brave enough. The *Ṛg Veda* exherts us to do so,[20] and thus inculcates a heroic outlook on life.[21]

Origin of the Concept of Dharma

This concept of Ṛta, however, could not develop to its

18. E.O. James, *The Ancient Gods*, pp. 260-66 and 279-80; also refer to Keith, *Religion and Philosophy of the Veda and Upanisads*, Vol. I, 1.83.
19. Gokhale, *Indian Thought Through the Ages* (Asia Publishing House, 1961), p. 95.
20. *Ṛg*. X. 53.8.
21. A.C. Bose, *op. cit.*, p. 51.

fulness in India. Keith points out that the idea of Ṛta is "one which, like the moral elevation of Varuna, has no future history in India, pointing irresistibly to the view that it was not an Indian creation but an inheritance which dit not long survive in its new milieu."[22] Ṛta did not, however, entirely disappear in India, rather it was transformed into the concept of Dharma.[23] In the *Vedas*, along with Ṛta, we also find the use of the word 'Dharma'. But it is very difficult to say what the exact meaning of the word Dharma was in the earliest period of the Vedic language.[24] It is, however, certainly derived from the root 'dhṛ' (to uphold: to support, to nourish) and at some places it means 'upholder, or supporter or sustainer'.[25] In most cases it means 'religious ordinances or rites'.[26] At other places, and in rare cases, it means 'fixed principles or rules of conduct'.[27] Thus in some passages of the *Ṛg Veda* the word Dharma means 'upholder or supporter', but in most other Ṛg Vedic passages it means 'religious ordinances and rites'. In rare cases it means 'fixed principles or rules of conduct.'[28] The *Atharvaveda* bespeaks of earth as 'upheld by Dharma'. (Pṛthivim dharmanā dhṛtam).[29] It also mentions the six fundamental principles of Dharma *viz.* truth, gratefulness, consecration, austerity, prayer and sacrifice (ritual), which uphold the earth.[30]

During the Vedic period the two concepts of Ṛta and Dharma were distinct and gradually the concept of Ṛta became less important. The moral implication of the concept of Ṛta, however, got associated with the concept of Dharma, and Ṛta simply signified 'Truth' in later literature. How and

22. Keith, *Religion and Philosophy of the Veda and Upanisads*, Vol. 1, p. 35.
23. Gokhale, *op. cit.*, p. 25.
24. Kane, *History of the Dharma Sāstras*, Poona, 1930, Vol. I, p. 1.
25. *Ṛg*. I. 187.1, X. 92.2.
26. *Ṛg*. I. 22.18; V. 26.6; VIII, 43.24.
27. *Ṛg*. IV. 53.3; V.63.7; VI.70.1; VII.89.5 ;*op. cit.*, Vol. 1, p. 1.
28. Kane, *op. cit.*, Vol. I, p. 1.
29. *Ath*. XII, 1-17.
30. *Ath*. XII, 1.1.

why the change in the concepts came about is difficult to explain. Dr. V.P. Verma says:

> "It is difficult to trace the process through which the notion of Ṛta mingled with Dharma but the mixture was intensely important because it lent to Dharma some sort of moral meaning. During the Vedic period the word Dharma signified only ordinance and law but due to fusion with Ṛta it came also to signify virtue or morality."[31]

So far as the cause of change in its meaning and concept is concerned, Mees is of the opinion that the conception of Ṛta was the product of a natural age in which not much egoistic initiative was yet given to man. In this age even social happening was considered a natural outcome of a corresponding spiritual happening. But soon the conditions changed. Man drifted away from nature, and hence his contact with nature ceased to be an inner one, rather it came to be based upon outer ceremonial form. Ṛta, therefore, ceased to be a cosmic power and became a mere rita. "A new conception was needed, a new name had to be found for the living experience, and the old Ṛta was reborn in Dharma wh ch is free from trammels of ceremonial forms, though it clothes itself in any form it pleases."[32] He also points out that when the same happened to dharma, the conception of Nīti arose.[33] Keith is of the opinion that the concept of Ṛta was probably not an Indian creation, the Aryans brought it from their original home, and "It did not long survive in its new milieu.[34] It appears that as the complexity of social organisation grew, the old concept was found to be inadequate, whereas the concept of Dharma was able to answer practicably all the needs of the growing complex situations. Maybe that when

31. Var, V.P., *Studies in Hindu Politica. Thought and its Metaphysical Foundations* (Motilal Banarsidass, Delhi, 1959), p. 109.
32. Mees, *op. cit.*, p. 10; *op. cit.*, Vol. I, p. 35.
33. *Ibid.*, p. 10n.
34. Keith, *op. cit.*, Vol. I, p. 35.

the tribal order began to break up and society became organised in state, the older order of Ṛta, which bound and sustained the tribal society became obsolete and a new concept of Dharma arose which was more social in character than the Ṛta. In course of time the term Ṛta ceased to be in vogue.[34a] Whatever might have been the cause of the change in the meaning of the two concepts and the gradual lessening of the importance of Ṛta, it is a fact that the concept of Dharma superseded the concept of Ṛta in later literature of India.

The Origin of the Concept of the Varna Dharma

Along with this change we find another development of great significance in the later portions.[35] Of the Ṛg Veda—the division of society into four classes with distinctive functions for each and their hierarchical gradation. The doctrine of the divine creation of four classes is to be found for the first time in the Purusa Sūkta.[36] Here we are told how the four classes—Brāhmanas, Rājanya, Vaisya and Sūdra—were formed or were created out of the different limbs of the Parama Purusa—Brāhmanas from his mouth, Rājanyas from his hands, Vaisyas from his thighs and Sūdras from his feet.[37] The same story is again repeated in the *Atharva-Veda.*[38] In the later Vedic period, this division hardened into the well-known system of four castes or Varnas which is the most important feature of Hindu Society.

We may mark some very fundamental principles of social organisation in the above description of the divine origin of classes and their functions. It signifies that the society is not a man-made or artificial creation. Moreover, it also involves the separation of the four classes by virtue of

34a. It appears that along with the gradual lessening of the importance of Vedic gods like Varuna, Indra and Mitra etc. the concept of Ṛta also became obsolete.

35. Macdonnel, *op. cit.*, p. 37.

36. *Ṛg*. X. 90.

37. *Ṛg*. X. 90.12.

38. *Atharva*. XXX.6.61.

their distinctive functions and their gradation, in order of their descending importance and at the same time their organic unity. Betty Heimann says that from the earliest time of the *Ṛg Veda,* Hindu thought is based on the "law of functionalism." "Ṛta is the functional balance of already existent single phenomena of which each in its proper place functions in its own law of activity and all of them collectively balance each other in mutually retarding or accelerating limiting or expanding rhythm. Each single function is appropriate to the thing concerned, but serves at the same time to fulfil the purpose of the whole. Apparently independent objects submit to the general rhythm of the universe, interdependent objects as they are."[39] According to this very principle of functional cooperation, balance order and rhythm, a huge cosmic order is visualised in which certain functions are allotted to its head, to its arms, to its trunk and to its feet. In the social cosmos the head is the Brāhmana, the arms the Ksatriya, the trunk the Vaisya, and the feet the Sūdra. And "each of these original four main castes functions in its proper place for the smooth collaboration of the whole."[40]

The Concept of Dharma in the Brāhmanas and Upanisads

In the Brāhmanas also the Ṛg Vedic dogma of the divine origin of four classes out of the different limbs of the Purusa is maintained.[41] Moreover in them[42] the word 'Dharma', along with signifying 'the whole body of religious duties', also stands for the principles of social order and of the supremacy of law. The Ṛg Vedic conception of the cosmic or divine law (Ṛta) operating in the social order is maintained with the change in nomenclature "Dharma" being used in place of 'Ṛta'.[43] Moreover, the word 'Dharma' now gains a moral content, being fused with the

39. Heimann, B., *Facets of Indian Thought*, p. 37.
40. *Ibid.*, p. 38.
41. *Panca Vimsa Pr.* VI, 1.6-11.
42. *Ait Br.* VII, 17, also VIII, 13.
43. Ghoshal, U.N., *History of Indian Political Ideas*, (Oxford, 1959), p. 22.

concept of Ṛta. In the *Satapatha Brahmana*,[44] it is said that "the waters are the law (Dharma), hence whenever the waters come down to this world, everything here comes to have been accorded with Dharma; but whenever there is drought then the stronger seizes upon the weaker for the waters are Dharma." This passage identifies the State of Nature without law with anarchy represented as in later times by the law of jungle (mātsyanyāya) from which it may be concluded that Dharma or law is the 'foundation of individual and collective security'[45] and the basis of social order. If there is no Dharma, society would relapse into the state of anarchy, where only the law of jungle would operate. This social order is divinely instituted and is represented by the four classes, which are sustained by Dharma. It is for maintaining this Dharma that kingship is instituted. The king is the Dharma-sya-Gopta (protector of the law)[46] and is the upholder of Dharma.[47] Dharma is thus imbued with the idea of morality carried by the concept of Ṛta, which in the *Ṛg Veda* signifies the cosmic and the moral order. Though the term 'Ṛta' has been superseded by the term 'Dharma', still its moral implication is incorporated and retained in this new term.

The Upanisadic view of the term 'Dharma is that it is the foundation of the whole universe, for it is through Dharma that one drives away the evil. Everything is founded on it, and hence, it is called the highest good.[48] In the *Bṛhadāranyaka Upanisad*, it is stated that after creating the four Varnas Brahma did not feel absolutely certain that the things will be all right. He, therefore, created still further, a better form, Dharma, the most excellent one. Dharma is the Ksatra of Ksatra, therefore there is nothing higher than Dharma. It is through Dharma that the weak man hopes to control the strong man. Dharma is truth. It is on account of the reign of Dharma or law that there is peace and order and the strong

44. *Saiapatha Br.* VI. I.6.24.
45. Ghosal, *op. cit.*, p. 23.
46. *Ait. Br.* VIII. 12 and 23.
47. *Satpatha Br.* V. 4, 5; V. 3, 35.
48. *Taittirīya Āranyaka* 10, 79.

man has to yield to the weaker man.[49] Dharna here means the supreme law that makes the social order possible and binds both the ruler and the ruled. It is equated with the supremacy of truth. The law is identical with truth. It is only after this and on account of the superior potency of Dharma (Law) that heaven and earth are able to hold together.[50] Sankara in his Bhāsya explains the relation of Satya and Dharma. He says that Satya becomes Dharma when it is translated into action. Thus the metaphysical concept of truth, the principle of order in the cosmos, informs the social relation. It becomes the moral norm of society which guides the social and political life, and informs the social and political institution. The interlinking of Ṛta, Satya, Dharma and Brahma is the fundamental basis of Indian ethics.[51] Dharma is the divine institution, it is the guiding principle of social and political life as also the ultimate end of social and political institutions.

Another meaning of Dharma in the Upanisad is the duties of particular classes and orders. "Its most prominent significance came to be the privileges, duties and obligations of man, his standard of conduct as a member of one of the castes, as a person in a particular stage in life."[52] It is in this sense that the word has been probably used in the famous exhortation to the pupil in the *Taittirīya Upanisad.*[53] "Speak the truth and practise (your own) Dharma."[54] The principle of law is thus brought into clear relation with the social concept.[55] The divine creation of the four classes is integrated with the divine principles of Dharma. Dharma is both law and the social order based on Varnāsrama Vyavasthā. Dharma is now begun to be interpreted in terms

49. *Bṛhd.* 1.4.14.
50. Belvalkar and Ranade, *History of Indian Philosophy*, Vol. II, p. 186.
51. R.K. Mukherji, *The Culture and Art of India*, p. 59.
52. Kane, *op. cit.*, p. 2.
53. *Taitt. Up.* 1.11.
54. Cf. Kane, *op. cit.*, p. 2.
55. Ghoshal, *op. cit.*, p. 23.

of social order characterised by the Varna system. "So among gods Brahma appeared by means of Agni, among men as Brāhmana, as Ksatriya by means of the (divine) Ksatriya, as Vaisya by means of the (divine) Vaisya, as Sūdra by means of the (divine) Sūdra."[56] Here the *Upanisad* does not argue like the *Bhagvadgitā* that the castes or classes were created by God according to "qualities and works" rather maintains that the castes on the earth were created after the pattern of castes in the heaven. This theory explains the origin of the earthly caste system "on the pattern of heavenly caste system almost in the manner in which ectypes in Plato's theory of ideas are merely of the archetypes."[57] Though the *Upanisad* does not develop, but it assumes the theory that the Dharma or law (which is identical with truth) was created so that the classes or castes in heaven and earth obey the same for the full realization of life and its purpose.[58] Hence the *Upanisads* put forward "another meaning of Dharma—the duties of the particular castes and orders."[59]

Thus the Vedic concept of Dharma which originally signified only the religious ordinances and rites, fusing with the concept of Ṛta, developed into the concept of virtue and morality. Further it assumed two meanings, during the Upanisadic period : on the one hand it became identified with a moral view or an ethics of virtue on which Buddhism laid great stress; and on the other, it became identified with "the social duties of various castes and orders."[60] This latter aspect of Dharma is given more prominence by Hinduism. The performance of one's duties in one's station in life is regarded as morality, and the moral life is equated with doing one's duties in one's station in life.[61] In the *Mahābhārata* the moral view or ethics of virtue becomes the sāmānya Dharma and the social aspect of Dharma becomes Varnāsrama Dharma.

56. *Bṛhad.* 1.4.15.
57. Ranade, *A Constructive Survey of Upanisadic Philosophy*, p. 60.
58. Belvalkar and Ranade, *op. cit.*, p. 338.
59. Varma, *op. cit.*, p. 112.
60. *Ibid.*, p. 113.
61. *Ibid.*, p. 114.

According to the Buddhist, it is Dharma, which makes the differences between good and evil. Dharma is the ruler of rulers, the highest in the world.[62] For the Buddhists, the Dharma is the cosmic law of Righteousness in which everything dwells, and is fashioned and bound.[63] According to Buddha there is an automatic and universal law of causation (Dharma) which conditions the appearance of all events physical and mental. It is both cosmic and social. So far as the social and ethical aspect of the Buddhist concept of Dharma is concerned, "it is conformity to one's action to the commands of Śīla which brings about social adjustment and leads to the ultimate goal of Nirvāna."[64]

The Nature of Dharma

The concept of Dharma is the most important concept in Indian thought. It is the key to Hindi ethics, both, individual and social, and also the basis of individual progress and social welfare. Right through the ages it has permeated Indian thinking and life and has formulated a norm of thought and behaviour for the large majority of people in India. It embraced the whole life of man and "was not a creek or religion but a mode of life or a code of conduct which regulated man's work and activities as a member of society and an individual and was intended to bring about the gradual development of a man and to enable him to reach what was deemed to be the goal of human existence."[65]

Dharma seeks to resolve conflicts of human life.[66] It tries to reconcile the opposition between the individual good and social good. It lays down a way of life which aims at securing the material well-being, spiritual development and moral perfection, and the unhampered growth of both the

62. *Anguttara Nikāya*, III, p. 154; *Dīgha Nikāya*, III, p. 95.

63. Dharma Sangiti Sutra, *Siksasamuccaya*, pp. 322-23. Quoted in the *Sources of Indian Tradition*, pp. 182-83.

64. Varma, *op. cit.*, p. 116.

65. Kane, *Dharma Sastra*, Vol. II, p. 2.

66. Radhakrishnan, S., *Religion and Society*, pp. 105-106.

individual and society. Manu says that there is hardly any activity of man which is not permeated by Kāma or desire,[67] but to act solely on the urge of desire which is the outcome of Tamas is not praiseworthy,[68] and so to enable man to act properly by controlling his Tāmasic desires 'Dharma' is promulgated. To the extent society and the individual respect the Dharma, they are protected, and to the extent they make inroads into it, they are undermined.[69]

The full implication of Dharma cannot be conveyed by the English word 'religion' into which it is generally translated. It is a term of wide implications and conveys many ideas. Mees has analysed the concept of Dhạyma in his book *Dharma and Society* and has pointed out several implications and meanings of Dharma.[70] According to Benaya Kumar Sarkar there are at least five senses in which Dharma is used both in scientific treatises as well as in common parlance :

(i) Religion,
(ii) Virtue as opposed to vice or sin, a category of ethics,
(iii) law as category of jurisprudence,
(iv) justice and
(v) duty.[71]

Thus we see that the term Dharma is very çomprehensive and signifies various ideas which have accumulated around it in the course of centrism.

The term 'Dharma' is derived from the root 'dhṛ' which means to sustain, uphold or to hold together and nourish, i.e., it is the principle which sustains the moral law which sustains

67. *Manu*. II. 4.
68. *Ibid.*, II.2.
69. *Ibid.*, VIII. 15.
70. Mees, *op. cit.*, pp. 8-9.
71. Sarkar, B.K., *The Political Institutions and Theories of the Hindus* (Leizpig, 1922), p. 206.

the world, human society and the individual.[72] It is the principle which holds together signifying thereby the principle of order, social or moral. The world order is Dharma. It is that principle by which the Universe is upheld. "Without Dharma the cosmos would turn into chaos and the universe would fall to pieces and dissolve into nothingness", which, however, is not possible for, though sometimes there is disorder (Adharma) but it exists and can exist only locally for a time and in a particular part of the whole only. Order (Dharma) will, however, ultimately assert itself and prevail.[73] Dharma holds and sustains a thing and saves it from disintegration. It is the principle which is responsible for a thing or phenomenon functioning as it does and not in a different way. It is the nature of things, that which makes them what they are. We speak of anything of fire, or water, sun, moon, animal, man, etc. as behaving or functioning in particular way and having certain specific qualities of their own, e.g. the Dharma of fire is to burn, of water the flow, and so forth. But for its being rooted in its Dharma neither the universe nor any part thereof could function for a moment with any sense of certainty or reliability for man. The Dharma of man is the expression of the Universal in him, the 'idea' of man in the Platonic sense, the law of his own being which is essentially his own and not of any other object. It is the expression of the true being of things. But at the same time it is not only the law of each individual being but also of the whole and expresses the right relationship of each part to the whole. The Dharma of a thing is its intrinsic property, its real nature and its true being by virtue of which, it is what it is and ought to behave in a way it should. If it does otherwise, it is Adharma which will lead it to ultimate disintegration and death.[74] Dharma, therefore, sustains society. It permeates all.[75] What is contrary to it perishes.

Though the term Dharma is generally used to refer to

72. *Ṛg*. I. 187. I & X. 92.2; *Atharva*, XII.7; *Vajasaneyi Samhitā* XXXV III.17.
73. Woodroffe, *Sakti and Sākta* (Madras, 1965), p. 2.
74. *Ibid.*, p. 3.
75. *The Mahānārāyana Upanisad*, XVI. 6.

the religiously ordained duty, it also signifies morality, justice, right conduct, duty and the intrinsic nature of a thing. Besides, it also stands for a principle of Reason, the law of causality which is the law of Reason, that runs through the world. It is, however, 'a mystic force capable of rewarding and punishing human beings.''[76] And over and above these, it means one's duty in the station he is placed.[77]

Dharma, the Ultimate Goal of the Mahābhārata

The *Mahābhārata* is a very comprehensive work, a virtual Encyclopaedia, in which there is no major problem of life which has not been considered. The central concept, however, is Dharma, around which all other ideas revolve. It is Dharma or justice which has been again and again emphasized throughout its pages. The work itself is not to be regarded as a mere story of intrigues and battles but as an allegory of the struggle between good and evil, Dharma and Adharma and the ultimate triumph of the good. According to Sukthankar, "Yudhiṣṭhira's life is a categorical insistence on the paramouncy of moral rectitude and a fixed belief in the conservation of values."[78] He represents Dharma whereas his cousin Duryodhana is the embodiment of Adharma. Envy, jealousy, covetousness, duplicity, hate and demonic passions are the elements of the character. Wild demonic passion glows in Duryodhana which never allows him any peace."[79] Again, it presents "Dharma and Adharma in action, as it were, in the lives of the cousins."[80] "The conflict, he further says, between Dharma and Adharma is the everlasting conflict between the powers of light and darkness, between right and wrong. Though evil is allowed to flourish, even to dominate for a time, the epic wants to point out, its reign is short

76. Gokhale, *op. cit.*, p. 24.
77. Sukthankar, *On the Meaning of the Mahābhārata*, p. 80.
78. *Ibid.*, p. 77.
79. *Ibid.*, p. 77.
80. *Ibid.*, p. 77.

because it carries within itself the seeds of its own destruction."[81] Hence we must feel assured that goodness shall ultimately triumph (yato dharmas tato jayah). The *Gītā* says that whenever Dharma declines and Adharma uprises, the Lord creates Himself to protect the weak and destroy the wicked. To establish the Dharma firmly he comes into being again and again.[82] It is the function of God, the protector of the world to keep the world going on the lines of Dharma. He assumes birth in the world to uphold Dharma (right), when Adharma (wrong) prevails.

The Bhārata Sāvitrī which appears at the end of the *Mahābhārata* in the Svargārohana Parva, consisting of the four verses, is said to be the essence of the teaching of the *Mahābhārata*. In its first verse Vyāsa says :

> "With raised hands I cry aloud, nobody hears me. It is from Dharma that Artha and Kāma arise, why is Dharma not followed ?"

In the last verse, it is said :

> "Not out of passion or fear or averice, not even for the sake of life one should abandon Dharma. Dharma is everlasting, happiness and misery are transitory. The soul is eternal. That which embodies it is not eternal."[83]

Nīlakantha, the commentator of the *Mahābhārata*, declares that petty minded people pursue Dharma for the sake of wealth, but the high minded ones pursue Dharma for the sake of the purification of the mind. The epic lays down that the Dharma should be performed for the sake of Dharma only and not for the sake of enjoyment and desires. This, Nīlakantha says, is the essence of the *Mahābhārata*, the parting advice of mother Kunti to Yudhiṣṭhira may be taken to be the motto of the *Mahābhārata* :

81. Sukthankara, *op. cit.*, pp. 78-79.
82. *Gītā*, IV. 7-8.
83. Cf. V. 12-13.

"Let thy reason be fixed on Dharma.
Let thy mind be ever great."[84]

The *Mahābhārata* preaches the paramountcy of moral values—the Dharma.

Dharma, Its Definition and Meaning in the Mahābhārata

The *Mahābhārata* gives a general definition of Dharma in the Karna Parva as follows :

> "Dharma (morality) is so called, because it protects all. Indeed Dharma (morality) saves all creatures. Surely then that is Dharma (morality) which is capable of keeping off a creature from all injuries."[85]

Hence, the term means to 'maintain' or to 'sustain' and has the general significance of upholding the stability of society, the maintenance of social order (in which no one is injured) and the welfare of mankind. Again, in the Śānti Parva, the *Mahābhārata* means by Dharma that principle which produces the welfare of mankind, that which brings about advancement and growth is Dharma.[86] Dharma has been preached to prevent creatures from injuring one another. Therefore, Dharma is that which prevents injury to creatures.[87] The world is stable and worth living because of Dharma, people prosper because of Dharma and Dharma destroys sin and sustains everything.[88]

Yudhiṣṭhira, being in doubt about the nature of Dharma asked Bhīsma to explain its nature and origin and also to enlighten as to whether Dharma is for this world or the next.[89]

84. *Mbh.* XV. 17.21.
85. *Karna* 69.58; *op. cit.*, Śānti. 109.11.
86. XII. 109-10
87. *Mbh.* XII. 109-12.
88. *Mahānārāyanopanisad*, XXII, 1.
89. *Mhh.* XII. 259. 1.

Bhīsma, after explaining the difficulties in the way of defining it, gave some rules by which Dharma may be determined. Dharma, said he, was ordained for the advancement and growth of all creatures and, therefore, that which leads to advancement and growth is Dharma. Dharma was ordained for restricting creatures from injuring one another, and therefore, that which prevents injury to creatures is Dharma. Dharma is so called because it upholds all creatures and therefore, that is Dharma which is capable of upholding all creatures.[90] He says :

> "In both the worlds, here and hereafter, righteousness (Dharma) begets happiness as its fruit."[91]

Thus, according to the *Mahābhārata*, is that which conduces to the stability of society and the maintenance of social order and well-being.

In the *Mahābhārata* it is said that it is Dharma which puts an end to "Mātsyanyāyika Adharma" through the agency of state or Danda. Therefore, if there is no Dharma, people would fall into the stage of injustice and violence. Dharma destroyed, destroys, Dharma protected, protects.[92]

The epic always reminds us that Dharma is subtle. It is not simple and unitary but many-sided and complex. Dharma, in the sphere of an individual member of society, is the integration of his personality which requires the control of his passions by reason and his moral obligation to society. It lies in the performance of his Svadharma without attachment. Dharma, in the sphere of society, is the social solidarity which is brought about by Varnāsrama Vyavasthā which establishes an organic unity amongst the various classes of society and balances Pravṛti and Nivati. Dharma, in the sphere of law and politics, is the establishment of a political organisation which puts an end to injustice and brings about peace, order and security in the society and provides justice to each and all.

90. *Mbh.* XII. Chap. 259. cf. Sukthankar, *op. cit.*, p. 81.

91. *Mbh.* XII. 259.5.

92. *Mbh.* XII. 259.5.

Dharma, in the sphere of religion, is men's attempt to attain the *summum bonum* of life—the moksa. Dharma is therefore every body in every sphere and situation of life. Every form of life, every individual and every group of individuals has its dharma which is the law of its being. Dharma or morality is conformity to the truth of things, the true being of them, Adharma is the opposition to it. Moral evil is non-conformity to truth which upholds, sustains and controls the world; it is disharmony with the eternal law of justice and goodness. The duty of man is to know Dharma accurately and act according to it. If he does so, happiness is assured in his life here and hereafter.[93] The rules of Dharma have been sanctioned to conduct the world.[94] If these rules are followed, life would be happy, peaceful and secure. Man should look to the comforts of others. "A person should never do to others which he does not like to be done to himself by others, knowing how painful it is to himself."[95] This is the fundamental principle of Dharma. Dharma consists in the performance of objects by means of agreeable means.[96] This is the principle which holds the world together and brings about stability, order, advancement and growth.

The Concept of Varna Dharma in the Mahābhārata

The *Mahābhārata* accepts the divine origin of the Varna system and its hierarchical stratification[97] but at the same time it is also conscious of the injustice involved in such a social gradation based merely on birth; and therefore, it tries to justify it on metaphysical and ethical considerations. We have already seen how the four Varnas were created from the different organs of the Great Purusa. An allegorical meaning and significance is attached to the whole of the Purusasūkta,

93. *Mbh.* XII. 295.5.
94. *Mbh.* VII. 259.4.
95. *Mbh.* XII. 259.20.
96. *Mbh.* XII. 259.25.
97. *Mbh.* XII. 46.68; XII. 72. 4-5; XII. 188. 4-5. XII. 318.90; XII. 296. 5-6; X. 3.18-19; XIII. 48. 3; XIII. 141.30.

and it is suggested that the whole universe as well as the 'body social' is the Great Purusa.[98] The Purusa is described as being himself "whole universe, whatever has been and whatever shall be."[99] The moon came out of his mind, the sun from his eyes, Indra and Agni were created from his mouth, air or wind from his breath; and further from his navel arose atmosphere (antariksa), from his head the sky, from his feet the earth,and from ears the four quarters (disah). In this manner the worlds were created.[100] Thus, symbolically the microcosmic elements have been traced to, and identified with, the macrocosmic ones. Not only the Universe but "the whole social organisation is here conceived symbolically as one human being—the 'Body Social', we may say—with its limbs representing the social classes based on the principle of division of labour.[101] The *Mahābhārata* too, like the Purusa Sūkta of the *Ṛg Veda*, symbolically identifies different classes with the different limbs or the human body performing different functions suited to them. Thus the whole society is an organism, and every class is designed to perform a particular function in society so as to fulfil its obligation to the body social, as the different organs of the body do and thereby jointly share the constructive contribution to the social well-being and the privileges to certain Varnas are nothing but certain facilities provide to them to fulfil their obligations in an efficient way. Each class is an integral part of the whole fabric of society. The four classes of the society are supposed to stand in relation to the social organisation in the same relationship as the different organs of the primeval Man to his body. Varna Vyavasthā stands for an organic as against atomistic conception of society. The four classes[102] as described in the Purusa Sūkta, constituting the body-social as divinely ordained, may be said to be natural. It appears that the *Ṛg Veda* wants to convey

98. Prabhu, *Hindu Social Organisation* (Popular Prakashan, Bombay, 1963), p. 286.
99. *Ṛg*. X. 90.2.
100. *Ṛg*. X. 90. 13-14; Cf. *Mbh*. XII. 46.69.
101. Prabhu, *op. cit.*, p. 286.
102. Vedic Index, Vol. VI, p. 247; also refer to Kane, *op. cit.*, Vol. II, Part-I, p. 27.

the idea that the division of society into classes is natural. In the Anusāsana Parva of the *Mahābhārata* also, the natural character of Varna system based on natural disposition and qualities of man is emphasized.[103]

The Purusa Sükta does not directly refer to the gradation of the four classes which, however, can be imputed to it by implication. It is the Taittirīya Samhitā which ascribing the original of the four classes to the different limbs of the creator, adds an explanation of the gradation of the social status and says that Brāhmanas are declared to be the foremost, because they were created from the mouth, the Rājanyas were vigorous, because they were created from vigour; the Vaisyas were meant to be eaten (referring to their liability to excessive taxation), because they were created from the stomach; and as the Sūdras were created from the feet they are to be the 'footmen', the servants of other Varnas.[104] The *Mahābhārata* accepts this basis of gradation at several places.[105] It is maintained that the functions of the four orders are ordained by the creator just at the time of birth.[106] Thus the work, the pattern of behaviour and the hierarchy of gradation are pre-ordained by God in which the Brahmins are at the head and the Sūdras at the bottom. This appears to be the general acceptance in the *Mahābhārata*.[107]

But, as has already been pointed out, the epic is quite conscious of the injustice involved in this traditional theory.[108] At some places, therefore, the *Mahābhārata* explains and justifies the Varna system and its gradation on the basis of colour. In the dialogue between Bhṛgu and Bhāradvāja, the former says that originally there was no differentiation of Varnas. Being born from the Brahmā, the whole of the world consisted of Brāhmanas. Later on, however, due to

103. *Mbh*. XIII. 143.6.

104. *Taitt. Sam*. VII. 1.1.4-6.

105. *Mbh*. XII. 72.4-5; VIII. 23.32; X.3.18-20; XIII. 48.3.

106. *Mbh*. XII. 72. 5-8.

107. Dhairyabala P. Vora, *Evolution of Morals in the Epics* (Bombay, 1959), p. 126.

108. *Mbh*. XII. 188. 6-9.

differences in work, the Varnas evolved.[109] All were originally Brāhmanas and were white in colour but later on these Brāhmanas who left their own Dharma, indulged in enjoyments, became subject of anger and harshness and performed courageous deeds became 'red' and assumed Ksatriyahood. Those who adopted agriculture became 'Yellow' and were called Vaisya. Those who resorted to untruth, violence, and impiety became black and came to be called Sūdra.[110] Thus the four divisions of mankind—Brāhmanas, Ksatriyas, Vaisyas and Sūdras—assumed white, red, yellow and black complexions respectively.[111] Thus, falling away from their duties, some of the original Brāhmanas turned into the three lower Varnas.

Varnas Determined by Karma

Another explanation of the Varna is given on the basis of the theory of Karma. The Chandogya Upanisad[112] has already given an explanation of it on the basis of this theory. In the *Mahābhārata* it is said[113] that the Dvijas who do not regard this world to be a manifestation of Brahmā and avoid Dharma and follow different occupations are born in different Varnas as well as in different Yonis.

The reasons of one's being born in a low Varna is his previous Karma. It is difficult to evercome the consequences of one's past deeds. The birth in a lower class is caused by sins committed in one's former life.[114] In the Anusāsana Parva it is said that a person of lower Varna may attain the status of a higher Varna in the next birth by following his own Dharma in this life, and conversely, the person who does not follow his own Dharma will be born in a lower Várna.[115] The *Mahābhārata* wants to show that the status of every

109. *Mbh.* XII. 188. 10.
110. *Mbh.* XII. 188. 11-13.
111. *Mbh.* XII. 5.
112. *Chand.* X. 10.7.
113. *Mbh.* XII. 188. 16-17.
114. *Mbh.* 111. 208.2; 111. 208.11.
115. *Mbh.* XIII. 143. 7-14.

individual in life is determined by his Karma or action of his previous lives, and that his salvation depends on due observance of his Dharma, i.e., the practice of virtue and the performance of duty in the station of life in which he is placed.

The *Gītā* too upholds the theory that the traits of the individuals are inherent right from the beginning, based on their past deeds.[116] Even though a man does not want to do a particular type of work he is driven to do it by the compulsive power of his nature.[117] Thus the *Gītā* tries to justify the division of society into classes on the principle of Karma and swabhāva even though this theory fails to explain "how individuals at the very beginning of the creation came to be possessed of particular qualities and capacities."[118]

Gunas as the Basis of Varna System

Another theory by the help of which Varna system is explained and justified, is the theory of Gunas. The theory of Gunas was probably elaborated by Kapila the preceded Buddha by a century or so and preached the samkhya school of philosophy. In the *Atharva Veda*[119] also we find a trace of this theory. It is possible that this may be the first reference to the three Gunas. In the Chandogya Upanisad[120] we are told that behind all things there are really three colours: white, red and black and that it is only these which may really be said to exist while all other things which are constituted out of them are merely words, modifications, and names. In some other Upanisads we find a more elaborate treatment of the theory of Gunas. In the svetāsvatāra[121] and the Maitrāyani[122] Upanisads find several references to Gunas. According to the theory of Gunas, matter is constituted of

116. *Gītā*, VI. 41-46.
117. *Gītā*, XVIII. 60.
118. Ghurye, *Caste, Class and Occupation* (Bombay, 1961), p. 64.
119. *Atharva*, X. 8.43.
120. *Chand.* VI. 4.1.
121. *Sveta.* I. 4, IV. 5.
122. *Maitra*, III. 2; VI. 10.

three dispositions called Gunas—purity (Sattva), passion (Rajas) and darkness (Tamas). Sattva is light, revealing, happy and good, Rajas is active, restless, passionate and sorrowful; and Tamas heavy, stupid and obscuring. These Gunas are not only constituted in Nature or Matter but human nature too is constituted of them. Not only this, the three Gunas stand roughly for the preservative, creative, and destructive powers of God respectively.[123]

In the *Mahābhārata* we find two interpretations of the Guna theory. Firstly, it applies to the three primary ingredients of Prakrti, the Primal Matter. The Gunas are manifested in all created beings as well as things in varied proportions. Secondly, they represent various qualities manifested in human behaviour. In human beings one or the other of these three Gunas preponderate. As a result of this, the society is divided into classes which represent the preponderance of one or the other of the Gunas. Sattva Guna is said to be white in colour, Rajas red and Tamas dark; while a mixture of Rajas and Tamas is yellow in colour. These colours, representing different Gunas, are further attributed to the Varnas. The Brāhmanas possess sattvika temperament and hence they are said to be white in colour, the Ksatriyas possess Rajas temperament and hence they are said to be red in colour. Vaisyas possess a mixture of Rajas and Tamas temperament and hence they are said to be yellow in colour. Sūdras possess Tāmasika temperament and hence they are of the black colour.

"Of all the ideologies of the Hindu thinkers concerning social organisation on the Varna basis (Varna Vyavasthā), the statement made in the *Bhagavadgītā* is the most outstanding and specific."[124]

The *Gītā* classifies society into four classes on the basis of Svabhāva (Guna) and Karma. Since men have different mental constitutions, nature and dispositions, they all cannot be put in one class rather different classes have to be formed,

123. S.C. Chatterjee, *The Fundamentals of Hinduism*, p. 15, Radhakrishnan, *The Bhagawadgītā*, p. 317.

124. Prabhu, *op. cit.*, p. 314.

and their duties and works have to be determined best suited to their nature and temperament. Men have different psychic, different tendencies and capacities, different traits and characters, and therefore, the division of society into classes is natural. Hence, "Gunas may be said to be the psycho-moral based on Varna organisation."[125]

The word Dharma generally means the pattern or ideal of moral behaviour. But it also means 'property' and 'function' of a thing in the sense in which these terms are used in physics or chemistry. The function of a thing derives directly from the intrinsic quality or property of the thing concerned. This is why the *Gītā* defines *Dharma* as the innate law of an entity and the behaviour and action proceeding from and determined by that Svabhāva or inner nature (Svabhava Niya tam Karma).[126] But so far as inanimate things are concerned, the relationship between nature and function is direct and automatic, but in the case of human beings, the relationship between Svabhāva and Karma is not automatic. The Karma amongst human beings does not follow automatically from Svabhāva but has to be adjusted deliberately made to conform to it. Herein lies the necessity of Dharma in human world.[127]

Human society is a graded organisation because men have different mental constitution, different psychological make-up, different temperaments, different aptitudes, different capacities and different vocations. There must be, as a result of it, gradation of duty. The duty in one State of life, in one set of circumstances will not and cannot be that of another. Potentialities and limitations differ from man to man according to the different permutation and combination of the three Gunas in him. Hence, it is but natural that society is divided into different classes which can be grouped into four orders. Ideally the Varna organisation of the Hindu Society gives little basis for exclusiveness or distinction of superiority and inferiority. It only emphasizes that society is a partnership with a division of functions.

125. *Ibid.*, p. 315.
126. *Gītā*, XVIII, 47.
127. Krishna Chaitanya, *Sanskrit Poetics* (Asia Publishing House, 1965), p. 346.

This fact was accepted in Indian social organisation and was stressed by morality and religion from the very early times. Different rules of conduct and different duties for different types of men have always been prescribed. The *Gītā* stresses that man should realise this fact and shape his ideals according to the status to which he belongs and follow his Svadharma, that is, do his duty according to his temperament and the requirements of the society.

The activities of the four Varnas are distinguished in accordance with the qualities of their nature.[128] Thus the *Gītā* shifts the emphasis from birth to the nature of individual man. It is nature and quality that determine one's station in life. The Varna system recognises that different men should contribute to the general good in different ways. Society is a functional organisation and all functions which are essential for the well-being of society, are to be regarded as socially equal. Since all are equally necessary for society, hence there is nothing degrading or elevating so far as the different functions required for society are concerned. What matters is the right performance of duties. "Devoted each to his own duty man attains perfection[129] Within the power of our nature and being, true to our feelings and impulses we must fulfil our duties. Better is one's own Dharma, though imperfectly carried out, than the Dharma of another carried out perfectly. One does not incur sin, when one does the duties ordained by one's own nature.[130] One should not give up the work suited to one's nature, though it may be defective, for all enterprizes are clouded by defects as fire by smoke.[131]

The four-fold category of individual natures is not artificial. They are inherent in men. It is on this natural division that the *Gītā* builds the firm foundation of the four-fold order of society, the caturvarna. Lord Kṛṣṇa says, "The four-fold order was created by Mahābhārata according to the

128. *Gītā*, XVIII, 41.
129. *Gītā*, XVIII, 45.
130. *Gītā*, XVIII, 47.
131. *Gītā*, XVIII. 48; III. 35.

division of quality and work.[132] Thus in explaining the basis of the four-fold order of society the *Gitā* lays stress on Guna and Karma and not on birth. "The class determined by temperament and vocation is not a caste determined by birth and heredity."[133] The work of Brāhmin, Ksatriyas, Vaisyas and Sūdras says the *Gitā*, are divided according to the qualities (Gunas) born of their own inner nature, spiritual temperament and essential character (Svabhāva). "Serenity, self-control, austerity, purity, forbearance and uprightness, wisdom, knowledge and faith in religion, these are the duties of the Brāhmin, born of his inner nature. Heroism and vigour, steadiness, resourcefulness, not falling even in battle, generosity and leadership are the duties of Ksatriya born of his nature. Agriculture, tending of cattle and trade are the duties of Vaisya born of his nature; and work of the character of service is the duty of Sūdra born of his nature."[134] Society, according to the *Gītā*, is not a blind aggregate of individuals. It is an organism of which different grades (Varnas) perform different tasks. The four-fold order is organised like a pyramid at the top of which stands the Brāhmana, the man of purity. Others also can rise to the top, for others is no bar to their ascent.

Character, not Birth, the Basis of Varna

Thus it is character and Guna which are the determinant of Varna or class, and not birth. In the Chāndogyopanisad,[135] there is a story concerning satyakāma jābāla. When he went to Haridrumata Gautama and requested him to be his disciple, the latter asked him as to which Varna he belonged. Satya Kama said, "I do not know this, Sir, of what family I am. I asked my mother. She answered me 'in my youth when I went about a great deal serving as a maid I got you. So I do not know this of what family you are.' " To him, then, Gautama

132. *Gītā*, IV. 13.

133. Radha Krishnan, *Bhagwadgītā* (George Allen & Unwin, 1948), p. 161.

134. *Gītā*, XVIII. 42-44.

135. *Chand.* IV. 4.

said, "A non-Brāhmana would not be able to explain this. Bring the fuel, my dear, I will receive you as a pupil. You have not deviated from the truth." This story shows that it is character, which should be considered as the best tent to decide the Varna of a man, and not birth.

The *Mahābhārata* also at some places supports this theory. In the Dialogue between Yudhiṣṭhira and the Serpent in the Vana Parva, the serpent asks, "who is the Brāhmana ?" Yudhiṣṭhira replies, "know him to be Brāhmana, O best of the serpents, who is truthful, charitable, forgiving, gentle, soft, merciful and who behaves according to Dharma." The serpent, then, asks, "O Yudhiṣṭhira, Veda is truth and it maintains the Varna system. If these (Gunas) can be found even amongst the Sūdra, then will he also be considered a Brāhmana ?" Yudhiṣṭhira replies, "If a Sūdra shows these qualities and a Brāhmana does not show them, then that Sūdra is not Sūdra, neither that Brāhmana a Brāhmana. O Serpent, know him only to be a Brāhmana who reveals these characteristics and him to be a sūdra who does not reveal them." The serpent then asks, "If a Brāhmana is to be known by his behaviour then the whole system of Varna would be useless." To this Yudhiṣṭhira replies, "Men of all Varnas can produce children with the women of all Varnas, and hence all Varnas are but a mixture. Thus it is difficult to test the Varna of an individual. Moreover a man can beget children on any woman. Speech, sexual desire, birth and death are common characteristics of all human beings. So it is difficult to decide the Varna on these bases. A person with deep insight should consider character as the best thing to decide in respect of Varna. So, O best of the serpents, one who possesses the best of the behaviour and has gone through all the good sanskaras, is a Brāhmana."[136] Here, in this passage, the emphasis is shifted from heredity to character,[137] and this enabled the individual to raise himself higher in social gradation by virtue of his noble character. This could, no doubt, serve as the stimulus to the moral and spiritual development of the indivi-

136. *Mbh.* III. 180.

137. *Ibid.*, III. 180.33.

dual of a lower grade. Similarly, when an individual belonging to the higher class, knew that if there were lapses in his character, he might be degraded in social status, and so he would try to avoid it.

It should be noted here that according to the *Mahābhārata*, till one is initiated into the Vedas, every man is just like a Sūdra.[138] It, therefore, means that all the children are supposed to Sūdras in their infancy. It is after their initiation into education and after they have attained their Sīla and Sadācāra, that their Varna is determined. A man becomes Brāhmana only when he possesses requisite character and qualifications.[139]

In the *Parāsara Gītā*,[140] it is said that originally all human beings were born from Brahmā. How then, it is asked that there is differentiation of classes. Parāsara replies that distinction of Varna occurred due to want of Tapas, that is, an ascetic life involving high moral standard. He is of the opinion that the three higher Varnas are degraded, if they resort to "Viparita Karma".[141] Further, according to him, an enlightened Sūdra is like Prajāpati and Vishnu, because he looks after and serves others.[142]

In the Ādiparva[143] Duryodhana also maintains that the origin of the brave as well as of the river is difficult to locate, meaning thereby that it is the work which determines one's Varna and not his birth. Again, in the Śāntiparva, Ṛṣi Bhṛgu very explicitly maintains that Varnas depend on Dharmas and not *vice versa*. Here Bhāradwāja asks him that if the distinctions between four castes be made by means of colour only, then it seems that all the four orders have intermixed. Lust, anger, fear, cupidity, grief, anxiety, hunger, exhaustion possess and prevail over all men. How can men then be distinguished by the attributes ? The bodies of all men

138. *Ibid.*, III. 180.35.
139. *Ibid.*, III. 180. 36-37.
140. *Ibid.*, XII. 296. 1-3.
141. *Mbh.* VII. 296. 26.
142. *Ibid.*, XII. 296. 28.
143. *Ibid.*, I. 127. 10.

sweat and puss and have urine, phlegm, bile and blood. How then can men be divided into classes ?[144] Bhṛgu replies that there is in fact no distinction between different castes. The whole world at first consisted of Brāhmanas—created equal by Brahmā. Men have, on account of their acts, been divided into various castes.[145] Men assumed different Varnas by dint of their character, aptitudes and work.[146] "Divided by these occupations, Brāhmanas, falling away from their own order, became members of the other three classes. All the four Varnas, therefore, have the right to perform all pious rites and sacrifices. Thus, were the four castes, at first created equal by Brahmā who ordained for all of them the observances described in the Vedas, cupidity alone brought about the fall of many who were possessed by ignorance."[147] Further, it is said, "If these marks[148] are to be seen in a Sūdra, and if they are not seen in a Brāhmana, then such a Sūdra is no Sūdra and such a Brāhmana is no Brāhmana."[149] This is a clear statement that a man's Varna has to be determined by his deeds, character and mode of behaviour and not by birth. Instead of laying stress on differentiation, the *Mahābhārata* maintains that all the castes are holy and are allied to one another by blood. They have all originated from Brāhmanas. It is the Brāhmana who is manifested in the other three Varnas.[150]

Thus, we find that it is with the help of the theory of Karma and Guna that the *Mahābhārata* provides an explanation on the gradation of society into four classes. A man is born with certain good or bad qualities by virtue of his deeds of previous life. These inborn qualities of man and his inherent nature from the proper criterion for determining his

144. *Ibid.*, XII. 188. 6-8.
145. *Ibid.*, XII. 188. 10.
146. *Mbh.* XII. 188. 11-13.
147. *Ibid.*, XII. 188. 14-15.
148. Pertaining to Brāhmins, e.g., truth, purity, mercy, benevolence etc.
149. *Mbh.* XXI. 189. 8.
150. *Ibid.*, XII. 60, 47.

status in the society under the Varna system and for actions and duties suitable to that status are assigned to him. The inherent qualities of a man are the results of the karmas of his previous birth.

Now let us come to Āsramadharma.

Āsramadharma: The life of the individual was divided into four stages or āsramas, i.e., *Brahmacaryāsrama*, *Gṛhasthāsrama*, *Vanaprasthāsrama* and *Samnyāsāsrama*. The duties of the individual, which were determined by the different stages are very elaborately discussed in the epic. The *Brahmacaryāsrama* may be called the stage of the students, the *Gṛhasthāsrama*—the stage of the householders, the *Vanaprasthāsrama*—the stage of the hermits residing in the forest away from cities and villages, and the *Samnyāsāsrama*—the stage of ascetics leading a wandering life for spiritual enlightenment and *Moksa*.

The word *āsrama* is originally derived from the sanskrit root *srama* 'to exert oneself'; therefore, it may mean by derivation, (i) a place where exertions are performed, and (ii) the action of performing such exertions.[151] According to P.H. Valavalkar, "literally, an *āsrama* is a 'halting or resting place'. The word, therefore, signifies a halt, a stoppage or a stage in the journey of life just for the sake of, in a sense, rest in order to prepare oneself for further journey. The *āsramas*, then, are to be regarded as resting places during one's journey on the way to final liberation which is the final aim of life."[152] *Āsramas*, as halting places in the journey of life, seem to be more logical and convincing because we ourselves feel that we have different obligations in different stages of our life. We should perform only those duties which are prescribed for that particular period of life, A man belongs to one particular stage for a limited period. One cannot proceed from one stage to another according to one's own choice without caring for one's age which is the guiding factor of these stages. So, a man has to wait at one stage till his

151. Encyclopaedia of Religion and Ethics, Art. on *Āsrama* by Deussen.

152. Valavalkar, Pandharinath H., *Hindu Social Institutions*, pp. 70-71.

age permits him for the change of the āsrama from one to another.

The *Brahmacaryāsrama* is a period of learning and discipline. After initiation, the boy goes to a teacher called as 'guru' from whom he receives instructions and education. For the whole period, he lives with his 'guru' in a position of subordination to him. It has a significance because ii moulds and forms the boy's character. Here, a strict moral education is given to the boys. Saint Bhṛgu narrates the duties of the *Brahmacaryāsrama,* thus "He who is in this mode of life, should have his soul cleansed by purity of conduct, by Vedic rites, and by restraints and vows and humility. He should worship the morning and evening twilights, the Sun, his own sacred fire, and the deities. He should cast off procrastination and idleness. He should cleanse his soul by saluting his preceptor, by studying the *Vedas,* and by listening to his preceptor's instructions. He should perform his ablutions thrice, (viz., in the morning, noon, and evening). He should lead a life of celibacy : attend to his sacred fire; dutifully serve his preceptor; daily go out on a round of mendicancy (for supporting himself); and give ungrudgingly unto his preceptor the whole of what is obtained in alms. Willingly accomplishing everything that the commands of his preceptor may indicate, he should be ready to receive such Vedic instruction as his preceptor may give him as a favour."[153] At another place in the epic we notice almost the same duties of this stage observed by Mahesvara in the *Anuśāsanaparva.*[154]

When we analyse these duties mentioned in the epic, the life of a *Brahmacāri* seems to be the embodiment of these ethical elements of service, study, simplicity, self-control, self-sacrifice, obedience, physical and moral courage and endurance.

Service is the duty owned to God, to the 'guru', to the parents. The service to be rendered to God is worship. The service to the 'guru' is very much emphasized in the epic. In the *Śāntiparva* Bhīsma suggests that a *Brahmacāri* should

153. *Śānti,* 191, 8 (G.P.).

154. *Anu.* 141, 36.

always keep himself in service to his teacher.[155] The service to parents also forms an important part of this life. The main task of this stage is to study the *Vedas* and to know the nature of God, self, and world. Without studying them no one can judge actions as right or wrong and cannot choose the right path in life. Simple life is the important aspect of this stage. A *Brahmacāri* does not lead a luxurious life in the hut of the guru. He does not get luxurious cloth, bed and food at all. He has to live on the food which he receives as alms.

Similarly, obedience is the important virtue of this stage. A *Brahmacāri*, whether he is a prince or a pauper, must obey the orders of his 'guru'. He has to obey the order without any exception. It is because the *Brahmacāri* has such sincere regard for the 'guru' that he obeys guru's orders even at the cost of his life.

The qualities of physical capacity and moral courage are important characteristics of this stage. The first lesson the boy receives from his teacher is the lesson of endurance. Without this quality man cannot do any work, whether easy or difficult. Only by his endurance, one can face the difficulties and calamities which fall upon him in life.

Brahmacarya or control of the mind and sense-organs is the essential virtue of this *Brahmacaryāsrama*. This stage is named after this very virtue. Absolute chastity and absolute continence are necessary for student-life. It seems to be based on sound psychological moral reasons. During adolescence all the vital energy of the youth is required for his physical and psychological development.

Annie Besant very nicely concludes the ethical elements of *Brahmacaryāsrama* in this way, "Sometimes in England the phrase is used 'the three R's' and by this is meant the elements of education—Reading, wRiting, and aRithmetic. To teach 'the three R's' is to give a child elementary education. So we might call the elements of the Brahmacāri's life, the four S's—Service, Study, Simplicity, and Self-control."[156]

155. *Śānti*, 61, 20.

156. Besant, Annie, *Hindu Ideals*, p. 28.

The second *āsrama* is *Gṛhasthāsrama* or the life of a householder. The duties of this stage are also discussed very elaborately in the epic. The life of the householder comes when the student-life is completed. In this stage he weds a wife and produces children. Bhīsma enumerates the duties of the *Gṛhasthāsrama*, thus, "A *Gṛhastha* should remain satisfied with his wife with full affection. He should have sensual gratification with his wife in proper time. He should follow the orders of the scriptures. He should remain aloof from cruelty, enmity, and take limited food, and employ himself in praying to gods. He must express his gratitude to his benefactors, speak the truth, have affection and forgiveness for all."[157] Further that a *Gṛhastha* or a householder must control his sense-organs and obey the orders of the scriptures and the teachers. For the satisfaction of his parted souls and gods he must not forget to offer ritual sacrifices. He must engage himself in ritual sacrifices like *yajña* while giving food and other requirements to others of different *āsramas* remaining detached from enmity.[158] Mahesvara states in the *Anuśāsanaparva* that hospitality and protecting the three fires *gṛhapati* etc. are the duties of a householder. He must also look after the cattle.[159] He should take his meal only after the other members of his family have taken theirs. This is regarded as the special duty of a *Gṛhastha* in the epic.[160] The following description of duties has been given by Mahesvara in the *Anuśāsanaparva*. "To perform the five great sacrifices, namely the sacrifice to the *Devas* or Deities or gods, to the *Ṛṣis* or saints, to the *Pitṛs* or dead forefathers, to the men coming to the house and to the lower beings like cattle around and to keep the mind pure, are the duties of the householder. The householder is righteous who always speaks the truth, never sees the fault in others, offers gifts, respects the Brāhmins, keeps his own house neat and clean, gives up vanity and pride, lives with humbleness, speaks affectionately

157. *Śānti*, 61, 11.
158. *Ibid.*, 61, 12.
159. *Anu.*, 141, 40.
160. *Ibid.*, 141, 42.

or politely, engeges himself in the services of guests, eats grains residued from sacrifices, and offers footwears, water, seat, bed, light and shelter to the guests in accordance with the orders of the scriptures."[161]

Observing the different duties of the householder we may briefly sum up the different ethical elements of this stage as service, study, simplicity, self-control, diligence, self-restraint, sacrifices, courtesy, hospitality, tenderness and protection. They have been regarded as fundamental virtues for the householder.

The *Gṛhasthāsrama* is regarded as very important because of its philanthropic scope. The whole world has to depend on it for food, lodging and clothing. In the *Parāsaragītā*, Parāsara states, "The other three āsramas are maintained by householder."[162] It is most important also because the individual enters into society with different responsiblities towards wife, father, mother, family, village and people at large. As I.C. Sharma puts it :

> "The *Grihastha Āsrama*, or the order of the householder, is regarded as the most important because it is at this stage that the individual enters into the first unit of society, i.e., the family, and the responsibility of supporting his wife and children falls on him. As a husband and a father he must experience love and utilize the wealth he earns for the fulfilment of his desires as well as those of his family members."[163]

The third stage of life is called the *Vānaprasthāṣrama*. A man after completing the *Gṛhasthāsrama*, taking firm resolution and keeping his sense-organs under control enters the forest life. In the epic the duties of the *Vānaprastha* are to sleep on the earth, to wear hair in braids, beard and moustache, to wear deerskin and tattered garments (valkala), to offer hospitality to gods and guests, to worship gods even

161. *Ibid.*, 141, 71-73.
162. *Śānti*, 295, 39.
163. Sharma, I.C., *Ethical Philosophy of India*, p. 79.

after bearing the greatest troubles; to offer sacred fires and take bath thrice a day for it, to observe celibacy, forgiveness and purity (sauca) as their eternal duties.[164] In the epic Mahesvara suggests that the *Vānaprasthas* should live in the forest, walk on the path of the forest and should lead their lives in the shelter of the forest like the teacher or *guru*.[165] Bhṛgu in the *Śāntiparva* prescribes for a *Vānaprastha* to eat limited spontaneously grown grain, fruits, roots with leaves, giving up beautiful clothes, tasteful food and sensual gratification of the householders in the villages.[166] Mahesvara enumerates the duties of the *Vānaprasthas* thus, "Performing ablutions thrice a day, worshipping the *Pitṛs* and the deities, pouring libations on the sacred fire, performing of those sacrifices and rites that go by the name of *Isti-homa*, picking up the grains of *Nīvāra*-paddy, eating fruits and roots, and using oil that is pressed out from *Inguda* and castor seeds, are their duties."[167] He further states :

> "Observant of the excellent ordinances relating to yoga, sitting in summer in the midst of four fires on four sides with the sun overhead, duly practising what is called *Mandūka yoga*, and always seated in the attitude called *Vīrāsana*, and lying on bare rocks or the earth, these men, with hearts set upon righteousness, must expose themselves to cold and water and fire. They subsist upon water or air or moss. They use two pieces of stones only for husking their corn. Some of them use their teeth only for such a purpose. They do not keep utensils of any kind (for storing anything for the day to come). Some of them clothe themselves with rags and barks of trees or deerskins. Even thus do they pass their lives for the measure of time allotted to them, according to the ordinances (set forth in the scriptures).[168]

164. *Anu.*, 141, p. 5922 (G.P.).
165. *Ibid.*, 142, 13.
166. *Śānti*, 192, 1 (G.P.); 185-1 Cri. edi.
167. *Anu.* 142, 6-7.
168. *Anu.* 142, 7-12.

According to him, they must offer the *agnihotra* or the sacred fire and the five great sacrifices daily. They must constantly offer those five great sacrifices with various kinds as enjoined in the *Vedas*.[169]

In this stage the individual does not altogether retire from social or family life. But he entrusts the entire responsibility of the household management to his younger generations. He devotes his times to the study of the holy scriptures and meditation. His wife may accompany him in his mission. At times he is consulted by the members of his family. He may continue to give them guidance in worldly matters in accordance with Dharma.

In this stage, there is a gradual increment of rigour of the austerities in the life. A *Vānaprastha* gets aloof from the society and leads a life of seclusion. However, the sense of hospitality still continues. The prime duty of the *Vānaprastha* is to honour the guests and visitors who visit his hermitage with alms consisting of water, root and fruits of the forest. Self-control is always there. Bhīsma says that a *Vānaprastha* is permitted by the epic to live with his wife but he cannot have sensual gratification.[170] Thus here we find that life becomes more and more rigorous and the lust to cling to the objects of pleasure of the world vanishes from the mind. Thus, hospitality, self-control and renunciation of worldly objects are the highlights of the ethical values found in this stage. This stage is the third stepping stone to the highest goal of *Moksa* by renunciation observed by the *Samnyāsin.*

The fourth and the last order of life is that of *Samnyâsin* who completely renounces his house, wife, children, wealth and everything. He lives as an ascetic abandoning all sorts of attachment to earthly objects. First, the individual has to be rid of the sins committed by him by leading a well-disciplined and pure life to qualify himself for entering the *Samnyāsāsrama* which entails the supreme amount of self-sacrifice. In the *Mahābhārata*, Bhīsma advises that a *Samnyāsin* should live according to the rules of asceticism, controlling

169. *Ibid.*, 142, 14.

170. *Śānti*, 61, 4.

the mind and the sense-organs. He should not have lust for anything. He should not build a house or hut for himself. He should always be wandering alone and stay there where the sun sets. He should lead his life on things allotted to him.[171] He further states that a *Samnyāsin* must have the feeling of equity for all and must give up all sorts of hopes and desires. He should keep himself aloof from gratification and should not allow any ill-will (vikār) to crop up in his heart. For these reasons this stage is called *Ksemāsrama* or stage of attaining good. One who reaches this stage gets union with the eternal Brahman.[172] Mahesvara gives the description of the duties of the *Samnyāsin* in the *Anuśāsanaparva*. The *Samyāsin* should not accumulate anything for himself. He should live on alms and remain detached from worldly things. He should practise deep meditation with absolute purity of mind. He should have forgiveness for all, mercy on all and should keep his reason always engaged in metaphysical speculations.[173] In the *Śāntiparva* Bhṛgu narrates the duties of the *Samnyāsins* thus, "Freeing themselves from attachment to the sacred fire, wealth, spouse and children, and robes, seats, beds, and such other objects of enjoyment, and breaking the bonds of affection, they roam about, regarding with an equal eye a clump of earth or rock and gold. They never set their hearts on the acquisition or enjoyment of the triple aggregate. They cast an equal eye on foes and friends and neutrals or strangers. They never injure in thought, word, or deed, immobile things or creatures that are viviporous, or eviporous or born on filth, or called vegetables They have no homes. They roam over hills and mountains, upon shores of rivers or seas, under shades of trees. and among temples of deities. They may go to towns or villages for residence. In a town, however, they should not live for more than five nights, while in a village their residence should never exceed one night. Entering a town or a village, they should, for the support of life, repair to the abodes of only Brahmins of

171. *Ibid.*, 61, 8.
172. *Śānti*, 61, 9.
173. *Anu.* 141, p. 5952 (G.P.).

liberal deeds. They never ask for any alms except what is thrown into the (wooden) bowls they carry. They should free themselves from lust, wrath, pride, cupidity, delusion, miserliness, deceit, slander, vanity, and injury to living creatures."[174]

Thus we see that this state of renunciation is reached only when the individual has enjoyed wealth and affection and also practised and preached moral duty and is well inspired to go in quest of the ultimate reality. The *Samnyāsāsrama* is the stage of life devoted entirely to the attainment of salvation. It is the summum bonum of life because the individual devotes his entire time to learning scriptures, discussing the nature of the ultimate reality and meditating on to have communion with it. Thus, the highlights of the ethical element of this *āsrama* is complete renunciation of the worldy life to achieve liberation.

In this connection it must be mentioned, that the four ideals of human endeavour (Purusārthas) which we have discussed earlier are in consonance with these *āsramas*. Dharma, the first ideal of Purusārthas, is accepted as the ideal of the first *āsrama*. Similarly the *artha* and *kāma* are recognized as the ideals of the *Gṛhasthāsrama*. In the *Vānaprastha* and *Samnyāsāsramas* the *Moksa* principle is found supreme. So, we find that these four ideals are related to these four *āsramas*.

Radha Kumud Mookerji gives a graphic description of this fourfold *āsrama system*. He writes :

> "If we may use a metaphor, the different āsramas or stages of life are mutually related in the same way as the bud, the flower, and the fruit. The tender youth is first subjected to a process of rigorous discipline and training, the aim of which is to purge him of all the impurities and imperfections, physical and moral, which obstruct the free operation of the vital principles of growth of the individual. Thus endowed with a sound mind in a sound body, the budding youth blossoms into

174. *Śānti*, 192, 3 (G.P.); Cri. edi. 185, 3.

a noble manhood which then produces itself in the householder's stage and through the experience of an active life ripens into the fruit of mature wisdom and moral steadfastness which are dedicated in the third āsrama of life to the advancement not of the individual but the collective life. The *Vānaprastha* must detach himself from personal interests centering in his individual home and family. He must wander from home unto homeless, cut himself off from his old moorings of self-interest to sail on the open main towards the universal and the Absolute, and feel that one tough of Nature which makes the whole world kin."[175]

Dr. Radhakrishnan also advocates the necessity of this fourfold *āsrama* system for perfect human life. He observes :

"Every state is necessary and in so far as it is necessary it is good. The blossom does not deny the leaf and the leaf does not deny the stalk and the stalk the root."[176]

On another occasion he observes :

"While the individual and the social sides of karma are inseparably intertwined, the theory of varna or caste emphasizes the social aspect, and that of *āsrama* or stage of life the individual aspect. The four stages of *Brahmacarya* or the period of training, *Gārhasthya* or the period of work for the world as a householder, *Vānaprasthya* or the period of retreat for the loosening of the social bonds, and *Samnyāsa* or the period of renunciation and expectant awaiting of freedom indicates that life is a pilgrimage to the eternal life through different stages."[177]

175. Mookerji, Radhakumud, *Ancient Indian Education*, p. 326.
176. Radhakrishnan, *The Hindu View of Life*, pp. 91-92.
177. *Ibid.*, p. 82.

Dr. Brij Gopal Tiwari justifies the scheme of *āsramas* on the basis of modern knowledge of Child and Industrial Psychology. He says :

> "As regards the āsrama principle, the investigations of modern researches in child psychology and the psychology of adolescence amply support the Indian system of physical, mental and moral development and of mental hygiene. It is now recognised that the neglect of the formation of good moral habits, at an early stage, creates a deficiency in character, which cannot be made up by any amount of theoretical instruction in later stages. Industrial Psychology and Business Psychology, similarly reveal to us the strength of the instinct of acquisition and of the motive of social security, which mould the mind and the character of the worker and the householder; and they stress the necessity of our providing for the legitimate expression of the above instincts. As regards the third and fourth stages of the Hindu scheme of life, novelists, dramatists and other writers have given us dismal pictures of what Lamb calls "superannuated veterans", who cling too long to earthly power and have a hankering after the plums of life, which they cannot, really, enjoy. And we have, further in all times and climes, the pictures of the wise and dignified Samnyāsin—young or old—who has taken long swift strides in the path of self-realization."[178]

It cannot be denied that the organization of the four āsramas of life is established for the gradual ethical and metaphysical sublimation of an individual. The fourfold division of human life is in accordance with the man's biological growth. As a matter of fact, the first stage is the period of training and discipline. It seems to be essential for the preparation of the life of the plastic youth to a life of responsibility. The next stage is the period of *Gṛhastha*. It supports

178. Tiwari, Brij Gopal, *Secularism and Nationalism in Modern India*, pp. 190-91.

the entire world by the performance of reciprocal duties, obligations and responsibilities. It is a period of practice and performances. The prime end of the third period is to get rid of the noise and bustle of the worldly life and retiring to a peaceful life of the forest to meditate on the supreme spiritual problems. The last period is the period of complete renunciation of all ties and fetters of home and society, country or even the humanity at large. He has no mercy, love or hatred or any feeling for any one. His mind concentrates only on the spiritual freedom or salvation.

Thus we find that human life is dealt with a practical outlook in the epic. The entire edifice of the human life is based on this fourfold scheme of *āsramas* as its four walls. Even if a single wall is absent, the edifice cannot be erected for the realisation of the supreme human goal.

After having seen in detail the *varna* and *Āsramadharmas* separately it is essential to have a general view of these two dharmas together. The *Varnāsramadharma* in general, seems to have a very scientific explanation as described by Dr. Bhagvan Das. He tries to justify this system on scientific grounds. He writes :

> "This four-fold social organisation was based on a few fundamental, wide-reaching, principles of many sciences, biological, psychological, economic, sociological, educational, dietetic and sexological, hygienic and eugenic."[179]

> "It was intended, and for long it helped, to amalgamate the thousand of clans and tribes of India, and organise them into one great social whole, which gave to every individual all the needs, opportunity for developing his special personal good qualities and for finding self-expression, and at the same time made those special qualities serviceable to society by assigning to him an appropriate occupation."[180]

179. Das, Bhagvan, *The Science of Social Organisation or the Laws of Manu*, Vol. III, p. 779.
180. *Ibid.*, pp. 818-19.

K.V. Rangaswami Aiyangar also supports the system of *varna* and *āsrama*. He observes:

> "Indian society was kept from disintegration by the sublime conception of the scheme of *varna* and *āsrama*, which gave its women and men a clear vision of the spiritual winning post, and showed them how to order their lives and mould their actions in order that they may, in the fulness of time or even in this life itself, triumphantly reach it."[181]

At another place he says:

> "*Varnadharma* is the key stone of the arch of Indian social scheme. It has been the foundation of Hindu society through the ages . . . . It has concerned itself with men in large aggregates, not with individuals. Its scope has been universal. Its purposes have been both worldly and unworldly, concerned with this life and with after-life . . . . It has stressed individual responsibility as well as collective . . . . It aimed at a permanent solution of every side of the social problem; genetic, psychological, spiritual, and economic . . . . Their admiration has been for the elements in it which made for social balance and stability, the elasticity, which made it respond to changing needs and which kept it from disintegration in the numberless vicissitudes of foreign invasion, conflict with alien cultures and religions, and dissent within its own fold. It harmonised society, and spiritualised it. It made for harmonious development through co-operation of its elements. Its recognition of fundamental instincts to which man responds by his activity, and its scheme for canalising and transforming them to common purposes through the system of ashrama so as to raise both the individual and the mass, made for its success."[182]

181. Aiyangar, K.V. Rangaswami, *Our Social Heritage*, p. 39.
182. *Ibid.*, pp. 31-32.

While discussing *Varnāsramadharma* in the *Mahābhārata*, we are reminded of Bradley's famous moral dictum of 'My Station and its Duties'. The duties of an individual follow from the class and stage to which he belongs. Dr. T.M.P. Mahadevan writes :

> "The duties that are prescribed for the different castes, *Varnadharmas* as they are called, have for their aim the preservation of society. Each man has his station in the particular social group to which he belongs; and he should perform the duties that pertain to his station."[183]

Bradley's ethical doctrine of 'My station and its duties' is based on the organic view of society. He pleads that man is a social animal and that his sociability is mainly due to the effect of society on him. He observes :

> "In short, man is a social being; he is real only because he is social, and can realise himself only because it is as social that he realises himself. The mere individual is a delusion of theory; and the attempt to realise it in practice is the starvation and mutilation of human nature, with total sterility or the production of monstrosities."[184]

His doctrine of 'My station and its duties', therefore, attempts to develop the ideal conduct of an individual on the presupposition that he is an organ of such an organism. Therefore, every man must feel that his role is determined by his function in that social system and his duties are derived from reflection upon the station or the position that he occupies within it. He says :

> "To know what a man is (as we have seen) you must not take him in isolation. He is one of a people, he was

183. Mahadevan, T.M.P., *The Concept of Dharma in the Mahābhārata*, Pub. in *Vedant Kesari*, Vol. 37, p. 20.
184. Bradley, F.H., *Ethical Studies*, p. 174.

born in a family, he lives in a certain society, in a certain state. What he has to do depends on what his place is, what his function is, and that all comes from his station in the organism."[185]

He further states :

> "We much content ourselves by pointing out that there are such facts as the family, then in a middle position a man's own profession and society, and, overall, the larger community of the State. Leaving out of sight the question of a society wider than the state, we must say that a man's life with its moral duties is in the main filled up by his station in that system of whole which the State is, and that this, partly by its laws and institutions, and still more by its spirit, gives him the life which he does live and ought to live."[186]

It may not be necessary to go into further details about his theory, but this much is obvious that the ethical doctrine of Bradley resembles the morality expressed in terms of *Varnāsramadharma* in the *Mahābhārata*. In both the cases individuals' duties and obligations come from their respective positions and stations in life.

The concept of *Varnāsramadharma* is based on the organic theory of society. The ancient Indian seers introduced the system to keep society stable and to maintain the healthy development of the social organism.

The Ethics of Svadharma

The ethics of Svadharma propounded in the *Gītā*, is generally supported in the *Mahābhārata*. Accordingly, each class has its own act of duties and obligations and for the sake of the solidarity and progress of society as a whole each class or social unit is expected to act up to it. A man, whatever be

185. *Ibid.*, p. 173.
186. *Ibid.*, p. 174.

his caste or position, should discharge his duties to himself as well as to society according to his position in life. There is an organic relationship of classes to society in which each limb has to perform (his) its functions well in order to maintain the health of the body-social. If it does not do so, there occurs a distinction of the body-social in which not only the others starve and perish, but it itself meets the same fate, an individual realises himself by fulfilling the duties attached to him according to his station in life. "Devoted each to his own duty man attains the highest perfection", says the *Gītā*.[187] It again says, "To action alone thou hast a right and never at all to its fruits; let not the fruits of action be thy motive; neither let there be in thee any attachment to inaction.[188] It means that one should do his duty without attachment. This is what is called 'Niskāma Karma'—action, without attachment or desires for fruits.

The *Gītā*, however, does not advocate asceticism. It rather condemns the excessive practice of austerities in the name of Yoga.[189] It does not, all the same, support any hedonistic philosophy. It advocates neither the life of indulgence nor the complete suppression of senses. It rather preaches the sublimation of appetites and instinct by performing one's action without attachment. It corresponds substantially to the conception of the moral ideal—'one's station in life and its duties'.[190] This is the highest ethical ideal which everybody should try to follow.

In the *Gītā* there is an ethical idealisation of the Varna system, which does not emphasize the hierarchical gradation, the hereditary principles and the differences, rather stresses the important principle of interdependence. It conceives of society as an integrated whole which can prosper only when the various sections of it properly perform the functions assigned to them. The considerations of whether the function is high or low and to one's liking or not, is not important.

187. *Gītā*, XVIII, 45.

188. *Ibid.*, II, 47.

189. *Ibid.*, XVII, 5-6.

190. Cf. F.H. Bradley, *Ethical Studies*, Chap. 5.

Svadharma is the law of one's being and the fulfilment of one's nature. By proving true to one's self and to the society of which he is an integral part, one helps in the fulfilment of human destiny.

Like the *Gītā* the episode of Dharmavyādha and Tulādhāra also lays stress on Svadharma. Both Vyādha and Tulādhāra maintain that no occupation is mean. One should be satisfied with the lot ordained by the Creator in accordance with one's previous Karma and perform the duties to the best of one's capacity.[191] One should not be puffed up with joy, when one achieves success; nor should he feel sorry, when things are against him. In any case one should not leave one's Dharma.[192] The profession of a Vyādha is not regarded to be good, but still he follows it, because it is the profession adopted by his forefathers.[193] One who leaves his Svakarma, commits a sin. Those who follow their Svakarma, follow the Dharma.[194]

In the dialogue between Tulādhāra and Jājali, it is maintained that the highest form of Dharma consists in a living which is founded upon total harmlessness towards all creatures or, if it is not possible, upon the smallness of such harm.[195] Tulādhāra holds that Dharma consists in universal friendliness and beneficence to all creatures.[196] He upholds the principles of Niskāma Karma and non-attachment. The performance of one's acts and the fulfilment of one's duties without attachment constitute the real Dharma. This is the substance of the teaching of Tulādhāra.[197]

So far as the Dharma in the sphere of an individual's life is concerned, the *Mahābhārata* gives importance to 'Sadācāra' and 'Sīla'. It holds that ācāra is the main support of Dharma and that it consists in self-control.[198] Self-control

191. *Mbh.* III, 206. 21.
192. *Mbh.* III, 206. 43.
193. *Ibid.*, III, 207.8.
194. *Ibid*, III, 207.9.
195. *Ibid.*, XII, 262.6.
196. *Ibid.*, XII, 262.9.
197. *Ibid.*, XII, 262.10ff.
198. *Ibid.*, XII, 160.6.

leads to the highest merit. There is no greater Dharma than self-control.[199]

Through self-control a person enjoys the highest happiness, both in this world and the next. A man who is without self-control always suffers misery. Such a man brings upon himself many calamities, all begotten by his own faults. A self-controlled man is never fettered by attachments originating from earthly connections.[200]

The *Mahābhārata* holds that the three Gunas—Sattva, Rajas and Tamas—which are the three constituents of Prakṛti, from the material structure of the Universe and all the objects of the Universe are evolved from Prakṛti consisting of these three Gunas.[201] The manifold objects of the Universe, both physical and psychical, are possessed of these three Gunas. These are the material cause of the Psychic and Physical Universe, and they coexist and cohere in every object of the Universe, though on specific occasions one of them predominates over the others. In human mi d, Sattva expresses itself as tranquillity, purity and calmness; Rajas as passion, restlessness, aggressive activity; and Tamas as stupidity, laziness and inertia.[202] Rajas and Tamas drive man's mind towards evil,[203] and Sattva elevates him to a higher level and leads to goodness.[204]

In Chapter XIV of the *Gitā*, a detailed description of the Gunas has been given. The three Gunas are present in human beings. None is free from them. In each soul one or the other of the Gunas predominates which determines his character and nature. From Sattva arises knowledge and from Rajas greeds; negligence and error arises from Tamas. Those who are established in Sattva rise upwards, the passionate

199. *Ibid*, XII, 160. 10.
200. *Mbh.* XII, 160. 13ff.
201. *Ibid*, XII, 314. 1.
202. *Ibid.*, XII, 313. 17ff.
203. *Ibid*, XII, 254. 11.
204. *Ibid*, XII, 314. 3.

(Rājasic) remain in the middle and the dull (Tāmasic) steeped in lower tendencies sink downwards.[205] Arjuna asks in the *Gītā*, "By what is a man, impelled to commit sin, as if by force, even against his will." The Lord replies, "It is Kāma (desire or lust) and Krodha (anger) produced out of rajas quality. They are our inborn enemies.[206] Hence one should get rid of these by suppressing the Rājasic and Tāmasic elements in him.

The Higher and Lower Selves in Men

There are two selves in men—one, the higher and other, the lower. The lower self of man should be lifted up and purified by the higher self. That keeps us down in the scale of life is excessive attachment to the objects of senses actuated by the Rājasic and Tāmasic elements. Man is a dual being, a child of both earth and heaven. He belongs to the worlds—the natural world and the spiritual world. He has a body and mind which belongs to the former, and a soul which belongs to the latter. He has also a lower nature and a higher nature. The lower nature drives the man to earth and binds him to sensual life, the life of Rajas and Tamas. The Sattva in man elevates him and leads to the higher life of self-realisation. The *Mahābhārata* including the *Gītā*, preaches that one should control the Rājasika and Tāmasika elements in him and should develop the Sāttvika nature. There is, in man, a soul, his real self which is the purest of the pure. Our passions and senses, however, cloud our mental horizon and darken our vision as a result of which we do not realise its importance and confuse it with body and senses. This brings about the ego which is the root of all our conflicts of self-centredness, cruelty, greed, and other vices. In order to get rid of them we have to cultivate the virtue of self-control. It is by virtue of self-control that man keeps the Rajas and Tamas elements in check and becomes an integrated personality. The three Gunas—of Nature—are evidently to be found in all human

205. *Gītā*, XIV, 17-18.
206. *Ibid.*, III. 36-37.

beings. None is quite devoid of one or the other. All are active in him. All men have in them in some degrees the Sāttvika element of light and happiness, the Rājasika impulse of desire and activity and the Tāmasika in capacity and ignorance or nescience. But they are not constant in any man rather vary from time to time and men to men. They are in a continual state of mutual impact, interaction and displacement of one by another. Sometimes one is predominant and sometimes the other and each subjects us to its characteristic mode of behaviour. This being the nature of man, it is desirable that man should not allow himself to be swayed by the Rājasika and Tāmasika elements rather adhere to the Sāttvika elements in him which lead him to goodness and virtue and finally to salvation. There is in man a soul disguised in his body. It is his real eternal self. The body is an appendage, an instrument to serve the purpose of the soul. Hence one should confuse the body with the soul. The real purpose of the life is the tendence of the soul. This can be possible only by self-control—the control of Rajas and Tamas. The question is how to keep the soul pure while one is placed in and round the hard situations of life amidst jealousy and greed, provocations and allurements, unkindness and uncharity. The *Gītā* finds a way out, it prescribes Niskāma Karma, the performance of one's duty clear of all attachment, without any expectation of reward or fear of punishment. The duties have to be carried on without any attachment to objects or hope for gain. This is what Dharmavyādha and Tulādhāra say in the *Mahābhārata*. This can be possible only by self-control—by 'Indriya Nigraha'. For the worldly people, the *Gītā* advises not to suppress or annihilate desires completely because it is not possible and asks for their sublimation in everything that we do. It is by non-attachment only that man can live a happy and contented life. Non-attachment is not a negative state of mind but a positive state of self-control, discrimination and understanding. It is not a mechanical life, but a deliberate behaviour of man based on the understanding of the nature and purpose of the Universe.

5

The Law of Karma

In this chapter we would throw light on the problem of the Law of Karma. It may be regarded as one of the basic concepts of Indian philosophy. In fact, it is one of the pillars upon which the edifice of Indian Philosophy stands. It is accepted by almost all the system, save and except the materialistic school. It helps us to explain many inexplicable riddles of human-existence.

According to the Indian tradition, man is unified category of matter and consciousness and he is also placed in the midst of the physical environ which acts and reacts in his inner spirit. Peace of mind can be realised when there is a perfect harmony between his inner spiritual being and the outer physical world of which his own mind-body system is a part. There is a constant endeavour on the part of man to make the physical nature including his own body to adopt itself to the demands and needs of his spiritual being. This is, as it were, the action and interaction between man and nature. This is how karma comes into being as a result of the impact of human will on the material conditions of his existence. The life of an individual is not confined merely to the painful life of this empirical world. It also has a transcendental dimension which is a timeless truth of all that is happening in time. The spiritual being of man refers to this transcendental level of existence whereas the material covering is only an artificial adjunct loosely tagged to this spiritual being. Law of Karma is indispensable to account for both spiritual regeneration and degeneration of man because the spiritual evolution cannot be completed in one birth and therefore this evolution needs reincarnation to reap the fruits of Karma.

The doctrine of Karma is nothing but the causal law operating in the moral sphere. Just as every effect must have a cause in the physical world, in the same way, pleasures and pains of life are supposed to be the effects of human actions which are, therefore, the causes of wants, suffering and enjoyment of the wordly life.

Man is regarded as the architect of his own fortune. He has created his own destiny by dint of his own efforts. He is using his own powers and faculties to serve his various and varied purposes which may be either good or bad. He also experiences the effects of his present action in the present life in the form of pleasures and pains. Hence, the necessary connexion between an act and its fruits is a fact and not a mere fictitious belief.

According to the Law of Karma, every action, be it good or bad, springs from desire and results in impressions which become the seeds of future activities and desires. In other words, we can say that every action is followed by corresponding reaction. This law of action and reaction is called the Law of Karma or the Law of cause and effect. If a man performs good and virtuous actions his mind becomes free from the impurities of the viciousness and in course of time with a spiritual development he succeeds in performing disinterested actions which will lead to liberation. Virtuous actions are helpful for liberation only to a certain extent. Preparation for spiritual liberation starts within the framework of the Law of Karma, with the performance of virtuous actions. Of course, when the spirit reaches supra-moral stage, a man passes beyond the sphere of Karma and intentional performance of virtuous actions consequently becomes entirely meaningless for him. But so long as a man remains under the sway of this Law of Karma, he performs different kinds of actions and goes on weaving his own net of birth and death.

A good action produces pleasures and a bad action pains. Action that falls within the domain of the Law of Karma is a voluntary action which the agent undertakes after the deliberation, only with a view to doing some good to himself either directly or indirectly. Hence, it is just and proper that he alone should reap the fruits of all his actions, if not in this birth, then certainly in some other births as otherwise justice is violated. Thus, as a necessary corollary of the doctrine of Karma, the ancient saints and sages have formulated another doctrine of births and rebirths. They have tried to explain apparent anomalies of life through Karma and rebirth. In actual life virtuous are often found to suffer and grown under the heavy pain and miseries whereas vicious persons are found to prosper.

There is, no doubt, inescapable trap of the Law of Karma for those only who remain interested in the empirical existence and its pleasures and pains, still there is a hope for every body's salvation from sufferings and Karma which do not constitute the final destiny of human life. It is evident that the interested actions only lead to births and rebirths and fail to open the close doors of peace and perfection. There is, however, another kind of action which is niskāma (wholly unselfish). Since the agent of niskām karma has no selfish end in view, he has not to reap the fruits of his actions. The fruits are to benefit the whole of mankind, i.e. the agent follows the altruistic principles. According to the Law of Karma, an agent has to undergo the appropriate results of his interested voluntary actions only. As it is not possible for him to reap the fruits of so many Sakāma Karmas in a single life, he has to take repeated births to do the same. The Law of Karma can keep an individual in its iron grip only during the period when he remains under ignorancc and performs Sakāma Karma; but he becomes able to free himself from the yoke of the worldly life, and taste the nectar of immortality by dint of knowledge and niskāma Karma.

The most characteristic doctrine of Indian religion and philosophy is what is called the transmigration of souls, reincarnation, rebirth or metempsychosis. This doctrine does not, however, seem to be:

> "Imported by the aryan invaders for they are not clearly enunciated in the Rig Veda or formulated during the time of Upanisada".[1]

It is most probable that the doctrine is the contribution of the earlier inhabitants of India particularly the Dravidians belonging to the Mediterranean races.

Rebirth literally means birth after death. It means that the individual soul does not cease to exist at death, but is born again with a new body. The doctrine of rebirth presupposes the reality of a permanent eternal soul. Hindu philosophy, therefore, believes in the existence of permanent reality—the Ātman—in man, distinct from the body. It is essentially divine in nature. This doctrine is also connected with the idea of Karma. The kind of rebirth the soul takes and the lot that falls to it are determined by its own deeds. The power of the deeds done in the past life or lives determined the nature of our present existence. So the doctrine of rebirth and Karma has moral value because it teaches that our actions will not go unrewarded or unpunished. The life is not the end of soul's 'Journey' in the world. If there are some deeds which have not the recompence, the soul will have to be reborn again and reap the consequence of its deeds. The subtle body which sticks to the soul bears the mark of our deeds and makes it suffer the consequences no one can escape from them.

The doctrine of Karma gives a unique character to the Indian thought and its conception of the nature of the cosmos as a whole and man's position and role in it. This doctrine has the same importance and status in Indian thought which the laws of causation and uniformity of nature have in Science. According to physical sciences, nothing gets lost in the Universe. This principle is known as conservation of matter in chemistry and conservation of energy in physics,

1. Eliot, Sir Charles, *Hinduism and Buddhism* (Edwards Arnold and Co., London, 1921), pp. IV-VIII.

similarly, according to the doctrine of Karma whatever action is one man is not lost. This principle may be characterised as the conservation of values in ethics. There is no uncaused happening, nor is there any action without the fact.

The doctrine of Karma means that whatever deed is done by the individul, leaves behind an impression on the soul—the subtle body that accompanies the soul and ordains for him the joy or sorrow in accordance with the deeds, good or bad and determines the nature of our future life. If the fruits of action cannot be enjoyed in the present life, one has to take another birth in order to enjoy them. The act passes away as soon as it is done, but its moral effect is stored in potential form which fructifies in future. According to this doctrine, bodily death is not the end of human existence, but a stage in the long-drawn process becoming according to the law of conservation of the values.

> "Karma indicates originally nothing but the biological development of seed (Karma-bija) into its adequate fruit (Karma-Phala)."[2]

The law of Karma may, therefore, be regarded as the law of the conservation of moral values:

> "The law ensures that nothing befalls a man except as a result of his own actions and nothing merited by man by his actions, is lost unto him. All the values positive or negative, accruing from a man's notion remain conserved for him, and are capable of bringing him joys and sorrows in this or another life."[3]

According to the Hindu thinkers the moral foundation of life is based on the belief that the soul continues to exist after death. Life on earth is short and so one cannot

2. H. Betty, *Facets of Indian Thought*, George Allen and Unwin, London, 1964, p. 52.

3. *Ibid.*

experience all the consequences of one's actions in it, and hence they postulated the theory of rebirth. Hinduism sees man's life through the three stages of time. Past is mother of the present and the present is the mother of the future. Thus, all the stages of human existence are inter-connected. The present is the result of the past and it creates future. The Hindus, thus, postulate a rational system in the world and explain many of the mysteries of life. According to Max Weber, the

> "Karma doctrine transforms the world into a strictly rationally determined cosmos, it represents the most consistent theory ever produced."[4]

Perhaps no other concept has had such a profound far reaching influence on Indian thought and life as the concepts of Karma and rebirth. Buddhism and Jainism, the two other great religions of India also subscribe to this theory. The great epics *Rāmāyana* and *Mahābhārata* have thrown ample light on them. The concept of Karma and rebirth has not only influenced the religious thought and the philosophy of India but also its social theory. The whole Indian approach to life has been very much influenced by these two concepts. They are the very basis of Indian ethics and moral philosophy as well as of social and political thought.

By the theory of Karma and rebirth the ancient Indians tried to establish a system of ethics of Universal application. It has three aspects. It is a message of hope for man by dint of his own deeds and character in the past. Moreover, it works, as a deterrent to sins and crimes by making everybody conscious of the fact that his acts of sin and crime would eventually be punished even though they are committed in secret and the doer is not punished for them in this life by the temporal authorities. Thus, the theory of Karma and rebirth encourages morality and righteousness. According to Stanley Jast:

4. Weber, Max, *The Religion of India*, p. 121.

> "Reincarnation with its complementary doctrine of Karma affords the best, in truth, the only working explanation of the mysteries of life on earth without these illuminating ideas, life becomes just a meaningless jumble. Our coming and going, our changing contacts, the immense differences between man and man in character, capacity, opportunity and the ordinary tragic gravity and incompleteness of the single life, its successes, failures, futilities and frustrations and perhaps all, the absence of any understandable end, all this remains adequately explained."[5]

The doctrine of Karma is traced by some scholars to the Vedic concept of Ṛta, the unvarying, inviolable inexorable order of things. The Vedic seers conceive of an unchanging order in nature. It is this order which makes the existence of cosmos possible. The unchanging regularity of the natural phenomenon suggested to the Vedic seers the existence of a cosmic law in nature, which regulates all activities in the world. This cosmic law pervades the whole world which all men obey.[6] The unvarying cosmic law holds supreme everywhere in the universe. Varuna is the upholder of this cosmic order. It is the function of Varuna to see that there occurs no transgression of the cosmic order. This cosmic law is supposed to apply not only the world of nature, but it also brings about a moral and spiritual order. Maxmuller defines it as the

> "Straight line which in spite of many momentary deviations, was discovered to run through the whole realm of nature. We call that Ṛta that straight direct or right line when we apply it in a mere general sense, the law of Nature, and when we apply it to moral work, we try to express the same idea again by speaking of the Moral Law, the law on which our life is founded, the eternal law of Right and Reason or it may be that

5. Jast, *Reincarnation and Karma*, New York, 1956, p 9.
6. *Ṛg Veda*, 1. 24.

which makes for righteousness, both within us and without."[7]

This world was used to denote:

"The order in the moral world as 'Truth' and 'Right' and in the religious world a sacrifice or 'rite'."[8]

Sin results from the violation of the order in the moral sphere and virtue results from the obedience to this order. The Ṛta also denotes the unalterable law of producing effect.[9] It must work itself out.[10] Thus, it is the unalterable law of good and bad effects following from good and bad conduct. As in the physical world every phenomenon is followed by its effect in the form of another phenomenon, in the same way in the moral realm also all our deeds are followed by their consequence, which we must suffer:

"If by any chance its effects are not revealed here on earth they must be brought to fruition elsewhere. Where law is, disorder and injustice are only provisional and partial. The triumph of the wicked is not absolute. The shipwreck of the good need not cause despair".[11]

Thus, in the concept of Ṛta we find the first germ of the law of Karma which is so fundamental in the Indian system of thought.[12]

According to the doctrine of Karma, nothing gets lost, every action has its "Repercussion in a wider sphere of time and space beyond its immediate present. This immediate present is responsible for effects in wider unlimited future

7. Maxmuller, Hibbert Lectures, pp. 243-55, Quoted by Gokhale, Indian Thought through the Ages, p. 94.
8. Macdonnel, *Vedic Mythology*, p. 11.
9. Dasgupta, S.N., *A History of Indian Philosophy*, Vol. I, p. 22.
10. Radhakrishnan, S., *Indian Philosophy*, Vol. I, p. 109.
11. *Ibid*, p. 109.
12 Dasgupta, S.N., *op. cit.*, p. 22.

and, besides, every momentary present is already a result of the presiding past. This may give comfort for the inequities and present sufferings, the present being the consequence of former deeds of tendencies, yet this provides no easy excuse for irresponsibility for the present action, on the contrary it is based on the unbreakable law of developmnnt, the present negligible mistake has to be viewed with regards to its far reaching future results.[13]

In the Upanishads this doctrine of Karma was fully elaborated in association with the doctrine of transmigration of soul. The ethical doctrine of Karma connected with the doctrine of transmigration is fully developed in the *Bṛhadāranayak Upanishad*:

"One becomes good by good action".[14]

When one man dies two things accompany him they are Vidyā and Karma.[15] According as one acts, according as one conducts so does one become.[16] Desire becomes action and action determines the course of life which in its turn determines the future of our being. The fortune that awaits a man after death depends entirely upon the moral quality of the individual and this, in its turn, depends upon the deed which he performs. It is by these two doctrines of Karma and rebirth that Hinduism is able to explain the differences in men. The past deeds of the individuals determine the kind of body which he assumes... the family, the society, the caste and the position in which they may be born. A man is born in a high or low Varna according to his actions in the past births. The status of man, in any existence, depends upon no accident. It is essentially the working out of the deeds done in the previous birth. Every creature "is a creation of his past deeds. Nothing in the world, either in physical or moral

13. Betty, H., *op. cit*, p. 20.
14. Bṛhadāranayak Upanishad, III, 2. 13.
15. Bṛhadāranayak Uoanishad, IV, 4. 2.
16. Bṛhadāranayak Upanishad, IV, 4, 5.

sphere, happens as results of mere caprice or chance. Everything which exists, comes into being by an operation of an immutable law. Thus, the otherwise inexplicable vicissitudes of life and inequities among human beings are explained by the doctrine of Karma".[17]

In the *Mahābhārata* also, the law of Karma has become a vital force holding firmly the civilization of ancient India when this fact has been exemplified through immemorable stories. Clear indications of future life resulting from the acts performed by living beings in their previous births are found in the *Mahābhārata*.

Men are born in different categories of beings ranging from the higher to the lower as a result of their good and bad actions. When King Yudhiṣṭhira was having a discourse with the snake-incarnation of Nahusha, regarding actions and their fruits in the form of rewards and punishments the latter told him that living beings had to be born in the world in three forms namely, man, heavenly beings and lower animals according to the merits and demerits of their past actions.[18]

According to Nahusha, one goes to heaven by performing charity and other described ethical actions. But those who perform contrary acts are born as man or lower animals. 'Anger', lust, temptation etc, make one fall from the human state to the category of animals during reincarnation.[19] It has been said by the snake form of Nahusha that "The embodied spirit enchained by fate and enjoying the pleasure or suffering the pain consequent on its acts, takes birth repeatedly. But he that has lost touch of his actions, is conscious of his destiny of all born creature".[20]

Thus we find that taking birth in after-life, depends very much on the performance of good and bad actions. The destiny of an individual in his transmigration either as a human being or as a lower animal is determined by action and action alone.

17 Dandekar, R.N. in Religion of the Hindus (ed) by Morgan, New York, 1955 p. 128. Cf. *Mahābhārata*, XII, 288, 17-18.

18. *Vana Parva* 181-9.

19 *Ibid.*, 181-12.

20. *Ibid.*, 181-15.

The idea of attaining heaven and hell according to the good and bad actions performed in this world is also admitted in the *Mahābhārata.* Men who perform good deeds were supposed to go heaven after death. In the age of *Mahābhārata* also death was not considered to be the final termination of life. A life after death was also the key-note of that epic. Death was supposed simply to be an act of transference of souls from one body to another. The eternity of the soul was the characteristic feature of the cultural life of ancient India. It was not enough to clean and adorn the physical body with perfumes and ornaments. One has to clean and purify his mind and fill it up with moral excellences so that his pure feelings and emotions may find expressions in good action just as a noble birth is achievable by dint of virtuous deeds. In the same way, heaven also is attainable by the performance of good action springing from a desire to acquire moral merit.

It is only the knowledge of Brahman and capacity to control the sense that can make one free from rebirth. Sakāma Punya Karma, on the other hand, can only fetch rewards either in the form of good births in this world or in the form of attainment of heavenly bliss which the pious soul can enjoy as long as his merit lasts After that he again comes back to this world.

To court death in the battle-field is also a heroic act according to the *Mahābhārata* and attainment of heaven is supposed to be its final result. There are also other acts such as the study of the Vedas, charity leading to fame, penances etc. which are supposed to lead one to heaven, but for a Kshatriya, death in a fight is a sure means to heavenly existence.[21]

It is also stated in the Sabha Parva that a king who protects the four castes of people, attains heaven and reaches the abode of Indra.[22] The king should, therefore, act in a manner which will make all people of his kingdom happy and cheerful. He should look after the spiritual and material well-being of his people and by doing so, he will earn merit which

21. *Sabha Parva*, 22-18.
22. *Ibid.*, 5-129.

will help him to gain heaven after death. One can also attain heaven by performing the four noble acts, bestowal of alms on deserving persons, endearing words, truthfulness, and uninviousness.[23]

Death, according to the *Mahābhārata*, is simply a change of form. It is so to say the outer cover of the inner body, just as when the clothes are worn off they need change. Similarly the body when it is worn off falls down and this separation of the body from the soul is called death. This idea of death as simply a change of form of transformation of the physical frame, has been expressed in Bhrigu-Bharadvaja dialogue. The living creature as well as its acts are never destroyed.[24] The living creature which survives after the dissolution of the physical body is not seen just as fire is not visible after the consumption of the fuel.[25] That is, it mixes with the space and hence becomes imperceptible. Similarly the living creature after it renounces the body definitely lives in space but is invisible, because of its subtlety.[26]

The living creature here refers to the soul because it is the Soul only which never dies. People who hold that the living creature dies along with the body can be said to have little of intelligence because the living creature simply goes from one body to another after the dissolution of the physical body.[27] Sceptics who hold that after death nothing remains, do not possess correct knowledge just as when we speak loudly, our voice resounds in the air and is gradually lost in the space and is not totally diminished. Similarly, the inner spirit which leaves the body is evidently not diminished. It simply becomes very subtle and consequently is not visible through our naked eyes. In the *Mahābhārata* it is stated that Yama "The god of death took out the thumb-sized soul along with the subtle body with which it is associated by force

23. *Vana Parva*, 181-2
24. *Śānti Parva*, 187-1.
25. *Ibid.*, 187-2.
26. *Ibid*, 187-6.
27. *Śānti Parva*, 187-27.

from the person of Satyavāna leaving his gross body devoid of consciousness on the ground."[28]

According to most systems, Soul is not affected by Karma. Karma affects only the subtle body which clothes the Soul and accompanies it through different worldly lives.

In the *Mahābhārata*, it is stated that one cannot get the fruits of his actions in the absence of any off-springs. Even those who attain success in ascetic penance, go to the reason of 'Pitris' but do not get the fruits of their actions if they have no off-springs. Therefore begetting a child is absolutely necessary to enjoy the fruits of actions.[29] The idea of transmigration depending on Karma-vāda is also linked with the idea of biological immortality. The father has to separate himself from the mortal body but he is eager to live in the life of his son who is a part of himself. Hence, begetting children in the stage of a householder is regarded as a sacred duty. Such an idea is present in the Upanishads as well. In the Bṛhadāranyaka Upanishad it is stated that at the time of death the father passes all his obligations to his son because he will then continue to live in the life of his son.[30] The Kaustaki Upanishad says that at the time of death the father passes his deeds, pleasures, pains, etc. to his son along with his speech, vital his etc.

This linking of the fruits of actions with begetting of off-springs is also a justifiable ground for holding the view that in the epic age, the attitude of the ancient thinkers towards social life was positive. The worldly life is not insignificant, it is not an obstacle in the way of responsible manner and should marry and beget children. Renunciation of worldly life should be practised only in the Vānaprastha and the Sanyāsa āśramas of life. This also proves that the four-fold scheme of life of the Hindus have gained considerable ground in the epic age and domestic virtues are glorified and a philosophy of practical life has been formulated.

28. *Vana Parva*, 297-17.
29. *Ādi Parva*, 231-7-13.
30. Bṛhadāranyaka Upanishad, 1.5.17.

The idea that actions performed under whatever circumstances get their fruit, finds place in the *Mahābhārata*[31] where Krishna has suggested such an idea when he along with Arjuna and Bhima has entered Jarasandha's house with an intention to kill him. Krishna has also emphasized that killing a person with the intention of helping the distressed people and bringing prosperity of race,[32] such performance of action is also rewarded.

It can be said that the motive and intention of performing actions, if bad, will not get any reward. Then the doer of such action will be punished for these acts. So, taking into consideration the higher ideals of life all actions should be performed with a view to helping the suffering humanity. The Celestial Sabha of Sukra was obtained by him as the fruit of his actions.

In the *Mahābhārata*, we find that the conception of the soul surviving the body and thereby entering into different bodies through the process of rebirths had gained adequate ground. The soul is considered to be the only indestructible principle but it is found to undergo a series of births and deaths if it suffers from ignorance. Vaśiṣṭha has remarked :

> "It is, thus, on account of his ignorance and his association with others who are invested with ignorance, that individual soul passes through millions and millions of births every one of which has dissolution in the end."[33]

Legends in the epic also suggest that in new births, there can be a change of form either from human to non-human or the other way round due to curse or boon.

The king of Hastinapur who was the king Mahavisha in his previous birth was required to lead a moral life on the earth, because of the curse of Brahma. Brahma cursed the king that he would first be born on the earth and later on attain to the heavenly regions.[34] Similarly it is because Ganga

31. *Sabha Parva*, 22-13.
32. *Ibid.*, 22-14.
33. *Ibid*, 304-1.
34. *Ādi Parva*, 96-9.

had a weakness for the king Mahavisha and had unfulfilled desires in her heart, that she was required to take birth again in the next life. Again the Vasus were required to be born as men as a result of the curse of Vaśiṣṭha,[35] in anger. These Vasus in due course were born in the womb of Ganga in her second birth as the wife of Śāntanu, the son of Pratipa and ultimately were freed from the clutches, of course, after they were born and thrown into the river. Rishi Ruru had earlier decided to destroy the serpent race; but once while he entered a forest and was about to kill an old dunduva snake, the latter told him that he was Rishi Sahasrapath in its previous birth and that because of the curse of the Brāhmanas he had become a snake.[36] It would be apparent from the aforesaid details that the curse of Brāhmanas, Saints and the Celestial beings had much significance in shaping the destiny of the individual in one of his future births.

Even the god of justice, Dharma was supposed to have been like Vidur, the brother of Pandu in the womb of Sūdra woman because of the curse of a certain Brāhman known as Mandavya.[37]

Again, the daughter of an illustrious Rishi though handsome did not have a groom. So she gratified Lord Shankara by her asceticism. As she addressed the Lord five times saying 'give me a husband', she was given a boon by the Lord that she would be fulfilled of her wishes in one of her future births.[38] This daughter of the Rishi was later on born as Draupadi, the daughter of King Drupad and was the wife of the five sons of Pandu. Vyasa explained all this to Drupad when the latter wanted to know from him if it was a sin to have five husbands. Vyasa further told him that it was not a sinful act. She was rather created for this purpose by Brahma, the creator.

Here, also the person who was receiving the boon or the curse was either pleasing or displeasing a sage or a god by

35. *Ibid.*, 96-14.
36. *Ibid.*, 10-7.
37. *Ibid.*, 107-16.
38. *Ibid.*, 196-50.

means of his action. So it was his action which was operative in determining his birth in a higher or a lower yoni.

It has been stated clearly in the *Mahābhārata* that there is no bar to attain liberation in order to be freed from the snare of rebirth. But only such persons can free themselves who are of controlled passions and who perform actions simply for the purpose of maintaining the body.[39] People who wish to lead a good life have to follow either of the two paths leading to happiness in worldly life or liberation. Those who wish to be blessed with a happy life in the world and do not hanker after liberation should practise the ordinary socio-moral virtues like truthfulness, self-sacrifice, patience, love etc. to attain human excellences. Again those who are eager for liberation should first of all practise all those socio-moral virtues and then should pass beyond through Yogabhyasa and Upasana to the realization of the Truth eternal. This will make them free from the clutches of Karma and rebirth.

The *Mahābhārata* exhibits a strong faith in the theory of Karma and rebirth. When a man dies his physical body disintegrates and dissolves into different elements but the subtle body sticks to the soul and leads it to new birth to a new body.[40] The nature of the new birth which the soul gets is determined by its Karma. It enjoys or suffers the fruits of its actions; good and bad deeds accompany the soul and make it suffer the fruits of its action[41] As the calf recognises its mother, even amidst the thousand cows, in the same way past deeds also catch hold of the doer and make him suffer the fruits of his actions.[42] A creature enjoys or suffers happiness or the misery that has been ordained for him by his own acts.[43] A man must suffer the consequences of his deeds done knowingly or unknowingly, openly or secretly.[44]

In the Vana Parva there is a long description of the

39. *Śānti Parva*, 214-24, 25.
40. *Mahābhārata*, XII. 202. 19; XII. 211. 14.
41. *Ibid.*, 202. 22.
42. *Ibid.*, 181. 16.
43. *Ibid.*, 181. 14.
44. *Ibid.*, 291. 14-15.

blessings and enjoyments in paradise where people enjoy the fruits of their righteous Karma after death.[45] As soon as rewards in proportions to deeds are enjoyed, the individual falls from heaven.[46] The soul is born again with its accumulated lead of Karma The soul does not die at the time of death. It leaves one body which disintegrates and is born in another new body.[47] Men must enjoy or suffer the fruits of his Karma, no else than he is to suffer it. The accumulated lead of Karma follows the doer and lead him to take new birth. Whatever we see in this world is the result of Karmas only. The righteous man is born in good Yoni and the wicked in bad Yoni.[48]

The law of Karma also explains why sometimes persons who should deserve happiness and success in life as judged by their deeds in this life are met with failures and unhappiness while the undeserving seem to succeed. The most intelligent and diligent men get failures in spite of his great efforts during this life, whereas, as a result of his past Karma, the wicked seems to enjoy a happy life in this world.[49]

In the Anuśāsana Parva sage Brihaspati teaches Yudhiṣṭhra that after death a man's virtuous and vicious Karmas follow him and determine his fate in the next birth; one should, therefore, try to do righteous Karma Dharma which alone is his friend in the next world and which determines his happiness and sorrow in the next birth.[50] Man is sure to reap as he sows.[51] The people who are ignorant of this law of Karma severely abuse the high powers, when they suffer and are unlucky. They do not know that their ill-luck is the result of their own evil Karmas.[52]

No one can be the dispenser of one's destiny according to one's sweet will; the Karmas done in the former life are

45. *Mahābhārata*, III. 261. 12, 28.
46. *Ibid.*, 261. 261. 29.
47. *Ibid.*, 209. 26.
48. *Ibid.*, 209. 27-31.
49. *Ibid.*, 209. 9-12.
50. *Ibid.*, 111. 14-18.
51. *Ibid.*, XIII. 6. 6.
52. *Ibid.*, III. 209. 5-6.

seen to produce fruits in this life.[53] "The acts that one does follow him even when he runs fast. Whatever acts one does lie down with the doer when the doer lays himself down. Indeed the sins one commits, sits when the doer sits and runs when the doer runs. The sin acts when the doer acts and indeed follow the doer like his shadow. Whatever the acts one does, by whatever means, are sure to be enjoyed and suffered by the doer in his next life."[54] The acts one has done in the past life appear at the proper time. Honour and dishonour, profit and loss, destruction and growth all are the fruits of one's actions. "The sorrow one suffers in the outcome of one's deeds. The happiness one enjoys originates from his deeds. From the time one lies in the mother's womb one begins to enjoy and suffer his pristine deeds."[55] In this world people enjoy and obtain food and cloth and other acquisitions acquired either by their parents or themselves. This is the result of the acts of pristine lives, for nothing can be had in this life which is not the result of the past.[56] A creature, when born, enjoys or suffers the fruits of deeds, done by him in his pristine lives. There is nothing agreeable or disagreeable which one enjoys or suffers without its being the result of the deeds and has done in his previous lives.[57]

Thus is becomes crystal clear after close inspection that the most significant and profoundly prevalent thought in Hindu culture and tradition is the conception of Karma. This Karma has influenced the Eastern Civilization very much as a law. Though it has been interpreted in various and varied ways, the core of the meaning is everywhere the same.

The Hindu thought and culture is based on not a remote metaphysics but on the practical conduct which in turn definitely leads to the understanding of the metaphysics. Metaphysics makes an attempt to discover a scheme in the physical world. The very meaning of the creation depends on

53. *Ibid*, III. 209. 22.
54. *Ibid.*, XII. 322. 14.
55. *Ibid*, XII. 322. 14.
56. *Ibid.*, XII. 288. 17.
57. *Ibid*, XII. 50.

such a scheme. But traditional Hindu culture finds its basis not in such a metaphysics, but in a metaphysics which is ethically perceptive. It is not only the viewpoint of Hindu thought but in the Genesis also we find the same idea. Sri Aurobindo observes :

> "He is a worker in a universal work, the life of their is his life; world consequence and the world evolution are also his business for he is oneself with the selves of all other beings." Thus,
>
> "He is an eternal soul which, though limited for certain temporal purposes in its outward consciousness has to learn to enlarge itself out of those limits to find and make effective its unity with eternal spirit who informs and transcends the universal."[58]

Leslie Stephen says that "The non-consequences of an action must always be relevant to its morality."[59] T.H. Green says that "a true moral philosophy consists in the readiness to sacrifice every lower inclination in the desire to do right for the sake of doing it."[60]

So directly or indirectly it is Karma which is the inner significance of the world. The action is the law of the universe. In the Bhagavad Geeta it is said that work is a function of nature.[61]

The law is the principle of the world which brings harmony and uniformity therein. The harmony and uniformity is essential for the universe. The Karma is the law of action which brings forth the creation and order in it and the ultimate harmony among things which leads to the destiny. The state of inactivity is the state of 'Jaḍa' which is devoid of consciousness and lacks in the power of progress and such phenomena have got no cultural explanations as such.

58. Shri Aurobindo, *The Problem of Rebirth*, p. 110.
59. Stephen, Leslie, *Science of Ethics*, p. 369.
60. Green, T.H.. *Prolegomena to Ethics*, p. 379.
61. See, *Bhagavad Geeta*, Chapter XVIII-14.

Whatever may be the belief, the action is necessary. It is the Karma principle by which humanity is born in this world of existence. This Karmavāda is the very foundation of the Hindu religion. This is a constricted law which evolves out the phenomen as well as the true nature of man. Man's existence, endeavour achievement, all are due to the Karma performed by him.

The law of Karma is a regularisation of the humanity which, gradually by performing good actions gives, wisdom and makes it realize its essence and the divinity. The law of Karma is the law of reaching to the Divine straightway. To reach the Divine there comes multiple factors beyond his control and which on the other way deviate man from the path of righteousness. Man is confronted with many temptations and for a mistake committed during his earthly life his soul must be punished to have chances to rectify his mistakes. And he can do it in this world by getting several births and deaths, i.e., the transmigration of the soul from one life to another.

The law of Karma not only functions in this life but also influences the lives to come. 'As we sow so we reap'. This is the law of Karma as the law of causality. In this life we are reaping what we have sown before. This faith not only gives a man fortitude, courage and calmness to face the trials and tribulations of life, but mitigates his bitterness toward others, whom he might otherwise hold responsible for his suffering. It also acts as an incentive toward habitual right conduct, because he realises that the secret of his future happiness lies in his resolve not to see anywhere.

The law of Karma, like the law of causation in nature is a law in the world of spirituality and its purification. There is the law in physical sphere that the evolution of the world follows a strict rule of the uniformity of nature. The coming of day and night, the heat and cold are never chaotic. This uniformity of nature is the underlying law. The gravitation, the relativity all are natural law of phenomena. The things are relative to one another and ultimately this relativity finds its meaning in the final Absolute.

Similarly the psychological sphere also entails certain laws. The essence of the consciousness is the same. That is why all souls are alike essentially. There is also uniformity in the order of consciousness, that is why souls have desires of the same type to take several migrations of life. The laws of the physical spheres and the psychological spheres are interdependent. One cannot exist without the other. The domain of the matter and the mind is intermingled from the viewpoint of the order of the universe.

There lies the harmony between man and the universe, the harmony between the individual and the cosmic order. The cosmic order will have no meaning if it is not appreciated by the individual and the whole of the mankind. The world will have no meaning so long it is not conceived by the human soul. It is not only in one life but through several lives in successions the individual soul finds the essence of the Real on this earth. The cosmos and the individual are two separate entities but the individual soul with a body resides in the cosmos to realise itself truly. Cosmos with the individual is not a chaos, both are approaching forward towards the same goal and apprehened the same reality.

Karma is condition not a destiny.[62] It is our past Karma that determines our status and environment in which we are placed. But subject to these limitations we have freedom of choice, "Our life is a mixture of necessity and freedom, chance and choice. By exercising our choice properly we control steadily all the elements and eliminate all together the determinism of nature."[63] The doctrine of Karma has two aspects. One refers to the past Karma which has determined our present and the other is an indication of the future which will be determined by our present Karmas. In both the aspects the stress is laid on the fact that it is man who is the architect of his fortune. It is he who is responsible for what he is and for what he will become.

The *Mahābhārata* also discusses how far life is governed by fate or destiny and how far by one's own efforts. In full

62. Radhakrishnan, S., *The Bhagavad Geeta*, p. 48.
63. *Ibid*, p. 49.

one chapter[64] in Anuśāsana Parva of the *Mahābhārata* the question has been discussed, wherein it is said that one's own efforts or strivings or exertions are like the seed while destiny or fate is comparable to the soil and the harvest thrives from the union of the two.[65] Just as without the seed the soil though tilled does not yield any fruit, in the same way without human efforts destiny does get fulfilled.[66] Destiny alone cannot give anything to anyone who lacks efforts.[67] On the other hand everything can be attained by efforts or exertion.[68] One's own self is his friend and his enemy.[69] Good and evil appear through Karma.[70] But, as by the diminution of oil in the lamp its light goes out, in the same way by the abetment of exertion or effort the influence of destiny also diminishes.[71] Thus by the influence of destiny and by the showing of personal exertion do men attain to heaven. The combined help of destiny and exertion becomes fruitful.[72]

Thus the doctrine of Karma should not be interpreted as implying a denial of human freedom which is regarded as the basis of ethical values. The law of Karma, when rightly viewed, is not opposed to human freedom rather it stresses the responsibility of man. It is a scientific principle which displaces belief in chance occurrences or arbitrariness in the Universe. It stresses the fact that the course of nature is not determined by prejudices or whims of a deity but by the operation of immutable laws according to which all our actions are duly rewarded or punished. None of our deeds goes scot-free or remains unaccounted for. There is the operation of necessity which maintains the balance in the Universe. The doctrine of Karma recognises the operation

64. *Mahābhārata*, XIII. 6.
65. *Ibid.*, XIII. 6. 8.
66. *Ibid.*, XIII. 6. 7.
67. *Ibid.*, XIII. 6. 22.
68. *Ibid.*, XIII. 6. 12-13.
69. *Ibid.*, XIII. 6. 27.
70. *Ibid.*, XIII. 6. 28.
71. *Ibid.*, XIII. 6. 44.
72. *Ibid.*, XIII. 6. 49.

of the rule of law not only in nature and physical world but also in the moral world. The Ṛta operates equally in nature and in human society. The law of Karma recognises the primacy of the rule of law which invariably makes us enjoy or suffer the fruits of our deeds. Thus, it stresses the primacy of ethical principle. It, therefore, should nct be regardad as a mechanical principle but a principle of Justice and ethical necessity. "Every act, every thought is weighed in the visible but Universal balance-scales of justice. The day of judgement is not in the remote future, but here and now and none can escape it."[73]

"Of the two things that govern human life, fate and personal initiative, 'I have no doubt', says Bhiṣma that personal effort is absolutely superior, for fate is only a matter of influence. The concept of Karma far from making a man contented with the position as being the result of his past actions, provides him with a motive for continuous effort for the betterment of his life and future destiny." In Hindu belief life is only a hyphen linking two eternities. "The need to stress the past and future of man is as relevant as the emphasis on personal and social obligations."[74]

73. Radhakrishnan, S., *The Hindu View of Life*, George Allen and Unwin, 1960, p. 53.

74. Aiyangar, Ranga Swami, *Some Aspects of Hindu View of Life*, p. 26.

6

The Standards of Morality

In this chapter we propose to discuss the different standards of morality as found in *Mahābhārata*. With the definition of the Moral Standard as being the ethical question proper, there are many definitions of the moral standard in Hindu Philosophy, some from biological, some from social and some from internal and other standpoints. We shall follow the undermentioned classifications as far as practicable:

1. The Standard as Custom and Tradition
2. The Standard as a Social Category
3. The Standard as an End
4. The Standard as Law
5. Purity of Motive
6. The Standard as Self-Realization

I. THE STANDARD AS CUSTOM AND TRADITION

In the *Nyāyamañjari* in discussing the moral standards the author, Jayanta Bhatta, refers to *Lokopadesa*, and *Lokaprasiddhi*, as the criteria of right and wrong. *Lokopadesa* is the standard according to those who hold that morality consists in the longstanding customs and usages that obtain amongst peoples. It thus differs from *Lokaprasiddhi*, which is the standard according to those who insist on universal agreement of belief as the criterion of right and wrong. A distinction is thus made between Tradition and Consensus, the assumption being that as there are conflicting traditions obtaining amongst different peoples there cannot be anything certain or fixed in them to ensure that universal validity as the standard of right and wrong. Hence it is not enduring or longstanding customs that constitute the criteria of morality, but customs that are universally accepted as authoritative, i.e., in respect of which there is consensus or universal agreement of belief.

In the *Mahābhārata* at several occasions we find that right and wrong actions are judged on several occasions by the prevailing customs and traditions of the community. Naturally, they are regarded as a standard of morality in the epic. S.K. Maitra defines tradition as a standard of morality in this way, "Lokopadesa, Tradition, is the standard according to those who hold that morality consists in the longstanding customs and usages that obtain amongst people."[1] In the fifth chapter of the *Ādiparva* when the question whether Pulomā's husband is saint Bhṛgu or the giant named Pulomā, Agni gives his verdict in favour of the saint. Agni regards their marriage as legal and justified because it has taken place traditionally and according to the custom by uttering *Mantras*. Agni states, "This Pulomā was, indeed first chosen by thee, O Rākṣasa, but she was not taken by thee with holy rites and invocations. But this far-famed lady was bestowed by her father on Bṛhgu as a gift from desire of blessing. She was not bestowed on thee. O Rākṣasa this lady was duly made by the Ṛṣi Bhṛgu his wife with Vedic rites in my presence. This is she—I know her."[2] In the same parva we notice that the forefathers of Jaratakāru are lying in hell only because he is not celebrating his marriage ceremony which is the convention and he is destroying the tradition.[3]

1. Maitra, S.K., *The Ethics of the Hindus*, p. 292.
2. *Ādi.*, 5, 32-33-34.
3. *Ādi.*, 13, 24, 25-26.

Sometimes it becomes difficult to choose the right path of morality when two of them disagree. In such situations we have to take the help of tradition and custom to avoid wrong path. In the *Mahābhārata* we observe so many occasions when without taking the help of this standard we cannot pass moral judgement over actions. As for instance, it becomes troublesome to decide whether all the five Pāndavas are justified in marrying Draupadī simultaneously following the wishes of their mother Kunti. King Drupada, father of Draupadī and her brother Dhṛṣṭadyumna are against such marriage. Drupada states:

> "In my opinion this marriage is adharma in contravention of morality because it is antagonistic to the *Vedas* and customs. There is no custom like this that so many persons should keep one wife."[4]

Thus Drupada takes it as immoral action. But Yudhiṣṭhira justifies their polyandry. Both take their stand on time-honoured customs and traditions. Yudhiṣṭhira says:

> "The courage or nature of Dharma is very subtle, so we do not know the dharma's course, but we must follow our forefathers."[5]

He quotes a precedent from the *Purānas* that a most pious girl named Jatilā was married to seven saints at a time.[6] He cites another example of Varksī daughter of saint Kandu who was married to ten persons, all brothers and having the same name.[7] On the basis of these evidences, he says that the marriage of Draupadī with Pāndavas is sanctioned by tradition and therefore unimpeachable.

The life of the people in the epic period was supposed to be governed by the traditions and customs prevailing in society. These traditions and customs were in keeping with

4. *Ādi*, 195, 7.
5. *Ibid.*, 194, 29.
6. *Ibid.*, 195, 4.
7. *Ibid.*, 195, 15.

the status and conditions of the persons concerned. A king had to follow the traditions of his royal family, otherwise his actions would be condemned. Similarly a Brāhmin had to observe the customs and traditions of his *varna.* In the *Śāntiparva,* we find that some Brāhmin boys of rich families leave their home and start to lead a saintly life in the forest. One day Indra comes in the form of a golden bird and asks them to go back home. He states that there is a provision of duties pertaining to varna and sacraments or *Samskāras* with *Mantras* for the Brāhmins. As long as they live, they should perform their *Samskāras.* Even after their death the *Samskāras* or ritual ceremonies of burning the dead bodies and other *Samskāras* like *Śrāddha* should be performed in accordance with the Vedic customs.[8]

In the *Śāntiparva* Bhīmasena advised Yudhiṣṭhira to follow the custom and tradition of their forefathers when Yudhiṣṭhira after battle wants to renounce the world and decides not to rule the kingdom. Bhīmasena says:

> "Applying the intellect to this, and ascertaining that right and the wrong paths of creatures, follow thou the course adopted by thy sire before thee and govern properly thy kingdom."[9]

On the same occasion Arjuna requests his eldest brother to rule the kingdom observing the course of the world.[10]

When we go through the different *Parvas* of the epic dealing with military operations, we find that from its beginning to end, the majority of the performances were observed in accordance with the customs of warfare. In the *Śāntiparva* Bhīsma asks Yudhiṣṭhira to follow the path of his grand-father and great grand-father. He observes:

> "Follow the conduct of thy sire and grandsire. Kings should never adopt that conduct which thou desirest to adopt."[11]

8. *Śānti,* 11, 12.
9. *Ibid.,* 15, 5.
10 *Ibid.,* 16, 27.
11. *Ibid.,* 75, 20.

It may be mentioned in this context, that the customs and traditions of the *Mahābhārata* are derived mostly from the *Vedas* and *Smṛtis*. They are usually in the form of rigid conventions. Sometimes they also conflict with each other. Customs and traditions are the determinants of actions when other criteria fail.

2. THE STANDARD AS A SOCIAL CATEGORY

In the preceding section we considered the moral standard regarded as Tradition and Custom. It was assumed that established usage of long standing has an authority in itself which validates its acceptance as the standard of right and wrong in the moral life. There is however no appeal here to social good as the ultimate criterion of the validity of custom though such reference may be indirectly implied. There are others however who insist on this test of social utility as the essential factor in the determination of right and wrong so that custom, tradition, etc., are authoritative only in a secondary sense as being resolvable into this ultimate test of social good. Thus the "Nyāyamañjari" notices also the following conceptions of the moral standard, viz., (1) the standard as *Lokasthiti* or Maintenance of the Social Equilibrium, and (2) the standard as *Lokasiddhi* or Realisation of the Social Good.

It is to be seen that the conception of *Lokasthiti* or Social Stability is more compatible with moral order than moral progress while that of *Lokasiddhi*, i.e., Realisation of the Social End or purpose provides both for order and progress. It is also to be noted that the standard of *Lokasthiti* or Social Stability implies a relativism in the moral life which impairs its authority by depriving it of its absoluteness and necessity.

This relativism in the conception of *Lokasthiti* is very clearly brought out by Āryadeva in the "Catuhsatika." It is pointed out that there being nothing durable or immutable in popular morality, it hardly inspires confidence in men's minds. Why? Because as righteousness (*Dharma*) is nothing but what maintains social stability, the social life is evidently superior to morality and determines the nature of the latter. Thus whatever is laid down by society for the regulation of family ties and relationships and of citizenship within specific territorial zones, e.g., what is laid down in regard to marriage and the like, is regarded as constituting morality. Morality and immorality are thus social convenventions varying from zone to zone and age to age. There is nothing constant or eternal in righteousness, nothing that is fixed immutably by Nature, morality being merely a means of social conservation, the content of which must vary according to the changing circumstances, conditions and the particular organisation of the society which is to be conserved.

On account of this relativism in the conception of *Lokasthiti*, the "Mahānirvānatantra" recommends *Lokā-Sreya*, Social Good, as the moral standard, as distinguished from *Lokasthiti* or Social Stability. An attempt is thus made not only to get beyond the limitations of communal and regional morality but also to provide for moral progress besides moral order.

Another important standard of morality in the epic is the achievement of social good. The ideal of social good occupies a prominent position in the *Mahābhārata*. This ideal can be attained only when social equilibrium is maintained, i.e., the four classes of society and the four stages of life should be maintained properly. Social stability is essential for the physical and moral and spiritual growth of the individual. It is stated in the *Śāntiparva* that for the growth and advancement of the creatures Dharma is essential, "*Prabhavarthaya bhutana dharmapravacanam Kṛtam.*"[12] It is also stated by Utathya in the epic that Brahmā created Dharma for the welfare of all creatures.[13]

Very often social good is regarded as an essential factor in the determination of right and wrong. Naturally other standards like customs and traditions, law and duty, etc., become secondary as they may be easily included in the prime test of social good. In the *Vanaparva* it is stated by the virtuous fowler that untruth sometimes leads to the triumph of

12. *Śānti*, 109, 10.
13. *Ibid.*, 90, 19.

truth, and the latter dwindles into untruth. Whichever conduces most to the good of all creatures is considered to be truth.[14] Nārada states to Gālaba that he regards welfare of the creatures as truth.[15] It appears from the above illustrations that the criterion of truth is the welfare of creatures. Thus the content of morality is changeable. It changes in accordance with the needs of changing situations in the society.

Morality is supposed to be related with the welfare of the society. The individual and the society are mutually inter-dependent. We have discussed that Dharma leads to *Abhyudaya* and *Nihsreyasa* of the individuals. The prosperity of the individual is useless and meaningless without society. Individual's prosperity has significance only when society progresses and prospers. Society is supposed to be an organism and its individuals are different limbs. Can working of the organs be active when the organism itself becomes inactive? The answer is in the negative. Similarly, without the good of society, without maintaining welfare of society, no good or welfare of the particular individual can be maintained. Hence, social equilibrium and social stability are supposed to be essential for the betterment of the individual when he takes his birth, receives his education and discharges all sorts of duties in life. Keeping it in view, Bhīsma states in the *Śāntiparva* that great sages and seers have established Dharma for *Lokayātrā* or the maintenance of society.[16] Again it is observed in the *Śāntiparva* by Utathya '*dharma tisthati bhūtāni*,' i.e., even all beings are supported in their existence by Dharma.[17]

Morality is the guiding principle of the society. If it is withdrawn, society as such will cease to exist and there will be anarchy. Balgangadhara Tilak observes:

> "When this Dharma ceases to be observed, the binding ropes of society may be said to have become loose, and

14. Vana, 208, 3-4 (P.C. Roy); 209 (G.P.).
15. *Śānti*, 287, 22.
16. *Ibid.*, 259, 54.
17. *Ibid.*, 90, 5.

> when these binding ropes are loosened, society will be in the same position as the planetary system consisting of the Sun and the planets would be in the sky without the binding force of gravitation or as a ship would be on the ocean without a rudder."[18]

In this connection, Mr. S.K. Patcliffe states:

> "Dharma includes the whole social conception of law and conduct and worship. Dharma is the force or principle that binds together; the union of traditional thought and faith of common custom, loyalty and understanding, that makes of society as an organic or religious whole."[19]

So, Dharma is the cementing force for social unity. It is essential for the good functioning of society as a whole.

Dr. Surama Das Gupta, while summarizing the different standards of morality in the *Mahābhārata*, recognizes social good as one of them. According to her, there are three types of standards of morality in the epic. She takes the advancement of society, maintenance of social order, preservation of traditions and customs as the first type while final liberation as the second and rules of guidance for the people in abnormal times as the third. She states :

> "The first type is concerned with the well-being of society and the individual, with which the third is also in full consonance, as it aims at the preservation of life and its well-being in times of danger, disorder and anarchy; while the second type is quite different from them; it has as its aim, the freedom of the individual from the bondage of the world (*samsāra*) and, therefore, of society, so to speak. While the first and third ones aim at social welfare and its stability, the second is confined to

18. Tilak, B.G., *Gītā Rahasya*, pp. 90-91.
19. Nivedita, Sister, Preface, *Religion and Dharma*.

individual liberation, which is something beyond society, and therefore, may be taken as supra-social."[20]

From the above account it is clear that Dr. Das Gupta takes the ethics of the *Mahābhārata* to be pre-eminently social in character. To her, morality is necessary for social well-being. She states, "Dharma has been defined as that which supports and sustains the world."[21] Further she states, "The definition is so elastic that whatever is conducive to the good of the people can be regarded as right and virtue."[22] Thus the concept of Dharma is a social phenomenon having its sway over social working and social betterment.

Much significance is attached to the *Varnāsrama-dharma* in the *Mahābhārata*. They are emphasized because if the Brāhmin, Ksatriya, Vaisyas and the Sūdras do not perform their duties, the maintenance of society, stability of social order will disappear and there will be all chaos and confusion. Barbarism and anarchy will prevail in society. Thus it appears that the main aim of the ancient Hindu literatures like the *Vedas*, *Smṛtis*, *Dharmasāstras* and of the *Mahābhārata* is to propound such notion of Dharma which can maintain peace, plenty, progress of all individuals along with the social stability. The underlying idea is to achieve social good and progress in a harmonious manner. Each *varna*, while fulfilling its separate functions, fulfils automatically all the functions of society. Taken together, these *varnas* work for general welfare as they are related among themselves for the purpose of social unity. Pandhari Nath Valavalkar also has the same opinion when he holds:

> "The *varna scheme* could be said to promote social organisation in another direction also. It seeks to promote social equilibrium and solidarity through the economic organisation.... On the whole, therefore, the

20. Gupta, Surama Das, *Development of Moral Philosophy in India*, p. 2.
21. *Ibid.*
22. *Ibid.*, p. 22.

Varna-theory was devised with a view to engage the different types of human energies in different channels suitable to each of them and all towards the one end of social organisation and social stability."[23]

The implication of political morality is the maintenance of peace, justice, progress, law and order in society. Political institutions like kingship is required to establish social equilibrium and stability to help individuals in performing moral acts. It also helps man in achieving his goals through social order. For this reason it is stated in the *Mahābhārata* that the foremost duty of the king is to preserve and conserve the duties of the four *varnas*.[24]

Aurobindo observes that the earnest desire of the author of the epic is to concentrate upon the social problems like social stability and others. He says:

> "But Vyāsa has not only a high political and religious thought and deep-seeing social judgement, he deals not only with the massive aspects and worldwide issues of human conduct, but has a keen eye for the details of Government and society, the ceremonies, form and usages, the religious and social order on the due stability of which public welfare is governed."[25]

Now judging all these points, it is obvious that social good is given a great importance in the epic as a standard of morality.

3. THE STANDARD AS AN END

The Standard as End of Sukha

The hedonistic standard of pleasure also occupies an important place in the ethics of the Hindus. It is the Cārvākas

23. Valavalkar, Pandharinath H., *Hindu Social Institutions*, pp. 327-28.
24. *Śānti*, 57, 15.
25. Aurobindo, *Vyāsa and Vālmiki*, p. 53.

that are credited with this sensualistic standard of pleasure as the guiding principle in morality. The Cārvāka motto of life is : live for pleasure as you can, and even if life is a blend of pleasure and pain the wise man should so regulate his life as to enjoy the maximum of pleasure with the minimum of unavoidable pain. It is sheer folly to forego pleasure because it is mixed up with pain just as it is folly to give up eating fish to escape the trouble of removing the scales and fishbones, or to give up cooking the meal to escape the annoyance of beggars infesting and disturbing us. On the contrary, we should be reconciled to life as it is and should endeavour to curtail our suffering as much as possible. This is true morality which consists in so regulating life as to make it yield the maximum of pleasure. Similarly immorality consists in unnecessarily increasing the amount of avoidable suffering or pain. Hence rightness and wrongness are to be determined by reference to *upakāra*, Well-being and *apakāra*, Ill-being, i.e., by egoistic pleasure or happiness and egoistic pain or suffering, and as the body as consisting of the elementary particles of matter is all that we mean by the self, soul or spirit, it is the bodily or sensual pleasures that count, and it is only the fools that sacrifice physical pleasures in anticipation of supersensuous pleasures to come in a future life. In fact there is no future life, the soul perishing with the disintegration of the body so that the wise-regulated life is that which has made the most of this life so as to make it yield the maximum of pleasure. It is necessary therefore to live prudentially so as to increase our happiness and reduce our suffering in this life, and it is even proper to purchase the pleasures of life by incurring debts, and other similar means (*Ṛnam kriva ghṛtam pibet*).

It is to be seen that the Cārvāka hedonism is gross and sensualistic as well as egoistic. It is the happiness of the self that counts in the last resort and a prudential and tactful regard for others with a view to self-gratification is the only form of altruism that is recommended as rational and proper. Similarly any discrimination between sensual and refined pleasures in view of qualitative superiority is condemned as foolish.

The standard of *Sukhavāda* or Hedonism is recurrently found in the *Mahābhārata*. *Sukha* or pleasure of this world or of the other is primarily regarded as the summum bonum of life. In the dialogue between a bird named Pūjanī and King Brahmadatta, '*Sukha*' or happiness is accepted as an object of desire. The bird says : "All beings desire pleasure and seek to avoid pain."[26] Saint Bhṛgu also affirms that men always try to avoid pain, and everything is done only for the sake of pleasure. He thus says to Bharadvāja:

> "Happiness is said to be of two kinds, viz., bodily and mental. Both in this and the other world, the visible and invisible fruits (of actions) are specified (in the *Vedas*) for the sake of happiness. There is nothing more important than happiness and among the fruits or consequences of the triple aggregate (Artha, Dharma and Kāma), happiness is desirable. It is an attribute of the soul. Both Virtue and Profit are sought for its sake. Virtue is its root. This, indeed, is its origin. All acts have for their end the attainment of happiness."[27]

In the *Śāntiparva* Nārada states to Suka that it is not proper to lament about that unhappiness which is universal; instead of lamenting about the matter, one should use such means as available to him for deviating that unhappiness.[28] In the *Anusāsanaparva* Bṛhaspati says to Yudhiṣṭhira:

> "Endued with life, O King, jīva in this world, from the moment of his birth, enjoys and endures his own (previous) acts, depending upon righteousness (and its reverse). If jīva, according to the best of his power follows righteousness from the day of his birth, he then succeeds in enjoying, when reborn, happiness without interruption."[29]

26. *Śānti*, 139, 62.
27. *Ibid.*, 190, 7-9.
28. *Ibid.*, 330.
29. *Anusā*, 111. 37-38.

Hence to seek pleasures and avoid pain is repeatedly maintained in the epic. Pleasure and pain both come in the life but one tries to seek pleasure and avoid pain. Thus, the hedonistic ideal of life seems to occupy a prominent position in the epic. Dr. Radhakrishnan also opines, "Ethics as the pursuit of happiness is given an important place in the *Mahābhārata*."[30]

If we analyse the hedonistic elements in the *Mahābhārata* we find different shades of hedonism in it, e.g., psychological and ethical, egoistic and altruistic, gross and refined. The dialogue between the bird Pūjanī and King Brahmadatta shows that seeking of pleasure and avoiding of pain is the natural tendency of living creatures. The discourse between Bhṛgu and Bharadvāja also points pleasure as the normal object of desire. Such passages in the *Mahābhārata* clearly advocate psycho-hedonism.

In the *Śāntiparva* when Nārada advises Suka not to lament for unhappiness and to use all means to obviate pain, he does not regard it as a psychological and normal fact, rather he asked him that he should engage all means to avoid pain. Here the word 'should' is used. This is ethical hedonism. In the *Vanaparva*, it is stated that one should seek pleasure in the first portion of life, wealth in the second, and virtue in the last.[31]

When we examine the varions shades of hedonistic thought in the *Mahābhārata* we find elements of egoism as well as of altruism. In the *Anuśāsanaparva* Bhīsma advises Yudhiṣṭhira to seek his (Yudhiṣṭhira's) own self-interest. Bhīsma says that those practices that support society, the duties of righteousness and all those acts which are productive of benefit to one's own self, should be performed.[32] Here we find a synthesis of egoism and altruism. In the *Vanaparva* sage Mārkandeya also asks Yudhiṣṭhira to seek his own benefit. He says:

30. Radhakrishnan, S., *Indian Philosophy*, p. 505.
31. *Vana*, 33, 41.
32. *Anu*, 37, 16.

> "Good men having an eye to their own welfare, as also virtue and the ways of the world, act in this way and thereby grow in virtue through endless ages."[33]

The egoistic nature of man is revealed in the fable of the rat and the cat. The rat 'Palita' states to the cat 'Lomasa' : "Nobody is anybody's foe, nobody is anybody's friend; persons become friends or foes only from motives of interest.... The father, the mother, the son, the maternal uncle, the sister's son, other relatives and kinsmen, are all guided by considerations of interest and profit.... This whole world of creatures is moved by the desire of gain (in some form or other). One never becomes dear to another (without cause). The friendship between two uterine brothers, the love between husband and wife, depend upon interest. I do not know any kind of affection in any person that does not rest upon some motive of self-interest."[34] This may be compared to a similar trend of thought found in the *Bṛhadāranyakopanishad*. Yājñavalkya states to his wife Maitreyi :

> "O Maitreyi, the husband is loved by the wife, not for the sake of the husband, but for the sake of her own *ātman*; in the same way, the son is not loved by us for his own sake; we love him for our own sake.... We like all things for the sake of our self (*ātman*)."[35]

In the *Anusāsanaprva* Bṛhaspati says to Yudhiṣṭhira that in refusals and gifts, happiness and pain, in the agreeable and the disagreeable, one should judge of their effects by a reference to one's own self."[36]

But though there are occasional references to self-interest here and there, the ethical trend of thought in *Mahābhārata* is pronouncedly altruistic. The epic emphasises the other—regarding virtue of 'Do as you would be done by', as the golden rule of life. Vidura enjoins in the *Śāntiparva* that one

33. *Vana*, 206, 90.
34. *Śānti*, 138, 110, 143, 152-53.
35. *Br. Upanisad*, 2, 4; 4, 5.
36. *Anu*, 113, 9.

should also behave towards all creatures as he should towards himself.[37] This principle is also maintained in the Viduranīti: "That which is antagonistic (adverse) to one's own self should never be applied in respect of another."[38] Bhīsma observes it:

> "Knowing how painful it is to himself, a person should never do that to others which he dislikes when done to him by others.... How can one who to draw breath himself think of preventing another by a murderous act from doing the same ? Whatever wishes one entertains with respect to one's oneself, one should certainly cherish with respect to another."[39]

From the above verses it is obvious that the principle of self-identification with others is the main cause underlying welfare of others. Self-identification is the basis of altruism. So egoism gives way to altruism. To do good or welfare is regarded as one of the important aspects of Dharma. In the *Vanaparva*, Draupadī says that whichever conduces most to the good of all creatures is considered to be truth.[40] At another place in the *Śāntiparva*, Dhṛtarāstra, after narrating the stories of Prahlāda and Indra, tells his son Duryodhana: "The act or exertion by which others are not benefited, or that act in consequence of which one has to feel shame, should not be done."[41] Here in place of 'pleasure' we find 'benefit of others' which determines actions to be done or not. If any act is not beneficial to others, it should not be performed. The intellectual discourse between Tulādhāra and Jājali also shows the importance to the welfare of others. Tulādhāra says:

> "He, O Jājali, is said to know what morality or righteousness is, who is always the friend of all creatures

37. *Śānti*, 167, 9.
38. *Udyoga*, 39, 71.
39. *Śānti*, 259, 20, 22.
40, *Vana*, 206, 4; P.C. Roy, 208.
41. *Śānti*, 124, 67.

and who is always engaged in the good of all creatures, in thought, word, and deed."[42]

S.N. Gajendragadkar observes in this connection ;

"It is clear that Tulādhāra is expounding Dharma which has a universal appeal in that. It aims at human welfare, peace in society and personal tranquillity."[43]

In the *Śāntiparva* Nārada says to sage Gālaba :

"Truthfulness of speech is excellent. The knowledge, however, of truth, is very difficult of acquisition. I say that that is truth which is exceedingly beneficial to creatures."[44]

The same principle is reiterated by Nārada in his talk to Suka.[45]

In the *Gītā* also we find stress on the welfare of all beings. At one place Kṛṣṇa says to Arjuna :

"Those *Ṛṣis*, who have lost the sense of duality (that is, who have realised the principle that there is only one Parmesvara in all places), whose sins have been dissolved, and who have become engrossed in achieving the welfare of the entire creation by means of self-control, attain Release in the shape of Brahma-nirvāna."[46]

Again at another place Kṛṣṇa says :

"After having controlled their senses and become equable-minded towards everything, such (persons too),

42. *Śānti*, 261, 9.
43. Gajendragadkar, S.N., Roving Mendicant in the *Mahābhārata*, Journal of the Asiatic Society of Bombay, Vol. 30, 1955, Pt. I, p. 48.
44. *Śānti*, 287, 20.
45. *Ibid.*, 329, 13.
46. *Gītā*, 5, 25.

> who are engrossed in the welfare of all beings, also come and reach Me."[47]

Thus we find that the stress is not on the welfare of human beings only but on the welfare of all living creatures. The altruism of the epic is wide enough to cover the whole universe within its scope.

Pleasure is sometimes divided into sensual and intellectual. In the *Mahābhārata* we find some passages in support of sensualistic hedonism. Bhīma requests his eldest brother Yudhiṣṭhira not to renounce but to enjoy damsels. He says :

> "Approaching beautiful damsels attired in excellent robes, adorned with every ornament, and exhibited with sweet wines, do thou sport with them. Kāma, O king, should be the foremost of the three (Artha, Dharma and Kāma) with us."[48]

This reminds us of the gross egoistic hedonism of Aristippus. In the epic we also find some verses advocating preference of present to future pleasure. It is stated that the abandonment of present happiness and the pursuit of that which is yet to come is never the policy of a person possessed of intelligence.[49] It suggests the philosophy of 'eat, drink and be merry for tomorrow you may die'. Thus it can be said that some elements of gross hedonism are traceable in the epic.

We have observed that Bhṛgu makes a distinction between boyily and mental pleasure.[50] A similar distinction is found in the philosophy of Epicuream philosophy.[51] It is regarded as refined hedonism because it prefers mental pleasure to physical. Happiness, achieved through reason, is regarded as greater than that achieved through the senses.

47. *Ibid.*, 12, 4 (Gita Rahasya).
48. *Ibid.*, 67, 38.
49. *Ibid.*, 140, 36.
50. *Ibid* , 190. 9.
51. Sharma, I.C., *Ethical Philosophy of India*, p. 110.

The *Gītā* enjoins, "That happiness is the most beautific happiness which being obtainable only by means of Reason, is independent of the organ."[52]

We find three kinds of *Sukha* in the *Gītā-Sattva, Rajasa* and *Tamasa.* "That in which one finds enjoyment only through practice (of Bhajana, meditation and worship) and whereby one reaches the end of sorrow,—nay, that which appears like poison in the beginning (i.e., when the practices are started), but tastes as nectar in the end, born of the placidity of mind brought about by meditation on God, such a joy is said to be *Sāttvika.*"[53] "The joy which is derived from the contact of the senses with their objects, though appearing like nectar in the beginning (at the time of enjoyment), proves to be mischievous like poison in the end. That is why such a joy is said to be *Rājasika.*"[54] "The joy which deadens the soul, both in the beginning and in the end, and which is derived from sleep, indolence and carelessness is said to be *Tāmasika.*"[55] The first kind of happiness is regarded as the best.

In the *Mahābhārata* there is a distinction between worldly pleasure and heavenly pleasure. Earthly pleasure is mixed with pain whereas heavenly pleasure is unalloyed or unmixed. We feel that everybody is constantly struggling with a view to obtain happiness. He wants pleasure on the one hand and less pain, as much as possible, on the other hand. As a matter of fact he does not succeed in achieving pleasure without pain and suffering. It is stated in the *Mahābhārata* that in this world, pain is mixed with happiness.[56] In the *Śāntiparva* we find an analogical description that the happiness and sorrow of human beings are revolving like a wheel. Sorrow comes after joy and joy after sorrow.[57] It is stated by Sampāka that diverse kinds of sorrow and happiness overtake, from the day of birth of the person that is born on the

52. *Gītā*, 6, 21.
53. *Ibid.*, 18, 36-37, G. P.
54. *Ibid.*, 18, 38, G.P.
55, *Ibid.*, 18, 39, G.P.
56. *Śānti*, 199, 14.
57. *Ibid.*, 174, 19 and 25, 23.

earth.[58] Draupadī appears correct when she states to Satyabhāmā that happiness never comes out of happiness. In order that a saintly woman should experience happiness, she must experience pain and sufferings.[59] Pain and sufferings are of many kinds. The bird Pūjanī says to King Brahmadatta that misery arises from various sources. Decrepitude is misery. The loss of wealth is misery. The adjacence of anything disagreeable or evil is misery. Separation or dissociation from friends and agreeable objects is misery.[60] In the *Śāntiparva* Bhṛgu says that there are both pleasure and pain in this world. They are mixed together. There is unmixed pleasure only in heaven. And the real pleasure is the very nature of the supreme Brāhman.[61] Bhṛgu further says that diverse kinds of physical and mental evils are never found in heaven. Pleasure in heaven is permanent and immutable. In heaven delicious breezes blow. There is also perpetual fragrance. There is no hunger, no thirst, no decrepitude, no sin.[62]

Thus according to the epic, the happiness of heaven is pure and superior to worldly pleasure. The former is unalloyed.

4. THE STANDARD AS LAW

The moral Standard is also conceived by the Hindus as a Law or Command which again is regarded either as a Personal Prescription of a superior to an inferior being (*pauruseya*) or again as impersonal Law (*apauruseya*) without a law-giver.

A. *The Standard as Personal Moral Law*

i.e., as the prescription of a superior to an inferior spirit. This is how the Standard is conceived by the Cārvākas,

58. *Ibid.*, 176, 4.
59. *Vana*, 234, 4.
60. *Sānti*, 139, 63.
61. *Ibid.*, 190, 14.
62. *Ibid.*, 190, 12-13.

the Jainas, the Bauddhas, the Rāmānujists and the Naiyayikas. Thus :

(a) According to the Cārvākas, the standard is the law imposed by the king, who is the highest earthly authority. The king's injunctions constitute duties just as the king's prohibitions constitute the opposed.

Thus according to the Cārvākas, the will of the sovereign determines right and wrong, but this is analysed into the pleasures and pains of the individual. As pleasure is the only real good and pain is the only real evil, the will of the sovereign is the Moral Law for the sovereign is the highest earthly authority and the dispenser of all happiness and suffering. (*Sukhameva purusārthah, duhkhameva narakam, lokasiddho raja paramesvarah.*)

(b) According to the Jainas and Bauddhas, however, it is not the prescriptions of the king, but the injunctions and prohibitions of Arhats and Buddhas that constitute right and wrong. The earthly sovereign is an imperfect being like ourselves and his authority is based on brute force. Obedience to such authority is prudential and not moral, being based on the hope of reward and fear of punishment. But the authority of the Moral Law is spiritual and not physical, and can be vested only in the Seer, i.e., the Spiritual Expert that has attained perfection by self-culture. The earthly king is as much subject to the prescriptions of these moral experts, Arhats or Buddhas, as other imperfect beings.

It is to be seen that the appeal here is to the verdict of spiritual experts and not merely to sheer authority. It is thus to be distinguished from the prudential morality of the Cārvākas which is based on the hope of reward and fear of punishment. At the same time no eternally perfect being is recognised as in theism. The authority of the Moral Law arises indeed from the spiritual perfection of Arhats and Buddhas who possess the proper insight into things and thus are able to prescribe the right modes of conduct, but this spiritual perfection is itself an acquisition in time and not an eternally accomplished fact as theists assume. The objection that on this assumption the Arhats would be themselves without spiritual preceptors to guide them is met by the conception of a chain of Arhats and Buddhas which is without beginning in time—a chain in which the preceding Arhats act as preceptors to their successors.

(c) The Nyāya-Vaisesikas, the Rāmānujists and other theists however content that the Moral Standard is the law of righteousness as prescribed by God who is the Creator and Moral Governor of the world. Thus in the "Nyāya, parisuddhi" of Vankatesa we have :

Right and wrong are determined by the injunctions and prohibitions of scripture. Like the commands of the earthly king, these scriptural injunctions and prohibitions are prescribed by God with a view to the governance of sentient beings and represent His beneficent purpose. Hence right and wrong embody the conscious purpose and intelligence of God, i.e., they are not arbitrary prescriptions of the Divine Will but represent God's rational purpose and end in this world. Right is that which the Divine Intelligence recognises as good and beneficent and wrong is that which it considers pernicious and evil. (*Dharmādharmau vihitanisiddhakriyāsadhyatayā abhimatau āgñāvato rājña iva sarvaprasāsituh isvarasyānugrahanigrahākhya-buddhivisesar ūpau.*)

Right and wrong are thus *buddhivesesas*, i.e., forms of the divine purpose and not objective categories. Further the divine purpose is not an arbitrary fiat of the divine will, but the revelation of the divine intelligence. Hence *Vidhi* as the command of God does not constitute the Moral law but merely reveals it—it is not law-making, but law-revealing.

According to the Nyāya-Vaisesikas, however, the Divine Command as embodies in scriptural prescription is not merely declaratory (*jñāpaka*) of the moral code but also constitutes it (*kāraka*). The analogy is drawn from positive law which depends on the will of the sovereign. Moral causation is thus conceived after physical causation and the authority of duty is regarded as a form of physical impulsion or force.

Thus far we have considered the following theories of the Moral Standard regarded as Personal Moral Law, viz.,

(a) *Vidhi* as the command of the king.

(b) *Vidhi* as *anusāsana*, i.e., as declaratory of the Seer's experiences in the *Pāramārthika* plane.

(c) *Vidhi* as command of God conceived, after positive law, as constituting and not merely declaring or revealing what is right or wrong.

(d) *Vidhi* as God's command regarded as merely revealing and not constituting the Moral Law.

(e) There is yet another conception of *Vidhi* as the Moral Standard, the view which finds favour with a certain class of Vedāntists. According to these, *Vidhi* is *Brahman* or the Absolute itself and not the mere prescription of a superior or perfect person. For the essence of *Vidhi* lies in its obligatoriness as Moral Law which means that *Vidhi* has *Pramāna*, validity or self-evidencing authority as Law which makes it binding on the individual moral agent. But *Vidhi* could not validate itself without being itself a self-validating experience, for the validity of the valid is only this that it posits itself in consciousness. *Vidhi* as *Pramāna* is thus *Cidātmaka*, i.e., a self-establishing experience whose authority on the moral agent is nothing but its self-accomplished character reflecting itself in the consciousness of the individual as something to be accomplished. Hence *Vidhi* is *Brahman* itself which is accomplished (*Siddha*) from eternity. In the consciousness of the individual it appears indeed as *sādhya*, as a thing to be accomplished, but in so far as it validates itself it is essentially *Pratibhāsamātra*, mere position in consciousness. As a matter of fact, the essence of *Pramānya*, validation, is nothing but this position in consciousness and *Param Brahma*, the self-positing Absolute Consciousness, is thus the only *Pramāna*, the various cognitive processes being regarded as *Pramāna* only by courtesy, their validity being ultimately nothing but this self-evidencing Consciousness which is the Absolute in the light of which they appear. In so far therefore as *Vidhi* has *Pramānya*, validity or authority, it is nothing but the self-accomplishing Absolute Experience which presents itself as something to be accomplished.

This is a new form of the conception of *Vidhi* as the Moral Standard which is to be distinguished alike from the conception of it as the prescription of a personal being like God and from that of an Impersonal Law without a law-giver. It identifies *Vidhi* with the Absolute which is not personal being but the self-establishing suprapersonal consciousness that lights up all experience. The authority of the *Vidhi* is nothing but the self-fulled reality of the Absolute Thought presenting itself in empirical consciousness as a thing to be realised in time. The close analogy of this view with Sankara's Transcendentalism is obvious enough. But while Sankara conceives the Transcendental Life as the negation of the empirical, the latter being annulled altogether in the consciousness of *Brahman*, it is urged here that the validity which attaches to *Vidhi* in empirical consciousness is nothing but the self-affirmation of the Absolute as self-validating experience. Hence according to this view the empirical moral life reflects the nature of the Absolute in a way though it does not manifest in its completeness and purity, while according to Sankara, the empirical life is the negation of the transcendental life in *Brahman* which is to be reached only by total cancellation of the moral life in the state of *Karmasannyāsa* or freedom from the bond of duty. It is remarkable, however, that in spite of this underestimation of the empirical life, the Sankarites not only recognise the value of morality in empirical life but also offer the original and novel conception of a gradation of moral standards and moral codes in accordance with the ascending stages of the spiritual life of the individual.

(f) Thus according to Sankara, the moral code as constituted by the Vedic prescriptions is impersonal in the sense that the Communicator (*vaktā*) of the Vedas only declares the Law and does not create it by his fiat. This Communicator is *īsvara*, *Brahmā* or the Lord and is thus to be distinguished from the Spiritual Expert or *Āptapurusa* of Jainism and Buddhism. In fact, it is eternally omniscient (*nityasarvajña*) and is also *Sṛṣṭi-Sthiti-Laya-Kartā*, the Creator, Maintainer and Destroyer of the world, which theistic characters are lacking in the *āptas* and *arhats* of Buddhism and Jainism. But the *vaktā*, the Communicator, of the Vedas, does not create but merely promulgates the Vedas as they existed in a previous cycle. Some of the Sankarites admit that some of the scriptures have a personal source such as Manu, *Mahābhārata*, etc., but they are all traced back ultimately to the impersonal (*apauruseya*) Vedas. But even the Vedas themselves are empirical, i.e. true in a *vyāvahārika* or relative sense and untrue in a *pāramārthika* or absolute sense. They are thus all *mithyā*, untrue, and are to be cancelled, but the Vedic *mithyā* is to be used in overcoming the grosser or lower untruths, and the Vedas themselves are to be transcended by *Brahmātmaikatvavijñāna*, the realisation of the identity of the Self and *Brahman*. Now in the course of this process of *sādhanā* or discipline for liberation the ethical standard may assume a different character according to the particular stage of the *sādhanā* or training of the individual. In the stage of the worship of *Saguna-Brahma* or Qualified Absolute, the standard is *isvarājñā*, the Command of the Lord. In the more advanced statge of *sādhana-catustaya* when external codes and external authority give way to internal sanctions *ātmasantosa* and *ātmalābha* may take the place of *isvarājñā*.

Thus according to Sankara, even though ethical codes and disciplines are relative and empirical, there is an order obtaining in this sphere of illusion to which the moral agent must conform through a gradation of the moral standards according to the different stages. The ultimate goal indeed is the transcendence of the empirical moral life of the Absolute, but this is to be realised by cancellation of the illusion of the phenomenal life in successive stages in which the lower illusion is to be cancelled at last by the intuition of the absolute. This, it will be seen, implies at once the transcendental unreality of the ethical codes as well as their metaphysical and moral necessity within the sphere of Illusion. It further implies a gradation in the sphere of the illusory empirical life in which specific codes with their specific moral standards have validity according to their proper sphere. It thus differs from the Hegelian conception of a progressive unfolding of the spiritual life in which the higher stage does not simply annul the lower but re-affirms the latter in a new synthesis by absorbing the element of truth contained in the lower view. It further differs from the Hegelian view in that while recognising a certain order in the empirical life which must be conformed to in subduing it, it makes it the absolute negation of the transcendental which is therefore to be reached not by the transfiguration of the empirical but by its total cancellation in the intuition of *Brahman.*

B. The Standard as Impersonal Moral Law

The moral standard is also conceived as Impersonal Prescription in some systems of Hindu Philosophy. Thus the Purvamimamsakas interpret *Vidhi* as Impersonal Law, which does not derive its authority or force from the will of a Personal Being, but is authoritative in and by itself independently of any personal origin. In fact, according to the Mimamsakas, the reference to a Personal source is absolutely unnecessary: *Vidhi* need not be presented as the command of God in order to be authoritative and may simply be verity of the supersensuous order, a law without a law-giver.

'Vidhi' or 'Law' is also taken as a standard of morality in the *Mahābhārata.* An action is right if it agrees with the law and it is wrong when it violates the law. From the earliest period of our life we find ourselves amidst rules or laws which are prescribed by parents, teachers, guardians, priests and rulers. The term 'law' includes political law, social law, religious law and moral law in itself. Almost all human conduct appears to be regulated and governed by these laws. Our behaviour to be right and moral, must be in conformity with these laws. In the *Mahābhārata* we come across such laws as commands of kings, seers and saints, divines, and of the *Vedas.*

'Vidhi' as the Command of the King: The rule of law imposed by the king, who was the highest earthly authority was taken as the standard of political morality. The royal injunctions constituted duties just as the king's prohibition constituted the opposite. The king by his 'Dandanīti' or Law of Punishment or chastisement keeps everything on

right track.[63] It is stated by Arjuna that "*Dande sthitāh Prajāh*", i e., the people are maintained and sustained by this *Danda*.[64] In the same parva he observes that a sinner does not commit sin for fear of being punished.[65] He further states that chastisement is ordained by the creator himself for protecting religion and profit for the happiness of all four orders, and for making righteous and modest.[66] It is also stated by him that law governs the people and also safeguards their interests.[67]

This reminds us of the Cārvāka view: "*Lokasiddho bhavedrāja Pareso nāparah smṛtah*", i.e., the earthly king is the only king, there is no lord or God other than him.[68] The will of the sovereign determines right and wrong as the king is the highest authority. The *Mahābhārata*, however, is pronouncedly theistic and takes the king as a representative of God.

Commands of Seers and Saints: In the *Mahābhārata*, the injunctions of the great men, seers, and saints are very often taken as guiding principles to decide the moral conflicts and determine the path of performing righteousness Seers like Vyāsa, Bṛhaspati, Vidura, Bhīsma, King Janaka are taken as authorities and their injunctions are regarded as standards of moral judgement.

According to the Buddhists and Jainas also, it is not the prescriptions of the king, but the injunctions and prohibitions of Arhats and Buddhas that constitute right and wrong. The authority of moral law is spiritual and not physical, and can be vested only in the seer, i.e., the spiritual expert that has attained perfection by self-culture.[69]

Vidhi as Divine Command: In the *Mahābhārata* we not only get materials in support of royal command and the

63. *Sānti*, 15, 34.
64. *Ibid.* 15, 43.
65. *Ibid.*, 15, 5.
66. *Ibid.*, 15, 25.
67. *Ibid.*, 15, 2.
68. Abhyankar, Vasudev Shastri, *Sarva-Darsana Samgraha*, *Cārvāka-darsana*, p. 7.
69. Maitra, S.K., *The Ethics of the Hindus*, p. 316.

commands of saints and seers, but also instances in support of divine law. Like *Nyāya-vaisesikas*, Rāmānujists and other theists, the *Mahābhārata* also admits the law of righteousness prescribed by God who is the Creator and moral Governor of the world. Right and wrong, good and bad are determined by the injunctions and prohibitions of scriptures. *Vidhi* as divine command embodied in scriptural prescriptions constitutes the moral code. It is observed by Bhīsma in the *Śāntiparva* that when Dharma decayed and the people gave up studies of the Vedas, and all *Vedic* knowledge disappeared and all ritual sacrifices vanished, then Brahmā himself composed a moral code named *Nītisāstra* in which he dealt with all the ends and means—*Dharma*, *Artha*, *Kāma* and *Moksa.* It was composed in one lakh chapters.[70] After that Samkara condensed the *Nītisāstra* in ten thousand chapters and was called '*Vaisālāksa*'.[71] Then again it was condensed by Indra in five thousand chapters which was called '*Bāhudantaka*'.[72] Again Bṛhaspati abridged it in three thousand chapters which was called *Nītisāstra* of Bṛhaspati.[73] Again it was shortened by Sukrācārya in one thousand chapters.[74] Thus for the benefit and longer life of the people the great saints summarised this *Sāstra*.[75] So *Nītisāstra* is the outcome of the labour of both deities and great saints and seers. Hence it has been given a divine status.

'Vidhi' as Command of the Vedas: The commands or injunctions of the *Vedas* constitute the moral code. According to the *Mahābhārata*, people were living peacefully according to their Dharma. They had been following their Dharma without any external pressure.[76] But a question arises from where does Dharma come ? In reply to this question, the epic asserts that the *Vedas* are the sources of law. Second to the *Vedas*, *Smṛtis* are the sources of law. And when the *Smṛtis*

70. *Sānti*, 59, 29.
71. *Ibid.*, 59, 81, 814.
72. *Ibid.*, 59, 83.
73. *Ibid.*, 59, 84.
74. *Ibid.*, 59, 85.
75. *Ibid.*, 59, 86.
76. *Ibid.*, 59, 15.

are silent, the path led by the great men is its sources.[77] It is also observed by Bhīsma in the *Śāntiparva* that Dharmas prevailing in society will be destroyed when the *Vedas* and rules of punishment are destroyed.[78] So all these laws governing human actions in society were derived from the *Vedas*.

Though the *Mahābhārata* is itself sometimes regarded as the source of law, it is not the primary source in itself. It is the impersonal *Vedas* which are the ultimate source of these *Vidhis*.[79]

The *Vidhi* as commad of the *Vedas* is regarded as impersonal prescription. The communicator of the *Vedas* only declares the law and does not create it by his will. *Vidhi* as command of king or saints and seers is of the nature of personal prescription. To S.K. Maitra, the standard is also conceived by the Hindus as a law or command which again is regarded either as a personal prescription of a superior to an inferior being (Paurseya) or again as impersonal law (apaurseya) without a law-giver.[80] Thus, *Vidhi* as personal or impersonal prescription is an important standard of morality in the epic.

Might is Right: The next standard in the epic is 'might is right'. When we say 'might is right' it means whatever a stronger man does it is right. In the primal state of Nature issues were decided by physical strength. "They will take who have the power and those will keep who can." There was no moral sanction of any kind. People devoured one another and no one had a sense of security of life and property. The stronger would swallow the weaker as stronger fishes eat the weaker ones and a bigger one devours the smaller one in the high water. This is called *Matsya Nyāya*. Arjuna finds this state of nature in every society. He observes :

77. *Anu.*, 141, 65.
78. *Sānti*, 63, 28.
79. Maitra, S.K., *The Ethics of the Hindus*, p. 320.
80. *Ibid.*, p. 315.

> "I do not behold any creature in this world that supports life without doing any act of injury to others. Animals live upon animals, the stronger upon the weaker."[81]

It is a state where there is no concept of justice. Right and wrong do not exist at all. This is a state of moral anarchy.

5₄ THE STANDARD AS PURITY OF THE MOTIVE

This is the theory of morality as enunciated by Samantabhadra in the Jaina-Kārikās and elaborated by Vidyānanda in his commentary thereon called the "Astasāhasrī". It is pointed out that righteousness cannot consist merely in the happiness of others and unhappiness of the self just as unrighteousness cannot consist in the unhappiness of others and happiness of the self.

Thus if righteousness were equivalent to happiness of others and unrighteousness to their unhappiness, then should we suppose that *acetana*, the non-sentient object, and *akasāya*, the taintless saint, are also in bondage, i.e., have moral bonds or obligations, as arising from their righteousness and unrighteousness, because in them there is also the *nimitta*, cause or ground, of happiness and unhappiness to others.

Again if righteousness consist in self-mortification, and unrighteousness in self-indulgence, then the dispassionate saint as practising self-restraint will have the bond of righteousness and the seer or sage as enjoying self-contentment will have the bond of unrighteousness.

Hence happiness and unhappiness, whether of self or of others, cannot of themselves constitute righteousness and unrighteousness. It is only when such happiness or unhappiness arises from the purity and impurity of the motives prompting the actions which cause them, that there is righteousness or unrighteousness. Otherwise the *Arhat* or Sage himself would be frustrated of his purpose, i.e., would not be free (mukta) as he would then be involved in the moral order by coming under the law of righteousness and unrighteousness.

81. *Sānti*, 15, 20.

The "Astasāhasrī" commenting on the above points out:

At two ends of the scale of being, there are no merit and demerit, even though there may be benefit or injury to others. Thus some are below merit and demerit, e.g., non-sentient objects (*acetanah*), and some are above merit and demerit, *viz.*, the dispassionate saints (*vitarāga*). Only sentient beings that are not free from desires are subject, through their activities, to merit and demerit.

It is therefore not the mere fact of causing happiness and unhappiness that constitutes merit and demerit. They must also be intentional in order that there may be merit or demerit. In the case of the dispassionate saint though there may be causes of happiness or unhappiness, yet the intention to cause them being absent on account of *tattvajñāna* or knowledge of reality, there are no merit and demerit.

Abhisandhi, intention, is thus a necessary condition of righteousness and unrighteousness, and not merely the consequences of happiness and unhappiness.

What, then, is the nature of this *Abhisandhi*, i.e., this intention or subjective attitude, as distinguished from objective consequences of happiness and unhappiness? It is pure in the case of *punya*, merit or righteousness, and impure in the case of *pāpa*, demerit or unrighteousness.

Samklesa, impurity (of the mind) again is either

(1) *Ārtta*, i.e., of an afflicting, distressing character, or

(2) *Raudra*, aggressive, violent.

(1) As *ārtta*, *samklesa* or subjective impurity manifests itself in

(a) The effort to escape from contact with the unpleasant;

(b) The effort to attain the pleasant (*manojña*) when separated from it;

(c) Absorption in the experience of pain and suffering (*vedanā*);

(d) Nidāna, the desire for the acquisition of power which is not yet acquired (*aprāptaisvaryaprāptisamkalpa*).

(2) As *raudra* or aggressive, *samklesa* takes the forms of

(a) *Himsā*, cruelty.

(b) *Anrta*, mendacity.

(c) *Steya*, unlawful appropriation.

(d) *Visayasamraksana*, aggressiveness in the maintenance of one's property.

Visuddhi, purity (of the mind) is also two-fold being :

(1) Either of the nature of contemplation based on the consciousness of duty (*dharmadhyānasvabhāvah*).

(2) Or of the nature of contemplation of the ideal of purity or perfection (*sukladhyānasvabhāvah*).

Hence right and wrong are to be determined not by the objective consequences but by the nature of the subjective intention of the agent. This therefore is an attempt to go beyond merely consequential morality to the intuitional principles of right and wrong with a view not merely to their enumeration but also their classification, and the basis of the two-fold classification is not anything external but is a state of internal determination of the self or *Ātman* or that which the *Ātman* becomes. The ultimate goal however is the realisation of the true nature of the self (*ātmani svarūpeavasthānam*), a consummation which is to be attained by purification through the successive phases of the contemplation of duty and perfection. Hence this is to be distinguished from the European goal of life which is one of ceaseless movement or progress as distinguished from rest in the self.

Purity of motive is also treated as a standard of morality in *Mahābhārata*. According to this standard, an action should not be judged by its result, but by the motive behind the action. Unlike hedonism which attaches significance to the consequences of the action, it gives importance to the intention of the doer. We find that the *Mahābhārata* suggests not only those standards of morality according to which moral judgements are based upon consequences but it also offers such standards which determine actions to be right or wrong on the basis of motives. It indicates that rightness does not depend merely on the happiness and goodness of others and of the self. Similarly, wrongness does not depend merely on the unhappiness of others and of the self. Rightness and wrongness proceed from the purity and impurity of motives which determine actions. S.K. Maitra puts it thus :

> "Hence happiness and unhappiness, whether of self or of others, cannot of themselves constitute righteousness and unrighteousness. It is only when such happiness or unhappiness arises from the purity and impurity of the motives prompting the actions which cause them that there is righteousness or unrighteousness."[82]

In the *Aśvamedikaparva* there is a story which brings out purity of motive as a standard of morality. When Yudhiṣṭhira performs the *Aśvamedha Yajña* and millions of people are satisfied and begin to praise the magnificant food and gifts, a blue-eyed mongoose (Nakula) with one side of his body changed into gold, comes there and speaks in a thunderous voice, "Ye king, this great sacrifice is not equal to a *prastha* of powdered barley given away by a liberal Brāhmin of Kuruksetra who is observing the *Unccha vow*."[83] The story is that a Brāhmin along with his wife, son and daughter-in-law offered their shares of *sattu* to a hungry guest (a mendicant) who came when they were to start to eat notwithstanding that they were without food for many days. The mongoose was turned golden when he had come into contact with the celestial flowers that had rained and with the particles of barley-powder which that good man gave away. As a result of the gift of that Brāhmin who was firm in truth and penances, half of the body of the mongoose became golden.

82. Maitra, S.K., *The Ethics of the Hindus*, p. 313.

83. *Aśva*, 90, 7.

But, the remaining half of the body could not be made golden. So, to the Brāhmins he states :

> "Hearing of this sacrifice of the Kuru King endued with great wisdom, I come hither with high hopes. I have not, however, been made gold. Ye foremost of Brāhmins, it is for this that I utter those words, viz., that this sacrifice can by no means compare with (the gift of) the *Prastha* of powdered barley. With the grains of that Prastha of powdered barley, I am made golden on that occasion. This great sacrifice, however, is not equal to those grains. Even this is my opinion."[84]

By means of this story, the epic suggests that not only performing great *yajñas* with substantial amount of wealth affecting large number of persons is commendable, but even small *yajña* like gift in accordance with the capacity of means, satisfying even a single individual, deserves credit. It is not possible for a poor man to perform *Rājasūya yajña* or *Aśvamedha yajña* but he can achieve all the merits of those great *yajñas* even by offering small gifts with purity of motives. It is evident from the above story that the poor Brāhmin was capable of a great act of self-sacrifice as he was impelled to save the life of the poor mendicant by genuine feelings of charity though he himself along with other members of the family was starving.

In the *Gītā* also, purity of mind is emphasized when Kṛṣṇa declares, "Whosoever offers to me with love a leaf, a flower, a fruit or even water, I appear in person before that disinterested devotee of purified intellect, and delightfully partake of that article offered by him with love."[85] Purity of motive is also stressed when god Dharma himself states to a Brāhmin that a man who owns a thousand, giving hundred, a man who owns a hundred giving ten, or some one according to his ability giving only a drink of water, all these acts are of the same merit and equally beneficial."[86]

84. *Ibid.*, 90. 115.
85. *Gītā*, 9, 26.
86. *Aśva*, 90, 96.

In this connection Swami Sivananda states :

"Purity of motive (Anupadha) is a *Sāmānya* dharma or common duty of every man. It is the motive that counts in the performance of an action. If an action is performed with a selfish motive it binds a man to the wheel of births and deaths. If it is done with a pure motive in a disinterested manner, it will purify the heart and lead to the attainment of the final liberation.... Right and wrong are determined not by the objective consequences but by subjective intention of the agent."[87]

Thus in the *Mahābhārata* purity of motive is also regarded as an important standard of morality.

6. SELF-REALISATION AS STANDARD OF MORALITY

In this section we shall consider Transcendental Satisfaction as the moral standard as distinguished from empirical pleasure which is the Cārvāka view, i.e., we shall consider the standard regarded as the *Sreyah* or Good as distinguished from the *Preyah*, the merely Attractive, Tempting or Pleasant. It is to be seen that the conception of Transcendental Bliss is a necessary supplement to the negative criticism of the Cārvāka Hedonism without which the latter would continue to hold its sway over the mind in spite of the pain and evil which it may bring with it.

This conception of Transcendental Bliss occurs not only in the Upanisads, but is also to be found in Manu and Sankara. Thus in the Upanisads a distinction is made between *sreyah* or what is intrinsically excellent and good for the individual, and *preyah* or what is merely pleasant. *Sreyah*, the Good, consists in *ātma santosa*, Self-contentment and Satisfaction, while *preyah*, the Pleasant, is connected with *visayasukha* or empirical pleasure. Every other pleasure is

87. Swami Sivananda, *Ethical Teaching*, p. 9.

a reflection of *ātmaprīti* or Bliss that characterises the self, and hence *ātmprīti* is the highest good and the standard of all good and evil. In fact whatever is done with a view to *ātmapriti* or Self-satisfaction so that *ātmapriti* is the highest good and the standard of all good and evil. It is this *Ātmakāma* or Love of the Self, says the "Bṛhadāranyaka Upanisad", that reflects itself into all other forms of Kāmanā, Attraction or Desire. Thus the husband is dear to the wife not because of the wife's love for the husband but for the love with which the wife loves her own true self. Similarly riches are desired not because riches are themselves objects of love but because of the love with which the individual loves his own self. (*Na vā are patyuh kāmāya patih priyo bhavāti, ātmanastu kāmāya patih priyo bhavati. Na vā are vitlasya kāmāya vittam priyam bhavati ātmanastu kāmāya vittam priyam bhavati.*)

Every particular desire is thus a reflection or mode of the desire for the realisation of one's true self which is the highest good, and this good, *Sreyah*, is to be distinguished from Empirical Pleasure, *Preyah*, which arises from external objects. Thus in the "Kathopanisad" we have : The good, *Sreyah*, is one and the pleasant, *Preyah*, is another. They attract the *Purusa* or individual in different ways by drawing them to different objects or ends. He who chooses *Sreyah* attains his highest good, and he who chooses *Preyah* is depriv-ed thereby of his ultimate good or end. (*Anyacca sreyo'nyadu-taiva preyaste ubhe nānārthe purusam sinitah. Tayoh sreya ādadānasya sādhu bhavati hiyate'arthād yah preyo vṛnite.*)

Sankara commenting on the above points out:

Good, *Sreyah*, means *summum bonum*, *Nihsreyasam*, Highest Good, and is to be distinguished from the merely pleasant. These two, viz , the good and the pleasant, being directed to different ends or objects, bind individuals in different ways with reference to their station in life. Of these, the good is constituted by truth, *Vidyā* or knowledge or reality while the pleasant is a mode of Nescience, error or *Avidyā*. Every individual is actuated to perform his duties under the influence of either of the two forces of *Vidyā* or knowledge and *Avidyā* or Nescience. The individual that desires immortality is actuated by the idea of the good to eschew the path of pleasures, because without eschewing the pleasant there is no attaining the good. By seeking the good the individual realises the perfection and nobility of his soul. But the short-sighted fool that chooses the path of pleasures is deprived thereby of his ultimate good.

It is to be seen that the original passage speaks merely of a moral struggle as arising from two different possible ends which man may propose to himself—*Sreyah*, the Good, and *Preyah*, empirical pleasure. Sankara however reduces this struggle to the metaphysical conflict between the Principle of Knowledge (Vidyā) and the Principle of Nescience (*Avidyā*). The choice of right as against pleasure brings in good while the opposite makes man lose his real good.

The psychological process underlying the choice of the good or the pleasurable is described. It is pointed out that the good and the pleasurable come to man in mixed forms, but the clear-sighted individual separates the good from the pleasurable, and then chooses the good in preference to the pleasurable. But the dull in intelligence chooses the pleasurable for the sake of material gain such as the attainment of the unattained (*yoga*) and the preservation of the attained (*ksema*). (*Sreyasca preyasca manusayam etah tau samparitya vivinaki dhirah Sreyohi dhirah abhipreyaso vṛnite*; *Preyo mando yogaksemāl vṛnite.*) *Sreyah*, the Good, is therefore mixed up in experience with *Preyah*, the Pleasant : in other words, in the same situation there are possibilities of *Sreyah*, as well as *Preyah*. The wise man therefore considers both sides carefully, weights or estimates the relative worth of the virtuous and the pleasurable course, and thus separates the one from the other. When the two different courses draw him different ways, the wise man chooses the virtuous course in preference to the pleasurable one. The foolish choose, on the contrary, the latter for prudential reasons.

Commenting on the above Sankara points out :

Though *Sreyah* as well as *Preyah* are under the control

of the moral individual, yet owing to cloudiness of the intelligence they come to us mixed up. But the wise man knows how to separate the one from the other even as the swan knows how to drink away the milk by separating it from the water. In short, the wise man discriminates the good from the pleasant and after comparing their relative worth chooses the former. But the dull in intelligence, being incapable of discrimination, is led away by prudential considerations and chooses the pleasurable course as consisting of physical comfort and material prosperity such as possession of cattle, joy of family life, etc.

Hence there are two kinds of satisfaction:

1. Transcendental Satisfaction arising from *Ātmalābha* or Self-attainment which is *Ātmasantosa* or Self-contentment; and
2. Empirical Pleasure arising from the possession of external objects.

In the "Sarvavedantasiddhantasangraha" the relation between empirical pleasure and one's true self whose essence is self-contentment, is explained in detail. It is pointed out that empirical pleasure is desired only as it is believed to be a means to the realisation of one's true self. In fact, it is the self which is the dearest of all objects to sentient beings. The self is one's own (*paramāntarah*) as distinguished from other objects which are external; its essence is *Ānanda*, Transcendental Bliss, and it is the most beloved of all objects of love.

In the "Upadesasāhasrī" (ascribed to Sankara) it is similarly pointed out that the Self is the end of all our activities, that there is no higher or better attainment than Self-attainment or Self-realisation, that all scriptural prescriptions and duties have this Self in view as the ultimate end.

But this is true not merely of scriptural actions and duties, it also holds good in the case of empirical actions from material motives. Even these latter have self-attainment (*ātmalābha*) as their ultimate end. But such actions whether prompted by motives of empirical pleasure or by the sense of duty or *dharma*, do not lead to unqualified happiness; the resulting happiness is impure, i.e., mixed with its opposite, viz., unhappiness (*viparyayah*); also such happiness is *anitya*, non-eternal, perishable. But the satisfaction arising from Self-attainment (*ātmalābha*) is eternal. Again the satisfaction of self-attainment is autonomous, *svayamlabdha*, while all other satisfactions are *Anyāpeksa*, dependent, adventitious, heteronomous.

Hence the satisfaction in Self-realisation is (1) Pure, (2) Eternal, and (3) *Svյamalabdha*, i.e., Autonomous, Self-evidencing and Self-dependent, while other satisfactions, whether of pleasure-seeking or of performances for the sake of merit, are (1) Impure, (2) Transitory and (3) *Anyāpeksa*, Attention to Things that are Non-spiritual.

This, it will be seen, is a new type of Edaemonism, a kind of Transcendental Edaemonism which radically differs from the Aristotelian Edaemonism of the co-ordination of empirical pleasures. Similarly the conception of Self-attainment or *Ātmalābha* is an original and unique form of the conception of Self-realisation which is to be distinguished alike from the Hegelian and Kantian conception of it in European Ethics.

Thus *Ātmasantosa*, Transcendental Satisfaction, is neither empirical pleasure nor the organisation of pleasures but represents the essential content and bliss that accompanies the eternally accomplished reality of the Self. Similarly *Ātmalābha* is neither the positing of the Self as empty Law of Reason (without presentation in experience), nor the realisation of it by the co-ordination of conflicting impulses but the rediscovery of an eternally fulfilled Self which was missed only under the influence of an original Illusion (*Māyā*).

There is thus an assential difference between Sankara's Transcendentalism and Kant's. Kant conceives the noumental self as realising its rational freedom in Moral Consciousness as the Categorical Imperative of the Moral Law. Because the self cannot realise itself in the blind matter of sense which will never express its unity completely and fully, it presents itself as self-determining reason in the Categorical Imperative of Moral Consciousness, independently of and despite the opposition of our sensuous nature. Hence the autonomous self realises itself as a supersensuous reality as the Moral Law or Ought of Moral Consciousness and not as a fact sensuously presented in experience. At the same time this Law or Imperative is not an arbitrary fiat or command but is the Law of Reason and thus implies rational necessity and not the freedom of indetermination. If now we compare Sankara's Transcendentalism with Kant's we find that in Sankara the negative attitude to empirical life is scarcely as pronounced as in Kant. In fact we shall see that some of the commentators have even tried to relieve the antagonism between the transcendental and the empirical by the conception of Pratibimba, reflection or copy, as we have in Plato. We thus see that in Sankara the transcendental is not merely the negation of the empirical but also in a sense its consummation and completion so that empirical values are the reflections, the imperfect and limited expressions, of the transcendental self. Hence the transcendental self is an accomplished reality from eternity and does not require to realise itself as Law in a specific act of the Self-legislating Reason. It is also autonomous in being essentially and independently real, i.e., in being non-dependent on anything other than itself. It follows from this that it is of the nature of an eternally fulfilled experience whose essence is this consciousness of complete realisation or fulfilment as expressed in the feeling of contentment or self-satisfaction, and which is therefore to be distinguished from the self-realising ought or law of moral consciousness which is the reality of the Rational Self according to Kant. And just because it is eternally fulfilled absolute experience embodying the quintessence of all reality it is the ultimate ground of all empirical reality, the source or fountain from which all other objects derive their reality.

This positive relation of the transcendental self to empirical life is brought out, as we have already stated, in the doctrine of *Pratibimba,* reflection or copy by Sankara's commentators. Thus in the "*Vedāntaparibhāsa*" we have a very interesting exposition of the doctrine as arising from the question of the true nature of *Sukha* or happiness. *Sukha,* happiness, says the "*Vedāntaparibhāsa*", is of two kinds :

(1) *Sātisayasukha*, relative or limited sukha, i.e., *sukha* or happiness which is capable of being exceeded, and (2) *Niratisayasukha*, Unexcelled Bliss or unlimited happiness. The latter is the assence of *Brahman* or the Absolute. The former, i.e., empirical pleasure, is a limited or partial manifestation of the latter, i.e., a limitation of Transcendental Bliss or Happiness. This limitation is due to the defects and inequalities of the psychic modes through which the latter has to reveal itself in empirical life—defects and differences which are themselves determined by the dissimilarities in the objects with which the *Antahkarana* or mind is connected on different occasions.

The "Sikhamani" commenting on the above observes :

Just as a particular psychosis, owing to the predominance of the essence of *Sattva* or medium of illumination, partially reflects the intelligence which constitutes *Caitanya* and thereby itself appears as a form of knowing, so also such a psychosis, by appropriating or reflecting in its essence of *Sattva* a ray of the Transcendental Bliss that constitutes *Brahman*, itself appears as a partial or limited manifestation of happiness. It may be proved by agreement and difference that these psychic modes characterised by happiness are connected with specific objects of enjoyment. Hence differences either in the degree or in the nature of all empirical happiness must be ascribed to differences in their objective causes or conditions.

An objection however may be raised. If empirical pleasure is thus the psychosis that reflects into itself the Transcendental Bliss that stands near it, why does it not reveal the transcendental felicity in its fulness in every case? But this does not happen as a matter of fact, for all pleasures would then be identical in nature and degree. The "*Sikhāmani*" disposes of this objection by pointing out that though this undivided Bliss always stands near the mind or *antahkarana* yet it cannot be reflected by the latter in its fulness and purity on account of the influence of *mūla avidyā*, an original Illusion.

As we have already pointed out this affords an interesting parallel to the transcendentalism of the Platonic metaphysics.

Plato also recognised an essential conflict between the pleasurable and the good, but instead of sharpening this conflict into positive opposition he sought to overcome the dualism by his theory of copies and his distinction of a sensuous and a supersensuous world. Thus the sensuous world is an imperfect copy of an ideal supersensuous world, and the transitory pleasures of this life are the reflections in matter of the Ideal and Perfect Satisfaction that constitutes the good which is the governing principle of the supersensuous world. It is on account of union with matter that there arise the conflict and incompatibility of pleasures and the consequent strife and wickedness of this world. But in the ideal world there is perfect harmony, every Idea in the ideal world being completely in agreement with the Idea of the Good and all pleasures being thus moments in the absolute satisfaction that constitutes the Good.

Hence with Plato as with Sankara empirical pleasure is a partial and imperfect manifestation of transcendental satisfaction, but while with Plato there is a harmonious co-ordination of specific pleasures in the supersensuous *Summum Bonum* or the Good which is thus a satisfaction constituted by a synthesis of individual pleasures, a synthesis which is lacking in the sensuous world of experience, with Sankara Transcendental Happiness is not a republic of pleasures with the element of conflict and discord resolved into harmony but is the infinite essence of the self representing its unqualified and undivided reality in its completeness and perfection. Hence the Infinite Satisfaction of Transcendental Bliss is a homogeneous undifferentiated infinite essence and not an organisation of partial pleasures—and infinite essence which is itself only imperfectly and partially manifested in empirical pleasures through the veil of *Avidyā* or Nescience. It is to be observed that Sankara ascribes the limitation of this transcendental happiness to *Mūla Avidyā*. i.e., an Original Principle of Illusion, a Power of Irrationality which limits the true essence of the self and thereby causes the appearance of the empirical world of evil and imperfection, while Plato ascribes all Limitation to *hyle* or matter which is an inert and inactive principle of division in which the ideas reflect themselves. In the *Mahābhārata* also Moksa is regarded as the summum bonum of life. It is the highest of the four Purusārthas. It is the goal which each and everyone of us must strive to attain. *Moksa* or Self-realisation is the object of all our ethical endeavour. The epic suggests the way to realise the real self.

In the *Śāntiparva* Bhṛgu explains to Bharadvāja the nature of individual self and absolute self thus, "When the *Ātman* is imprisoned within the body, it is called *ksetrajña* (or jīvātman, i.e., personal self). And when the same *Ātman* is released from these '*Prakṛta*' qualities, that is, from the qualities of matter or of the body, it is known as the *Paramātman* (Absolute self)."[88] In the *Gītā* Kṛṣṇa explains the nature of self as a part of the Absolute. He says:

> "The jivatman (soul in the body) is an eternal portion of Myself."[89]

It is the real and not an imaginary form of it. It is a limited manifestation of God. The individual self is supposed to be held in bondage when it differentiates itself from Brahman and also when it identifies itself with false self. Dr. Radhakrishnan puts it in the following manner:

> "When the ego is lost in a false identification with not-self and its forms, it is bound; but when through the development of proper understanding, it realises the true nature of the self and not-self and allows the apparatus produced by the not-self to be illumined completely by the self, then it is freed. This realisation is possible through proper functioning of buddhi or vijñāna."[90]

In the *Śāntiparva* Vishnu describes His own nature to Nārada thus:

88. *Śānti*, 187, 23.
89. *Gītā*, 15, 7.
90. Radhakrishnan, *Bhagavadgītā*, p. 45.

> "He that cannot be seen with eye, touched with the sense of touch, smelt with the sense of scent, and that is beyond the ken of the sense of taste. He whom the three attributes of Sattva, Rajas, and Tamas do not touch, who pervades all things and is the one Witness of the universe, and who is described as the Soul of the entire universe; He who is not destroyed upon the destruction of the bodies of all created things, who is unborn and unchangeable and eternal, who is freed from all attributes, who is indivisible and entire; He who transcends the twice twelve topics of enquiry and is regarded the Twentyfifth, who is called by the name of Purusa, who is inactive, and who is said to be apprehended by knowledge alone. He into whom the foremost of regenerate persons enter and become emancipate. He who is the eternal Supreme Soul and is known by the name of Vāsudeva."[91]

He further states:

> "It is from Me that the entire mobile and immobile universe springs. It is from Me O Nārada, that the indestructible and destructible, the existent and the non-existent, flow. They that are devoted to me enter into me and become emancipated.... I am, O Nārada, the Doer, I am Cause, and I am Effect. I am the sum-total of all living creatures. All living creatures have their refuge in me. Let not the thought be thine that thou hast seen the *Ksetrajña*. I pervade all things O Brāhmin, and am the *Jīva-soul* of all creatures. When the bodies of all creatures, however, are destroyed, I am not destroyed."[92]

In the words of Dr. Radhakrishnan, "When Brahman and Ātman are identified, the highest goal is declared to be unity with the self."[93] For self-realisation, terms like

91. *Śānti*, 339, 21-25.
92. *Ibid.*, 339, 42-43, 47-48.
93. Radhakrishnan, S., *Principal Upanisads*, p. 117.

emancipation, deliverance, salvation or Moksa have the same meaning. P.S. Sivaswami Aiyar in 'Evolution of Hindu Moral Ideals' observes:

> "It is not quite easy to identify the Hindu theory of the summum bonum exclusiveness with any of the theories which adopt happiness, perfection of self-realisation as the ultimate end. In so far as the condition of the emancipated soul is decribed as one of the ineffable bliss, it may be held that happiness is the ultimate end adopted in Hindu ethics. But in so far as, however, as emancipation requires a severe and arduous course of moral discipline, the control of the lower elements of our human nature by the higher and the realisation of the true self or Atman it may be equally correctly said that the summum bonum of the Hindus involves also perfection and self-realisation."[94]

In the *Anuśāsanaparva* of the *Mahābhārata*, Mahesvara mentions that nothing is superior to *Moksa*. The wise men regard this *Moksa* as ceaseless, great and supreme bliss. The learned men and even saints and divine beings regard it as superior to all knowledge. It is fascinating for even gods and demons as it is eternal, indestructible, unconquerable, everlasting and beneficial. And wise men must achieve it.[95] *Moksa* has been extolled at many places in the *Mahābhārata*. In the *Śāntiparva* Bhīsma advises Yudhiṣthira to strive for salvation as this world is full of defects and demerits.[96]

It appears from the fact that in the *Mahābhārata* the ultimate end of human life as envisaged in orthodox Indian Philosophy is not an object of the world but something transempirical or transcendental. The *Mahābhārata* also subscribes the Vedantic view that the worldly objects are momentary and have no permanent value. They are subject to change and decay. Behind this world of change there is

94. Aiyar, P.S. Sivaswami, *Evolution of Hindu Moral Ideals*, p. 53.
95. *Anu*, 145, p. 6008, Gita Press.
96. *Śānti*, 174, 5.

an ultimate reality which is beyond the limits of space and time. It is regarded as immutable, imperishable and all-pervading consciousness. This reality is known as Brahman. The human self is essentially identical with Universal Self. The *Ātman* and Brahman are one and the same. As Dr. Radhakrishnan puts it:

> "The Real is the supracosmic, eternal, spaceless, timeless Brahman who supports this cosmic manifestation in space and time. He is the Universal Spirit, *Paramātman*, who ensouls the cosmic forms and movements. He is the *Paramesvara* who presides over the individual souls and movements of nature and controls the cosmic becoming. He is also the *Purusottama*, the Supreme Person, whose dual nature is manifested in the evolution of the cosmos. He fills our being, illumines our understanding and sets in motion its hidden springs."[97]

The *Mahābhārata*, as we shall see, has drunk deep from the fountain of the Vedānta.

In the *Gītā* we find various names given to this highest ideal of life. In the second chapter this is described as '*Anāmayam*'[98] where man is freed from the shackles of birth and attains the blissful supreme state. In the third chapter it is described as '*Parama*'[99] a state when work is done without attachment. It is also called '*Param Śānti*[100] or the Supreme Peace'. It is a state when knowledge is attained and senses are controlled and devoted to spiritual practice. In the fifth chapter it is described as the state from where there is no return.[101] In the sixth chapter it is also called '*Param gatim*'[102] or a state of perfection. Thus it is described in many ways in the *Gītā*.

97. Radhakrishnan, S., *The Bhagavadgītā*, p. 27.
98. *Gītā*, 2, 51.
99. *Ibid*., 3, 19.
100. *Ibid*., 4, 39.
101. *Ibid*., 5, 17.
102. *Ibid*., 6, 45.

The *Mahābhārata* recognises the threefold paths leading to *Mokṣa* viz , path of knowledge (Jñāna Mārga), path of action (Karma Mārga) and path of devotion (Bhakti-Mārga). They have been elaborately discussed in the *Gītā*. Regarding the path of knowledge in the *Śāntiparva*, Suka is told by his father Vyāsa that by knowledge, however, one becomes emancipated.[103] He further remarks:

> "Through knowledge, however, one becomes transformed into that which is eternal, unmanifest, and immutable. By knowledge, one attains to that where there is no occasion for grief, where one becomes freed from both birth and death, where one is not subject to descrepitude, when one transcends the states of conscious existence; there is Brahman which is supreme, unmanifest, immutable, everexistent, imperceptible, above the reach of pain, immortal, and transcending destruction."[104]

There are numerous verses in the *Gītā* in praise of *jñāna*.[105]

Karmayoga is given a more exalted place in the *Gītā*. The path of action is the better way to attain self-realisation. He (Kṛṣṇa) thus states:

> "Knowledge is better than practice (carried on without proper insight), and a meditation is superior to knowledge, and renunciation of the fruit of actions is even superior to meditation, for peace immediately follows from renunciation."[106]

The *Gītā* suggests us to perform those duties without any attachment or expectation of the result of the action performed. Kṛṣṇa thus states:

103. *Śānti*, 241, 7.
104. *Ibid.*, 241, 8.
105. *Gītā*, 4, 36, 37, 38.
106. *Ibid.*, 12, 12,

> "When a man ceases to have any attachment either for the objects of senses or for actions and has renounced all thoughts of the world, he is said to have attained yoga."[107]

In the *Śāntiparva* also, Bhīsma emphasizes it. He says:

> "Living creatures, by being attached to objects of the senses which are always fraught with evil, become helpless. These high-souled persons, however, who are not attached to them, attain to the highest end."[108]

He further observes:

> "Being pure in speech, thought, and body and freed from pride of tranquil soul and possessed of knowledge, he should lead a life of mendicancy, and pursue happiness without being attached to any worldly object. Again, if attachment be seen to possess the mind in consequences of compassion for creatures, he should, seeing that the universe is the result of acts, show indifference in respect of compassion itself."[109]

In the *Śāntiparva* Manu states to Bṛhaspati:

> "It is by liberating oneself from acts that one succeeds in entering into Brahman. The ordinances about acts have flowed for that very end. The ordinances about acts tempt only those whose hearts are not free from desires. By liberating oneself from acts one acquires the highest state."[110]

Besides the paths of *Jñānayoga* and *Karmayoga*, the *Gītā* strongly recommends the path of devotion or *Bhakti-Mārga*

107. *Ibid.*, 6, 4.
108. *Śānti*, 215, 1.
109. *Ibid.*, 215, 1.
110. *Ibid.*, 201, 13.

which can deliver the highest goods to all. This path is easier to follow because a person who faithfully devotes himself to the Lord attains *Moksa* not only easily but quickly.[111] It is also stated that even a person who is of low origin, if he were to take refuge in the Lord, is emancipated.[112]

As regards *yoga* as a path to liberation Yâjñavalkya says to Janaka:

> "While in Samādhi, the yogin beholds Brahman which is supreme and immutable, and which is situated like a blazing effulgence in the midst of thick darkness. It is by this means that he attains, after many years, the emancipation after casting off this inanimate body. Even this is what the eternal *Smṛtis* declare. This is called the *yoga* of the yogins."[113]

All these different paths however lead to same goal. As Dr. Radhakrishnan puts it:

> "Whatever be the method we pursue, wisdom, love or service, the end reached is the same, union of the soul with the highest."[114]

Thus the epic maintains that *Moksa* or self-realisation is the supreme goal and it prescribes various means to realise it. The identity of individual self with Brahman is the object of self-realisation. This is of the greatest value in human life. The Upanisadic view that '*Preyah*' or empirically pleasant is inferior to '*Sreyah*', i.e., transcendentally good is strongly stressed in the epic. It becomes evident that Moksa is regarded as the ultimate goal of life.

111. *Gītā*, 12, 7.
112. *Ibid.*, 9, 32.
113. *Śānti*, 315, 25.
114. Radhakrishnan, S., *Indian Philosophy*, Vol. I, p. 574.

7

Conclusion

Mahābhārata is a great epic depicting the foundations of Indian culture and civilization. It depicts the trials and tribulations, hopes and aspirations of our ancestors. It is a code of life, a philosophy of social and ethical relations, an speculative thought on human problems that is hard to reveal. The aim of the epic is not only to describe the history of Kauravas and Pandavas, but it also presents the perfect and vast picture of Hindu religion. The Śānti Parva of *Mahābhārata* is a glaring example which has been solving the problems of humanity since thousand years. It is why this historical epic has become a religious epic which is very important and useful for modern people. The Ethics of Vidur has elucidated beautifully the laws of ethics and worldly affairs. It embodies our ancient wisdom par excellence. "Truth," says *Mahābhārata*, "is the essence of the Vedas; self-control is an essence of truth; and renunciation is the essence of self-control. These form the essential features of good conduct."[1]

There was a moral crisis when the *Mahābhārata* was written. The traditional morality had broken down, and materialism, individualism, hedonism, scepticism, agnosticism

1. *Mbh* , Vana Parva, 207.67.

and an unhealthy asceticism had gained currency and thrown a great challenge. They even threatened to disrupt the moral life and the stability of society and exposed the traditional value to criticism and created a situation of moral chaos. In such a critical time the author of the *Mahābhārata* sought to provide a rational foundation to morality and restore to its lost dignity and respect.

It is regarded as the encyclopaedia of Indian morality and culture. It has been exerting tremendous influence upon the character and civilization of the major populace of the world since times immemorial. It is not merely a narrative of battles but is predominantly dialectic in spirit. It becomes obvious that the central ethical teaching of the great epic is the establishment of the rule of Dharma in the world to help individuals to realise the summum bonum of life. "The observance of Dharma under any condition, or in any adversity, says Vaidya, is the duty which the *Mahābhārata* tries constantly to inculcate throughout its length."[2]

The *Mahābhārata*, as we have seen, conceives of human nature as constituted of three dispositions and tendencies. The lower elements of rajas and tamas compel men to unrighteousness and evil and sattva to good. Hence the rajas and tamas elements of human nature should be controlled and suppressed and the sattva element should be encouraged. There should be control over the bodily passions and appetites. The senses should not be let loose rather they should be controlled.[3] "Man, the subject should gain over man, the object."[4] There should be the integration of human personality which consists in the subjection of the lower dispositions of men to the higher one—the domination of the higher nature of man over the baser elements in him. Man is a combination of the divine and the earthly, and the divine should rule over the earthly. The divine is the principle of good in us and the earthly is the principle of evil. Hence the evil should be suppressed and the

2. Vaidya, C.V., *The Mahābhārata, A Criticism*, p. 53.
3. *Mbh.*, XII. 254.10.
4. Radhakrishnan, S., *Bhagvadgītā*, p. 47.

good promoted. The soul in us is the divine and the body the earthly, and hence one should care more for the tendency of the soul and not of the body. The soul is eternal and imperishable whereas the body is ephemeral and perishable, hence it is the soul which should be the object of our attention. Man has body and mind which bind him to the world to the sensual pleasures and material desires, natural impulses and worldly goods to the desires, hatred, selfishness, foolishness and infatuation. But there is in him the soul also which helps to rise above the limitations of the body. The *Gītā*, metaphorically, speaks of the human life as a 'peepal' tree (asvattham) with its roots above and branches below.[5] The soul in man springs forth from the Divine, the Supreme Spirit, and the destiny of the soul lies in the liberation from the modes of prakṛti and the final absorption with the supreme spirit. The Prakṛti and its modes are, however, the shackles, they bind the soul to the earth and make it move in the wheel of births and deaths. Hence man should not in such a way *that its (soul's) attachment* with the body may cease and it may attain final liberation. Rajas and Tamas create attachment and delusion, the sattva leads to non-attachment. Hence the two lower dispositions are to be discarded and the higher disposition of the sattva should be promoted.[6]

The *Mahābhārata*, however, does not prescribe asceticism and a negative approach to life. "The red garment, the vow of silence, the threefold staff, the water pot—these only lead astray,"—says the *Mahābhārata*.[7] The *Mahābhārata* prescribes a balanced life which combines both the Pravṛtti and Nivṛtti. It prescribes an ideal scheme of life consisting of the four stages—Brahmacarya, Gṛhastha, Vānaprastha and Samyāsa,[8] and the four ends of life—the four Purusārthas, Dharma, Artha, Kāma and Moksa. The first three are within the ambit of the sceiety knowledge and control and are grouped separately as Trivarga whereas the fourth is concerned with the life

5. *Gītā*, XIV. 1-3.
6. *Mbh.*, XII. 321.
7. *Ibid.*, XII. 320-47.
8. *Ibid.*, XII. 191-92; XII. 242-44.

hereafter, in the ascetic atmosphere of Buddhism and Jainism desire for pleasure of the physical kind was looked down upon as inferior in value. But in a completely balanced view of life which is concerned with both 'here' and 'hereafter,' its lowliness would be found groundless. Manu[9] has uttered the warning that bad overpowered by desire is not good, nor is the condition good which desire is rooted out.

The pursuit of material gain and pleasure (Artha and Kāma) are both natural and necessary for life, as no one can live without acquiring some material goods and the fulfilment of the natural urges. But they should be controlled by the considerations of Dharma. While material gains and Purushārthas (Artha and Kāma) refer to actuality, the Dharma refers to the ideal principle—a norm to which man should conform to activities and life in the world with reference to his self and to his fellow beings. Dharma is, therefore, assigned the first place in the Purusārthas, because it is the highest principle, in absence of which the material gains and pleasure (the Artha and Kāma) will lead man to ruin or conflict with fellow beings in society.[10] The *Mahābhārata* carries its burden. It states, in the end, in the four verses of Bharat Sāvitrī, the essence of its teaching as: "with uplifted arm I cry but none heeds, from Dharma material gains and pleasures flow, that way is not Dharma pursued? Neither for the sake of pleasure nor out of fear or avarice, no, not even for the sake of one's life should one give up Dharma. Dharma stands alone for all the pleasure and pain are transitory."[11] But the *Mahābhārata* does not preach abstinence from pleasure for all, or at all stages of life. It rather preaches the ideal of chastened pleasure regulated by the consideration of Dharma, the morality. In a well known passage in the *Bhagawadgītā* Lord Kṛṣṇa identifies Himself with such desire (Kāma) which is not contrary to Dharma.[12] The desire as such is not evil. It is the selfish desires which require to be rooted out. The *Mahābhārata* thus preaches a

9. *Manu.*, II. 2.
10. *Mbh* , XII. 123.
11. *Ibid.*, XVII. 3.59-'0.
12. *Gītā*, VII. 11.

balance view of life in which the desires are not to be rooted out completely rather they are to be sublimated and directed towards the fulfilment of human destiny. It preaches the subjection of the lower to the higher, the earthly to the divine, the transitory to the eternal; the passions and appetites to the reason, the rajas and tamas to the sattva and finally the body to the soul. It combines the Pravṛtti and Nivṛtti in its grand principle of Niskāma Karma which the *Gitā* sets forth in its teaching as the performance of one's duty without attachment.

According to the view of the *Mahābhārata*, neither 'Artha' nor 'Kāma' is supposed to be unworthy. Their inclusion in the scheme of Purusārthas is itself an expression of their necessity and importance. Without 'Kāma' there can be no domestic life and perpetuation of the race. Similarly 'artha' is also essential for the full development of human personality. Poverty in itself is a bane; therefore, wealth or 'artha' has been praised in the *Mahābhārata*. As life giving streams have source in the mountain so all the human activity finds its spring in the 'artha.' Life is impossible without it. Dharma, Kāma and heaven, joy, anger, learning, tranquillity, all spring from artha. In short, it is from wealth that Dharma itself emanates as rivers from the mountain.[13] At another place also it asserts that artha is the source of everything.[14]

But, all the same, the *Mahābhārata* does not support unchecked enjoyment of pleasure and wealth (kāma and artha). It thinks that some ascetic discipline is essential for the evolution of human personality and moral life. There is, no doubt, an atmosphere of asceticism and renunciation of wealth. But ascetic discipline and depreciation of acquisitive instinct is prescribed merely as a disciplinary measure. The authors of the *Mahābhārata* are conscious of the fact that 'kāma' and 'artha' are essential for a healthy social life. There is no possibility if family life without sex instinct, and society cannot be continued without procreation. Moreover, man is not a full man if he is physically or emotionally starved. There can be

13. *Mbh.*, XII.8.13-23.
14. *Ibid.*, XII.15.48.

no realisation of human personality without 'kāma' and 'artha'; that is required to put a limit over man's enjoyment in the interest of social as well as individual well-being and to avoid any mutual friction or conflict so that justice may be maintained.

The *Gītā* stresses the need of doing one's duty and not to shun the world. Man should get to work not for the sake of any material advantage or enjoyment but only for the sake of duty. The tone of the *Gītā* is against asceticism and self-torture. It teaches to strive after the inner freedom from the world. According to it, the world-and-life-negation is not the will of God nor is it practicable.[15] God himself practises activity in that he creates and maintains the world.[16] "Not by abstention from work does a man attain freedom from action nor by renunciation does he attain to this perfection."[17] What the *Gītā* prescribes is, that "without attachment perform always the work that has to be done, for man attains to the highest by doing work without attachment."[18] What is essential is not the renunciation but to avoid sense attachment and aversion. "Let no one come under their sway for they are his enemies."[19]

The *Mahābhārata* also does not ignore the world, even though it holds the belief that human existence in this world is not the final truth. But it believes that the liberation can be attained by performance of one's duty in a righteous way in the world. The *Mahābhārata* regards this world to be composed of the spiritual and the material, the changeless and the changeful, and thinks that the changeless can be attained through the material and the temporal.

The ethical teaching of the *Mahābhārata* is relative and changing. It does not believe in absolutistic morality. It is flexible and adaptable. Its main purpose is to bring about social cohesion, equilibrium and stability as well as the all

15. *Gītā*, III. 5.
16. *Ibid.*, III 22-24.
17. *Ibid.*, III.4.
18. *Ibid.*, III.19.
19. *Ibid.*, III. 34.

round development of individual personality. It appears that the observance of Dharma was not rigid but a flexible, modifiable and dynamic principle related to the exigencies of time, place and human needs. Dr. B.G. Gokhale rightly observes:

> "What the concepts of *kāla* and *desa* imply is that given the differences in outlooks and attitudes of different periods and climes the details of a scheme of human conduct be the same at all times and in all spaces. This prevented the concept of Dharma from becoming a stratified idea by leaving the possibility open for change in its institutionalised character."[20]

Although specific dharmas have been made for all the Varnas, there is room for deviation in exceptional situations. In extraordinary times modifications can be made in Varna-dharma as envisaged by *Mahābhārata* with varying situations and circumstances. One cannot stipulate what is absolutely good or evil for all men at all times. The *Mahābhārata* justifies the relative nature of dharma and takes absolute dharma as the cause of injustice and exploitation.

Thus we find that the main objective of the epic is to ensure social good in accordance with Dharma. It aims at the establishment of social cohesion by the conservation of moral values. The ethical message as enshrined in the *Mahābhārata* is relative, catholic and pragmatic. It is relevant for all ages to come.

According to the *Mahābhārata*, every situation has its own morals. It lays down a different moral code for times of distress. This has been called Āpaddharma. A study of Āpaddharma leads us to infer that the abnormal circumstances justify recourse to otherwise condemned and prohibited deeds. This is true of political morality as well as of social morality. This is in the fitness of things, because what is true of a healthy man can never be true of a diseased one and that is true of a normal person can never be applied to one, fallen in distress.

20. Gokhale, B.G., *Indian Thought Through the Ages*, p. 42.

To put briefly, politics and ethics in the *Mahābhārata* have one and the same end and that is the attainment of salvation, the summum bonum of life. This must be preceded by the ethical preparation. Politics creates the atmosphere wherein one can pursue the goals of life, as laid down by ethics. Hence politics and ethics are complimentary, closely correlated and interdependent.

The individual and the social morality, as depicted in the *Mahābhārata*, has no difference in the machiavellian sense. Dharma is at the basis of both of them and it is thus, same for both. Moral standards, which guide the life of individuals also guide the life of states, whose end was to help the individual in the attainment of salvation.

Bibliography

Atreya, B.L., *Bhartiya Niti Sastra Ka Itihasa*, 1st Edi., 1965.

Aiyangar, Rangaswami, *Indian Heritage*, Vol. III, 2nd edi., 1960.

Altekar, A.S., *Sources of Hinau Dharma in its Socio-Religious Aspect*, Solapur, 1952.

Besant, Annie, *Hindu Ideals*, Adyar, 1965.

Buch, Maganlal Amritlal, *The Spirit of Ancient Hindu Culture*, Baroda, 1921.

Bradley, F.H., *Ethical Studies*, 2nd edi., 1927.

Barth, A., *The Religion of Inaia*, London, 1882.

Broad, C.D., *Five Types of Ethical Theory*, London, 6th edi., 1951.

Bhattacharya, Sukhamaya, *Mahābhārata Kalina Samaja*, Allahabad, 1966. Translated by Puspa Jain.

Chatterji, Satischandra and Dutta, D.M., *An Introduction to Indian Philosophy*, 6th edi., 1960.

Dasgupta, Surma, *Development of Moral Philosophy in India*, 1st edi., 1961.

Dutt, Romesh Chandra, *The Early Hindu Civilization*, 4th edi., Calcutta, 1963.

Dixit, V.V., *Relation of the Epics to the Brahmana Literature*, Poona, 1956.

Farquhar, John Nicol, *The Crown of Hinduism*, Oxford University Press, 1915.

Foulder, R., *The Principles of Moral and Political Philosophy*, 9th edi., London, 1893.

Gandhi, M.K., *Hindu Dharma*, Ahmedabad, 1950.

Ghoshal, U.N., *A History of Indian Political Ideas*, Oxford University Press, 1959.

Gokhale, B.G., *Indian Thought Through the Ages*, Asia Publishing House, Bombay, 1961.

Hopkins, E.W., *Ethics of India*, U.S.A., 1924.

———, *The Mutual Relations of the Four Caste*s, Leipzing, 1881.

———, *Legends of India*, New Haven, 1928.

———, *India Old and New*, New York, 1901.

———, *The Religions of India*, London, 1896.

Hiriyanna, M., *Oulines of Indian Philosophy*, George Allen and Unwin, London, 1958.

———, *The Essentials of Indian Philosophy*, George Allen and Unwin, London, 1960.

Hobhouse, L.T., *Morals in Evolution*, Chapman and Pall, London, 1951.

———, *Metaphysical Theory of the State*, George Allen & Unwin Ltd., London, 1926.

Hopkins, E.W., *Epic Mythology*, Strassburg, 1915.

———, *The Great Epic of India*, Yale University Press, New Haven, 1920.

Hostings, J., *Encyclopaedia of Religion and Ethics*, Vols. V and VII, Y. & T. Clark, Edinburgh, 1912, 1915.

Haimann, B., *Facets of Indian Thought*, George Allen & Unwin, London, 1964.

Hutton, J.H., *Caste in India, Its Nature, Function and Origin*, Oxford University Press, 3rd edi., 1961.

Joad, C.M.E., *Guide to Philosophy of Morals and Politics*, London, 1940.

Jast, *Reincarnation and Karma*, New York, 1956.

Kane, P.V., *History of Dharmasastra*, Vol. I and Vol. II, Part I, B.O.R.I., Poona, 1941.

Kosambi, D.D.. *An Introduction To The Study of Indian History*, Popular Book Depot, Bombay, 1956.

———, *The Culture and Civilization of Ancient Indian In Historical Outline*, Routledge & Kegan Paul, London, 1965.

Mahadevan, T.M.P., *Outlines of Hinduism*, Bombay, 2nd edi., 1960.

Maitra, A.C., *Elements of Morals*, Cuttak, 1912.

Mazumdar, A.K., *Outlines of Moral Philosophy*, Calcutta, 1915.

Mazumdar, J.C., *Ethics of the Mahabharata*, Calcutta, 1953.

Majumdar, R.C., *Ancient India*.

Mullick, P.N., *The Mahabharata, as it was, is and shall be*, 1st edi., 1934, Calcutta.

Maitra, S.K., *The Meeting of the East And West In Sri Aurobindo's Philosophy*, Pondicherry, 1956.

———, *The Ethics of the Hindus*, Calcutta University, 1956.

Mackenzie, John S., *A Manual of Ethics* (Sixth Edition), University Tutorial Press Ltd., London.

———, *Hindu Ethics*, Oxford, 1922.

———, *Outlines of Social Philosophy*, Allen & Unwin, London, 1952.

Mees, G.H., *Dharma and Society*, Luzac and Co., London, W.C.I. 1935.

Mukerjee, R.K., *Hindu Civilisation*, 2 Vols., Bharatiya Vidya Bhawan, Bombay, 1931 & 1963.

Max Muller, *Heritage of India*, Suil Gupta Ltd., Calcutta, 1951.

———, *India, What Can It Teach Us?*, Munshi Ram Manohar Lal, Delhi, 1961.

———, *The Upanisads*, Part I, Dover Publications, New York, 1962.

———, *The Vedas*, Susil Gupta (India) Ltd., Calcutta, 1956.

Monior Williams, *Indian Wisdom*, Chawkhambha, Varanasi, 1967.

Mukerji, Radha Kamal, *The Culture And Art of India*, George Allen & Unwin, London, 1959.

———, *A History of Indian Civilization*, Hind Kitabs Ltd., Bombay, 1958.

Mehta, P.D., *Early Indian Religious Thought*, Luzac & Co. Limited, 1956.

Nikhilanand, *Hinduism*, George Allen and Unwin, London, 1959.

Niebuhr, Reinhold, *Moral Man and Immoral Society*, London, 1934.

Oldenberg, H., *Ancient India, Its Language and Religion*, Punthi Pustak, Calcutta, 1962.

Pusalkar, A.D., *Studies in the Epics and Puranas*, Bharatiya Vidya Bhawan, Chaupatty, Bombay, 1955.

Panikkar, K.M., *Hindu Society at Cross Roads*, Asia Publishing House, Bombay, 1st edi., 1955.

Paley, William, *The Principles of Moral and Political Philosophy*, London, New edi., 1928.

Pande, R.B., *Hindu Sanskaras*, Vikram Publication, Banaras.

Popper, K.R., *The Open Society And Its Enemies*, Vol. I, Routledge & Kegan Paul, London, 1962.

Prabhavananda, *The Spiritual Heritage of India*, George Allen & Unwin, London, 1962.

Prabhu, P.H., *Hindu Social Organisation*, Popular Prakashan, Bombay, 1963.

Prasad, Beni, *Hindustan Ki Purani Sabhyata*, Hindustani Academy, Allahabad, 1950.

———, *The State In Ancient India*, Indian Press, Allahabad, 1928.

Radhakrishnan, S., *Indian Philosophy* in two Vols, 1929, 1st. edi.

Radhakrishnan, S., *The Bhagvadgita*, George Allen & Unwin Ltd., London, 1948.

———, *East & West : Some Reflections*, Allen & Unwin, London, 1954.

———, *Eastern Religions and Western Thoughts*, Oxford University Press, 1940.

———, *Indian Philosophy*, in 2 Vols., George Allen & Unwin Ltd., London, 1920, 1931.

Radhakrishnan, S. and Others (Edited), *History of Philosophy: Eastern and Western*, II Vols., George Allen and Unwin Ltd., London, 1951.

Radhakrishnan, S., *An Idealistic View of Life*, Unwin Books, London, 1961.

Radhakrishnan, S., *The Hindu View of Life*, Unwin Books, London.

Radhakrishnan, S. and Moore, C.A., *A Source Book in Indian Philosophy*, Princeton, New Jersey, 1957.

Raghavan, V., *The Indian Heritage*, Indian Institute of Culture, Bangalore, 1956.

Rao, N.J., *The Age of the Mahabharata War*, Bezwada, 1931.

Rice, E.P., *The Mahābhārata : Analysis and Index*, Humphrey Milford, Oxford University Press, 1934.

Rogers, R.A.P., *Short History of Ethics* (Greek and Modern), Madmillan and Co. Ltd., St. Martin's Street, London, 1945.

Ranade, R.D., *A Constructive Survey of the Upanishadi Philosophy*, Oriental Book Agency, Poona, 1926.

Risley, H., *The People of India*, Calcutta, 1913.

Raju, P.T., *The Idealistic Thought of India*, George Allen & Unwin, London, 1933.

Rajagopalachari, C., *Mahābhārata*, Bhartiya Vidya Bhawan, Bombay, 7th edi., 1962.

Renou, Louis, *Hinduism*, New York, 1962.

Russell, Bertrand, *Human Society in Ethics and Politics*, London, 1954.

———, *An Outline of Philosophy*, George Allen and Unwin, 1948.

Sharma. D.S., *Hinduism Through the Ages*, 2nd edi., 1962, Bombay.

Sharma, C.D., *A Critical Survey of Indian Philosophy*, 1st edi., London, 1960.

Sukathankar, V.S , *On the Meaning of the Mahābhārata*, Asiatic Society of Bombay, 1957.

Sivaswamy Aiyar, P.S., *Evolution of Hindu Moral Ideals*, Calcutta, 1935.

Sen, K.M., *Hinduism*, 1st edi., 1961 (Penguin books).

Schweitzer, Albert, *Indian Thought and its Development*, London, 1951.

———, *Civilisation and Ethics*, Adam and Charles, London, W.I., 1949.

Saletore, B.A., *Ancient Indian Political Thought and Institutions*, Asia Publishing House, Bombay, 1963.

Sarkar, B.K., *The Political Institutians and Theories of the Hindus*, Chackerverty, Chatterji & Co. Ltd., Calcutta, 1939.

Sastri, K.N., *New Light on the Indus Civilization*, Atma Ram & Sons, Delhi 1.

Sharma, M.R., *Mahābhārata Aura Śrīkṛṣṇa*, *Bhisma & Bros.*, Patakapur, Kanpur, 1950.

Sharma, R.S., *Aspects of Political Indians & Institutions in Ancient India*, Motilal Banarasidas, Delhi, Varanasi, Patna, 1959.

Sharma, I.C., *Ethical Philosophies of India*, George Allen & Unwin Ltd., 1965.

Shukla, Devi Dutt, *Mahābhārata Mimansa*, Indian Press Ltd., Allahabad.

Shukla, L.R., Nitisāstra, Sanmārga Press, Banaras, 1949.

Smith, H.N., *Ethics*, Penguin Series, 1956.

Tiwari, Brij Gopal, *Secularism and Materialism in Modern India*, Jabalpur.

Vivekanand, Swami, *The Complete Work of Swamy Vivekanand*, Vol. IV, 1899.

Vora, D.P., *Evolution of Morals in the Epics*, Bombay, 1st edi., 1959.

Vankateswara, S.V., *Indian Culture Through the Ages*, 2 Vols., London, 1928, 1932.

Vaidya, C.V., *Mahābhārata : A Criticism*, The Bombay Book Depot, Girgaon, Bombay, 1904.

———, *The Epic India*, Bombay Book Depot, Bombay, 1933.

Valvalkar, P.H., *Hindu Social Institutions*, Longmans Green & Co. Ltd., Bombay, 1939.

Williams Monier, *Hinduism*, London, 1906.

———, *Religious Thought and Life in India*, London, 1883.

William, P., *The Principles of Morals & Political Philosophy*, 1910.

Willoughby, *The Ethical Basis oj Political Authority*, The Macmillen Co., 1930.

Winternity, M., *History of Indian Literatura*, English Trans. 2 Vols., University of Calcutta, Calcutta, 1927, 1933.

Wheeler, M., *The Indus Civilization*, Cambridge, 1953.

Wheeler, J.T., *Ancient and Hindu India*, Purthi Pustaka, Calcutta, 1961.

Zinner, H., *Philosopoies of India*, Routledge & Kegan Paul, London, 1953.

Index